monsoonbooks

T0023205

THE GLASS ISLANDS

Born in Tasmania, Australia, in 1957, Mark Heyward has spent the last thirty years living, travelling and working in Indonesia. He now lives with his wife and two children in Lombok. Mark currently works as an international education consultant. In his spare time he writes, makes music, and takes long walks in the hills. Mark's first book, *Crazy Little Heaven: An Indonesian Journey*, was widely praised in the media in Indonesia and Australia.

Praise for *The Glass Islands*

'*The Glass Islands* is a sensitive, insightful and warm-hearted account of life in Indonesia. What raises this book far above other expat memoirs is the depth of Mark Heyward's commitment to the country and the subtlety of his observations on its culture, society and history – a heartfelt love-song to the place he has made his home, and to his own Indonesian family.' Tim Hannigan, author of *Raffles and the British Invasion of Java* and *A Brief History of Indonesia*

'Mark Heyward has a beautiful way of unpacking local customs, traditions and religious practices.' Gill Westaway, translator, editor and Lombok resident

The Glass Islands

Mark Heyward

monsoon

monsoonbooks

First published in 2023
by Monsoon Books Ltd
www.monsoonbooks.co.uk

No.1 The Lodge, Burrough Court, Burrough on the Hill,
Melton Mowbray LE14 2QS, UK.

First edition.

ISBN (paperback): 9781915310163
ISBN (ebook): 9781915310170

Cover design by Cover Kitchen.

A Cataloguing-in-Publication data record is available from the British
Library.

Printed and bound in Great Britain by Clays Ltd, Elcograf S.p.A.
25 24 23   1 2 3

For my wife

ꦩꦩꦪꦸꦭꦪꦸꦁꦧꦮꦤ

Memayu hayuning bawana

Well, the sun is surely sinking down,
but the moon is slowly rising,
so this old world must still be spinning round,
and I still love you.

James Taylor, 1971

Acknowledgements

My sincere thanks to Derek Pugh, Simon Payne, Sue Heyward, Gill Westaway and Tim Hannigan, who commented on early drafts of this book. Thanks also to the team at Monsoon Books. Any remaining errors of language or fact are mine.

Thank you to those who have shared their stories and their lives with me, especially Peter, Ace, Andrew, Felicity, Agus, Rani, Wartono, Derek, Tarno, Tono, Diane, Sakinah, Iwan, Gregg, Leigh, Jacob, Will, Tari, Gert, Thomas, Fabien, Matt, Alan Leishman, Alan Wilson, Meryl, Ary, Dewi, Husein, Rus, and Scott. Special thanks to Sopan and her family: Bapak, Ibu, Sari, Slamet, Song, Longgar, Rika, and Ganjar; to my father, Oliver, my mother, Peggy; to Pete and Sue, and to my children, Oliver, Anna, Rory, and Harry. Some names have been changed. But I have tried to retell all your stories as accurately as possible, while capturing something of the flavour and meaning of the events as I experienced them. My apologies for any inaccuracies or unwitting offence caused.

An earlier version of the passage in this book about family in Yogyakarta appeared in the short story 'Love and Loyalty' in *Jakarta Post*, and a version of the passage about Japanese-occupied Lombok appeared in the article 'Operation Starfish: The Untold Story of Australian Commandos in Lombok, 1945' in *Indonesia Expat*.

Contents

Map of Central
and Eastern Indonesia

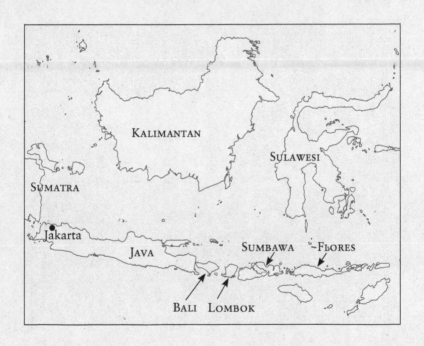

Prologue

In Lombok the seasons are changing. The winds have lost their way, the trees no longer know when to drop their leaves, the moths and grubs are confused, and the sea worms begin to forget when to spawn.

The seasons of men and women, too, are changing. The people are losing their way; their old kings and gods have failed them, and they are looking for new stories, for new rulers, new gods. The colonial days are long gone, Javanese and Balinese kingdoms have crumbled, Dutch and Japanese empires passed away. Today, the fading promise of Indonesian nationalism struggles against the sway of a new ideology, a new utopian dream: a return to the mythical golden age of Islam – reinstating God's rule on earth. This is the seduction of Islamism. And the indigenous Sasak share their island home with the Balinese, with Javanese, Arabs, Chinese, and a new breed – Western expatriates, with their own dreams, their own tropical fantasies.

But the earth still circles the sun; its moon still spins in the void. Night follows day, the call to prayer echoes in the valleys as the sun drops behind the island of Bali in the west. The oceans still answer to the tug of the moon, their tides following the old rhythms. The waves still embrace the sand, the seasons turn, the rains come and go. Some things never change. The love of a man for his wife, for his children; his desire to build, to create, to leave a mark on this good earth; his struggle to survive, his love of life, his fear of death.

THE BURNING SEASON

One

Together we stand on the hill. This is where we plan to put down roots. This is where we will build our Lombok home and raise a family.

It is dry. There is no road access, no water, no electricity. With a sweep of my arm, I create the picture. 'The main house will be here,' I declare, turning to the roughly terraced hillside behind us. 'Two storeys, with an external kitchen at the rear. We are standing where the front veranda will be.'

Across a small creek, on the slope behind a huge *waringin* tree with dangling aerial roots, we will reconstruct the Javanese *joglo* cottage we acquired in Yogyakarta. A second cottage will nestle beneath the tree in the little valley by the creek. And below us – I sketch with my hand – the pool.

'Are you sure we can afford all that?' laughs my wife, Laras. But there is no need for me to respond. We have had this conversation before.

The hill is scruffy, a mess of wild grass and acacia saplings. The earth looks thirsty. Its seeds lie dormant. But the day is young. A faint smell of dust, of cow dung and dew-damp dirt hangs in the air. A tribe of resident bulbuls chatters away. High in the coconut palms, the little birds are about their business, flitting this way and that in the early air. Smoke from a cooking fire in the valley filters through the trees, a low sun casting angled beams. The Lombok Strait glimmers, a distant curving expanse of blue. The early boat to Bali carves a rippled arc in Senggigi Bay. The point break curls, a little piece of faraway magic. And beyond that, across the Strait, Bali's holy mountain, the volcanic cone of Gunung Agung, rises from a sea mist to catch the sun's first rays.

I look down over the ridge up which we have just walked. By my reckoning, we are about a kilometre from the beach and the coast road; eighty metres above the valley floor – and a few more than that above sea level. The ocean stretches away to the south, hazy in the distance. The valley floor is carpeted with coconut palms, the occasional larger tree emerging like a shaggy yellow hillock from among the dark fronds. To the west we look across a green valley to the next ridge: a pale rusty brown row of *banten* trees, their leaves dry, limbs bare, outstretched, waiting for the rains. Past the ridge, the wide ocean disappears in a haze I know to be Bali.

'We'll have to cut some coconut palms to open up the view,' I comment.

'Why?' asks my wife, looking at me with a smile, a slight tilt to her head. 'It might be nice to leave them there and you can look at the view through the trees. Sometimes a view is improved with trees in the foreground.'

I look again. 'You may be right about that!' I say.

And then I see it. An image from my childhood, from a child's illustrated edition of Daniel Defoe's classic, *Robinson Crusoe*, which has stayed with me over the years. Crusoe and his faithful Man Friday peer down from their hideout, through a screen of coconut palms and tropical foliage and onto a white sand beach with an aqua sea beyond. There is a suggestion of danger as natives pull their dugout canoes ashore. It is curious how such images can shape a life. I realise in that moment, standing there on the coastal hills of Lombok, fifty years and five thousand kilometres from my first encounter with that childhood image in faraway Tasmania – I realise then that I am setting out to recreate that image, here in Lombok. We won't need to cut the palms.

**

And so it begins. It is July. Like many beginnings, this one takes place in the dry season – long before the rains arrive and the stringy banten trees turn a pale green with new life.

With an instinct for culture, Laras has arranged the *buka bumi* ceremony through her connections in the local Sasak community. Buka bumi, the breaking of the earth, is the first step in the construction of our Lombok home. The little group gathers on the terraced hillside where we plan to build our villa complex – a family home and two cottages. A congregation of just four: *Ibu* Laras is there with Ibu Elly, a local Sasak woman who has been helping in our house, and *Pak* Dul, a relative of Elly's and a village elder. Elly has been to the market. The necessary ingredients are assembled: a bottle of water, a woven *tikar* mat, flower offerings arranged in woven palm baskets, clusters of bright chrysanthemums and roses, fragrant *kananga* and frangipani – and a live chicken, its scrawny feet bound together with twine. The chicken lies unceremoniously in the dust, mute and compliant, a decent specimen, hopefully large enough to ensure the success of the event. Within the little group the talk is friendly but subdued, as befits the modest solemnity of the occasion.

'How are we going to do this?' asks Laras. 'I am Javanese, I'm not quite sure what to do here. I am also a Muslim.'

'No problem,' replies Pak Dul, with a cracked smile. 'I am Sasak, we'll do it my way. You pray in your way. We are all Muslims, so it'll be fine.'

The day was deemed auspicious, a day on which the dates of the Islamic calendar mysteriously intersected with those of the Javanese and modern Gregorian calendars. 'But every day is a good day!' Laras's father had declared when asked. 'You can build a house on any day you like – except the anniversaries of when my father and my mother passed away.'

Of course, like everything, it began long before this, but the scruffy little ritual marks the beginning for me. Pak Dul paces about, settling on a spot for the ceremony and marking out the four cardinal directions: north towards the foothills of Gunung Rinjani, south to the sea and the watery domain of Princess Mandalika, east to where the sun rises over the ridge, and west to the Lombok Strait and Bali beyond. We stand together; a quiet little clutch beneath the wide sky; looking inward, facing one another among the dry grasses and wild lantana weed. Then Pak Dul kneels to the west, towards the inconceivably distant desert city of Mecca. He opens with a series of muttered prayers, invocations. Qur'anic verses are recited in a gruff liturgical Arabic, the palms held outwards and upwards. And then, in the more familiar Sasak language, he seeks the blessing of the local gods, the permission of the earth, a hedge against misfortune. The muttering seems to go on for a long time, the rhythm of the words more important than their meaning.

Eventually the old man stops, takes the bottle, and with his right hand liberally sprinkles the flower petals with water before rising and casting them in the four directions: spidery green kananga to the north, little red roses to the south, creamy-white frangipani to the east, and orange-yellow chrysanthemums to the west. The morning sun shines. And after a brief pause, a grunt and a hefty swing of his short-handled hoe, the first wound is inflicted. The hard earth is turned, and the unfortunate chicken is slaughtered, its head held facing west, its thin neck sliced from below. Bright blood splashes on the freshly turned earth, a reminder of the old religion and an odd contrast to the innocent hues of the flower petals, a sacrificial offering to the Almighty, to the Fates, to the Universe and the old gods.

A handshake, smiles all round, and Pak Dul heads home with Elly, a fistful of rupiah that he says he will share with the orphans he sponsors in his village on the hill, and the chicken, which will make a fine meal. And with that, the construction formally begins.

**

By way of explanation, throughout Indonesia, it is normal and polite to use an honorific when addressing another person. This takes some getting used to. *Bapak*, or *Pak* for short, is used for men and literally translates as father. Unless, of course, it's a younger man, who is referred to in Java as *Mas* (elder brother), *Kakak* (shortened to *Kak*), for an older child or youngster, or *Adik* – sometimes shortened to *Dik* – for a younger person or a child. Similarly, women are generally referred to as *Ibu*, or *Bu* for short, meaning mother. Or *Mbak*, meaning elder sister. Once you get your head around this, you can begin to play with the regional and ethnic variations: *Kang*, for a mate in West Java, for example (*Neng* for a young woman); *Bung, Bang, Inaq, Nona, Om, Mama, Tante, Ci, Ko* ... and so it goes on. There is even an honorific for a Western gentleman, *Tuan* – though these days the English, 'Mister', is generally used – often without a name to follow, so it comes out as 'Hello, Mister!' It's simple really, all you have to do is determine the gender, relative age and status, regional background, and ethnicity of the person you are addressing – and then adjust for the level of formality the occasion demands – in order to get it right. But if, for some reason, you don't get it right, Indonesians are very forgiving.

***

Three months prior to the buka bumi ceremony, we had signed a contract with our builder, Pak Agus, and his wife, our architect, Ibu Rani. We met at our cottage in the village of Baruna Shanti in the valley below, the four of us sitting around the big teak table we had set up in an open terrace by the garden. And there, with smiles and handshakes and signatures, we sealed an agreement to work together to design and build a villa. But with this little ceremony on the hill we enter into different kind of contract, an agreement with the mountain, with the island, with the earth, with God.

Agus and Rani are Lombok Balinese, members of the Hindu minority of West Lombok. We were introduced by a mutual friend, Will, a New Zealander who lived in the valley below and was married to a Balinese lady. Agus is in his mid-thirties, tallish for an Indonesian and with the fine features typical of the Balinese. Not only had he built Will's house – a beautiful Bali-style courtyard villa – but he had worked on some impressive projects on the coast. This would be the first real build, the first project that he would manage independently. After a little shopping around, we decided that we liked Agus. We liked his work. But more importantly we liked him, his cheeky smile and intelligent eyes, the way he gave time and considered responses to our never-ending questions. And we liked it that he and his wife came as a package. Ibu Rani had studied architecture in Bali and was ready to work with us. A little more earnest than Agus, but with something of the same wry attitude, she is the brains of the outfit, Will told us.

In the end it was more of a hunch than a careful analysis of the options. But we decided to give them a go. We needed someone we could work with. Someone who would be ready to accommodate our off-beat ideas, to realise our quirky vision. Together we would make a fine team.

* * *

At the close of day, Laras and I sit outside our rented cottage in the valley, listening to the night sounds. Dogs bark, chickens crow, children squabble, and the occasional motorbike rattles past. The call of a mosque from up the valley signals sunset. The sounds of a village gamelan orchestra echo across the rooftops from somewhere near the beach. A Balinese temple ceremony.

'Do you think we're being a bit naïve about all this?' I ask. Laras looks up.

'We're basically acting on a hunch,' I laugh. 'But how else does one make major life choices?'

'What do you mean?' she asks.

'I'm not really sure,' I reply. 'But I'm not just talking about the contract with Agus and Rani.'

'Do you mean the buka bumi ritual?' Laras asks. But I don't mean this or the layered and rather messy belief system it represents – an uneasy but colourful mix of earthy Hinduism and local animism, topped off with a dash of austere imported Islam.

'No, I guess I mean the whole thing,' I reply. 'Building a villa in Lombok!'

'You think it's naïve?' Laras turns to me with a worried look. 'Maybe.'

'Well,' I respond. 'For a start, the land is not mine. You know what I mean. I'm Australian. As a foreigner I can't own land in Indonesia. It is your land.' As an Indonesian citizen, Laras is perfectly entitled to own the property. But I am not. And nothing is simple in this place, where laws and regulations shift with the winds and frequently contradict one another.

'Sometimes I just wonder,' I go on. 'My residency status here is temporary. It doesn't matter that I have spent nearly twenty years living and working in this country. All the financial, professional and personal investments I have made here, they don't seem to matter, either. My life's work to help improve the nation's education system, my marriage, my family, none of it counts. I am, and will always remain, a foreigner.'

Laras reaches out and takes my hand.

'So,' I take a deep breath, 'we are setting out to build our home in what, for me, is a foreign country, a country with rubbery laws, vague and unpredictable at best, and on land I don't own.'

She listens in silence. It is not the first time we have had this conversation, either.

'Then there is the process of building,' I continue, following a familiar script. 'Contracts can be slippery in Lombok; we have learned that from our friends. Everyone has a story to tell. Legally purchased land that turns out to belong to someone else. Promised access through a neighbouring block that doesn't eventuate.'

'True,' Laras chimes in. 'And don't forget the builders who run out of money – your money – before the job is finished. Prices marked up for materials and labour. Kickbacks to suppliers to falsify receipts. Informal payments to local officials for permits and approvals. Contractors who disappear overnight. Lawyers and notaries who steal your money.'

'And then there are the builders who skimp on the cement and bulk up the sand when mixing concrete,' I add, beginning to enjoy the game, 'the result being that your home begins to dissolve in the first monsoon rains. Undersized reinforcing steel. Creative accountants. Ghost workers receiving daily wages. Vanishing tools and equipment. Conmen posing as police officers and asking for bribes.'

'And all of this is before we consider the risk of crooked expatriates who shift land borders, break agreements and refuse to pay agreed accounts,' says Laras with a dry laugh.

'Yep, we've seen it all!' I laugh. 'Indonesia and Lombok are not for the faint hearted.'

'And what is the chance, do you think, of achieving what we intend,' I add with a raised eyebrow and a slightly more serious tone, 'of coming in under budget?' Agus and Rani have prepared an indicative budget for the project, but we are agreed that we will pay real costs for materials and labour, using a system of weekly payments, reconciliations and budgeting. This way we can keep on top of expenditure and avoid paying exorbitant overheads. We have a rough idea about how to pay for it all – hopefully from land sales, but, like everything in this world, nothing is certain.

'I guess you do have to be naïve to set out and build a villa in Lombok,' Laras says, finally. 'But if we weren't a little bit naïve, we wouldn't do anything, would we?'

Later that night, I reflect on our conversation as I drift off to sleep. I think about all the different kinds of naivety we need, just to live a life. Building a house, like writing a book, establishing a business or starting a family, is an act of faith. Without a blind faith in the future, in one's capacity to see it through, you would never begin.

'Fortunately,' I think, 'though my heart may be a little too faint for all this, blind faith is something I have in spades.' Among the many blessings I can count, one of the greatest is surely an upbringing which led me to believe in myself – and in the basic goodness of the world. I grew up in a period of confidence in a confident nation: Australia. My early years were spent on the island of Tasmania, that wonderful, forgotten corner of the Commonwealth. There were few threats to contend with, beyond bushfires, bull ants, bullish brothers and boring Sunday sermons. Life was sweet, and I was taught that I could do anything I turned my hand to. Climb a tree? Okay. Write a song? Why not? Hitchhike across the island? Sure. Stage an art exhibition or a comic review, publish an underground paper, join the revolution, change the world? No problem. Fine. Go ahead.

I did learn to avoid some pursuits. A little humility is not a bad thing, I reflect. Sport was never a success – not only due to lack of talent, but also lack of interest. If, by some misfortune, the ball ever came near me at the far end of the hockey field, I would usually be mentally absent, happily daydreaming or writing the next adolescent poem in my muddled head. I later crossed mechanics off my list of can-do things after spending one long summer holiday from university stripping back the engine of a clapped-out Peugeot 403 – only to have it function on just two of its four shiny cylinders when the job was done.

All of this thinking and reminiscing has woken me up. It is a warm night. Laras is still awake.

'You know,' I say quietly. 'I've been thinking about what we were talking about before.'

'Oh yes?' Laras looks up from her book.

'I think I learned to be naïve when I was a kid,' I begin. 'And I think I'm fortunate to have retained that naïve confidence I learned as a child; it's the kind of naivety that allows someone to set out on the adventure of building a villa in a foreign land. Naivety is a virtue, I reckon.'

'How can it be a virtue?' Laras sounds sceptical. She gives me that resigned look that says she is prepared to indulge me with this – but she doesn't believe it for a moment.

'Well,' I continue, 'naivety is a kind of faith, a kind of innocence; it's about having a certain trust in the world. That innocent trust in people, in places, in the world at large, has repaid me with a good life, a happy life.'

Laras laughs, but it is a good-natured laugh.

'Naivety requires a suspension of disbelief,' I press on. 'To maintain the faith, the innocence, that belief in the goodness of the world, you have to overlook the bad stuff: the illness, the corruption, selfishness, dishonesty. You have to ignore the fact that death is out there waiting for you, too.'

'But being naïve is basically being stupid,' Laras objects.

'True, at times I've been lied to, let down, betrayed. I've been hurt like everyone else. We all get hurt. It happens from time to time – and it surprises me whenever it does! And there are times when I disappoint myself – and sometimes the people I love. There have been times when I've let you down, too.'

I look at Laras; we exchange a knowing glance. No need to open old wounds.

'And one day,' I add, 'I'll end up feeding the worms. We all will – whether in Lombok or Tasmania remains to be seen.'

I smile in the darkness. But Laras has grown quiet. She covers her face with her hand and looks away.

'It's okay. Bear with me,' I say. 'You'd think that the opposite of naivety is sophistication, right? Children are naïve, grownups are sophisticated. But it seems to me that often it's not sophistication at all; that loss of innocence leads to a sort of ugliness; a rudeness, arrogance, a meanness. And I don't want to be like that. So, allow me my fantasies, my childish pride. Allow me my innocence – and let's do this. Let's build this house!'

Fortunately, my wife is less trusting than me. A good Javanese woman and a formidable line of defence against mischief, she knows well how to manage the money, how to keep the family together, how to deal with conniving contractors, dodgy civil servants and wayward staff. Without the checks and balances she has put in place, the adventure of building our villa may well end in tears. But perhaps without my innocence, my trust and naivety, we would never begin; we would never embark on this foolish journey together.

* * *

But first, a little history. I came to Indonesia to live in 1992, a long way from the Roaring Forties and the cold south-west of my home state, Tasmania, at the far south of Australia. I met my Javanese wife in 1995. She was teaching at an international school in a mining town in Kalimantan. Having moved around from Kalimantan to Jakarta and West Java, in late 1999 we decided to relocate with our infant son from the overcrowded island of Java to Lombok in the east. The traffic congestion and political turmoil of Jakarta had become tiresome.

'My wife and I had agreed that if McDonalds ever came to Lombok we would move further east,' quipped Peter, who invited us to help establish a school for Lombok's small international community. But when, inevitably, the fast-food chain did open an outlet on the island, Peter and family were too entrenched in the community to leave.

Peter's invitation came at a good time. The non-profit, community-based nature of the project appealed. And so did Lombok. Jakarta was a crazy place. After thirty-plus years in power, President Suharto had fallen from grace, his carefully constructed system of control and patronage finally collapsing under the weight of a monetary crisis and a surge of people power. The political vacuum that he left behind was filled with a mess of competing interests: students, reformists, old-guard, Young

Turks, democrats, military protagonists, and opportunists. The wreckage of the 1998 riots was still evident, the economy was shot, and the streets were clogged with daily protests.

But if Jakarta was a frying pan, Lombok turned out to be a fire. The peaceful community we had discovered in 1999, a tropical idyll in which Sasak Muslims and Balinese Hindus happily coexisted, was ripped apart by politically orchestrated riots in January 2000.

January 2000 was Lombok's burning season; it was the riot season, the season of the gun. An unlikely alliance of Suharto loyalists, Islamist hotheads and conservative military forces had stirred up the fight between the majority Muslim community and the tiny Christian minority, hoping to justify a military crackdown and create an excuse for the conservatives to seize power. Unfortunately, the day we had chosen to open our new school was also the day they had chosen for their riots. We began with just six students: a little gang of bright-eyed kids and keen teachers. By the end of the day, all but two of the children were gone, their families having fled the island. Our office manager, a Christian woman, had gone into hiding and our plans were in disarray.

That night a couple of guys with military haircuts turned up on a motorbike, apparently planning to torch the school buildings. We were presumably on the list as a suspect foreign – and possibly a Christian missionary – enterprise. Fortunately we had held a communal feast, an Islamic *selamatan*, after Friday prayers the previous week, and the local Sasak community turned them away. The would-be arsonists crossed us off their list and, after a day off, we resumed classes in the nearby family home of the two remaining kids. Adam and Soraya were the children of the school's co-founders: Peter, a British expatriate who had grown up in the countryside of Pakistan and lived his life in South-East Asia, and his wife, Ibu Ace (pronounced 'ah-chay'), a businesswoman, who traces her ancestry to Bandung in West Java and Bima in Sumbawa, the next island to the east. The couple had built a grand family home on the coast and a successful business exporting Lombok pottery and arranging house removals for expatriates locating to and from a large American copper mine on Sumbawa. The school was their new venture.

The attempt to stir up trouble and seize power was a failure. The Christian community went to ground and efforts to provoke the Balinese Hindus failed. But the cost to Lombok was high. The commotion was all over in three days, but it left the place in shock. As the dust settled and the smoke drifted away from burnt-out Chinese shophouses, stories began to emerge; people began to try and make sense of what had happened. The streets were empty, the atmosphere surreal, a palpable mix of nervous tension and bewilderment. The overwhelming reaction amongst locals of all persuasions was along the lines of 'What the hell was that all about?' and 'We must never, ever, let anything like that happen again!'

Normal services had ceased while everyone began cautiously to put their lives back together. But there were no tourists in the tourist town of Senggigi. Locals and expatriates alike were mainly at home behind locked gates. Or had fled. Laras and I called into a Padang restaurant in Ampenan to buy some local takeaway – a package of rice, spicy vegetables and chicken. The little group of patrons looked up in surprise to see a foreigner. A young man glared at me, his faced creased with residual rage. As we made to leave, he shouted the Islamic greeting, *'Assalamu'alaikum!'*

'Wa'alaikum'salam,' I responded with a nervous smile and what I hoped sounded like authentic Arabic, as I left the restaurant.

The following day we had a weird, Pythonesque kind of experience when we decided to chance a meal at the aptly named 'Coco Loko', a little restaurant down behind the deserted art market on Senggigi Beach. The place was empty but for a single forlorn-looking waiter. We worked our way through the entire menu, patiently ordering, item by item, everything on the list in order of preference, while the waiter checked item by item in the kitchen, emerging a minute or two later each time to declare *Habis!* – Finished! We eventually ran out of things to order.

'Well, just get me a bowl of steamed rice, then,' said Laras, exasperated but polite as ever.

'Sorry, we're out of rice!' came the response after the waiter once more checked in the kitchen.

They did have cold beer, though. And hot potato fries. And the following day we discovered one of the school's original six students still in Lombok. The girl's mother was the general manager of the Holiday Inn, a resort hotel up the coast at Mangsit.

'I'm not willing to take the risk of sending my daughter to school down at your place,' she said, 'but why don't you run the school here for a couple of weeks? It's not as if we have a lot of guests.'

So, for the next fortnight we conducted daily classes at the Holiday Inn. It was wonderful! Learn to swim in the big resort pool, lunch in the empty restaurant, science lessons on the beach, and classes in a small meeting room. There was just one guest in the hotel, an American expatriate on leave from his job in Thailand. 'This is great!' he enthused. 'I have the whole place to myself. Nobody to bother me. I think I'll make a habit of holidaying in hotspots!'

After a week, a local lad with big worried eyes joined our little group, the son of an Indonesian woman involved in the pearl industry, grandson of a former mayor. We now had four teachers and four kids. Eventually, as Lombok crept back to some semblance of normality and the numbers grew, we reluctantly moved back into the school buildings about ten kilometres down the coast.

Laras and I had been staying in a friend's house when the riots took place. Andrew is an Irish tobacco farmer from Zimbabwe who had settled in Lombok with his wife and family; a white African refugee from the Mugabe regime. A fit early-middle-aged man with intense eyes, a perpetual frown and a crown of tight curls, we had met a few times the previous year at school planning meetings.

'We'll be away on holidays,' he told us. 'Why don't you house-sit for us while you look for somewhere to rent?'

But when the riots erupted, Peter suggested that we move in with them for a time. It felt too risky to be driving around town, and Peter and Ace lived close by the school. There was a lot of looting going on. We packed up Andrew's stuff and bundled it into the back of a pickup to be taken for safekeeping to a tobacco warehouse in central Lombok – and we moved in with Peter and Ace. Then, when after a fortnight of staying at Peter and Ace's home and running classes at the Holiday Inn we shifted operations back to the school, Laras and I moved there too. With only four students, there was plenty of room, so we took over a couple of classrooms at the rear of the building – and there we set up house with our six-month-old son, Rory.

* * *

Peter took me for a drive to the south coast, where the annual festival of Bau Nyale was underway. It was a few weeks since the riots, things had settled down a little, and we all needed to let off some steam. Kuta Beach, an hour or so from Senggigi, is a long crescent of white coral sand and sparkling blue ocean with an offshore surf break. The beach leads at the eastern end to a grassy, green knob. A place of stunning beauty. Behind the knob, as we drove in past mud-caked buffalo grazing waterlogged fields, we found the festival and the smaller Seger Beach. A mass of local people had gathered for the event which was due to climax the following morning with a hunt for the slippery green and purplish sea worms known as *nyale* that annually emerge from the coral with the waning moon.

Around a thousand people were happily milling about in the late afternoon light. Security for the event was provided by a light contingent of armed police, supplemented by larger groups of local militia – community vigilante groups which had become so numerous and so powerful during the years of unrest following Suharto's fall, that the authorities thought it wise to work with them rather than against them. Parking was organised by the blue shirts, known as Bujak, and general security by the larger group of orange-shirted Amphibi. An uneasy truce had been declared between the two groups. The former, Pemburu Jejak (or

'Tracker'), shortened to 'Bujak', was formed to combat crime – and specifically to retrieve stolen goods – an important community service in this period. Unfortunately, it seemed that many of the members were criminals themselves – and used their positions to extort money and goods from others. The island is known, among other things, for petty crime, and, while some villages in Central Lombok are famous for their pottery and some for their weaving, others are known for their thievery. It is apparently impossible for a young man from such a village to attract a wife unless he has pulled off at least one substantial heist.

The second group, Amphibi, was established by an Islamic preacher and his psychic brother in East Lombok, in part to combat the first. Their numbers far exceeded Bujak's. Reportedly over a hundred thousand had joined, mainly villagers hoping to secure their property, and particularly their livestock and crops. Cattle rustling was rife at the time – and without security a farmer could lose an entire tobacco crop overnight. For the sum of one hundred thousand rupiah (about twenty dollars, at the time), he could buy the protection of the group, along with a magically charged orange-camouflage 'invulnerability jacket' – and, if he rose up through the ranks, a walkie-talkie and an attitude. While Bujak was concerned with recovering 'lost' goods (for a fee, no doubt), Amphibi was after the criminals – and dished out rough justice when it succeeded in catching one. Summary executions were not uncommon, with beheading the preferred method of dispatch. A few months prior to the festival, the tension between the two militia groups erupted in a full-scale turf war, a bloody battle. The effort to bring them together to provide security for Bau Nyale was significant, if risky.

None of this was evident as Peter and I strolled around, mingling with the crowds, the only foreigners there. Peter had arranged an outing for his neighbours, bussing the fishing kampung families – mums, dads, kids and grandparents – to the festival. Occasionally he would spot a familiar face in the crowd, but for the most part we simply wandered about enjoying the festive atmosphere. Kids ran around, flocks of young men and young women promenaded, eyeing one another off and giggling in a self-conscious way, the odd motorbike roared past, and we headed for a row of makeshift foodstalls called *warung*, where we could get a cold drink and a bowl of noodles.

A stage had been erected for the festival princess, a Sasak beauty chosen to enact the role of Putri Mandalika. According to local legend, a classic tale of love and sacrifice, the princess's beauty was the cause of her downfall. Rival princes from kingdoms far and wide vied for her hand in marriage. The princess was unable to choose without causing offence. Her father, the king, in an effort to resolve the situation, called all the kingdoms together and instructed his daughter to choose a husband before sunrise. Princess Mandalika announced that her love for her parents, her people and her country was too great to risk causing a war between the kingdoms. Instead of choosing a suitor she threw herself into the sea, promising that she would never leave her subjects, that each year she would return to remind them of her love for them. The people searched the seas and the beaches, but all they found were the colourful sea worms: the princess had been transformed.

The serious part of the festival took place in the small hours of the following morning – long after Peter and I had returned home. A local shaman, or *dukun*, waded out into the shallow sea at Seger Beach to observe the spawning nyale and predict the rice harvest based on the number of sea worms. It was a good omen. The people needed some good news and the size of the catch promised a rich harvest. At low tide that morning, the wide bay was crowded with locals, each with a bag or a bucket and a net, each bent over the task of scooping up the worms.

***

Sometime later, I attended the Pasola festival on the island of Sumba, east of Lombok. An extraordinary event. I was dressed in traditional gear for the occasion; wrapped in heavy hand-woven cloth, with a short sword tucked into my waist band and a cloth headdress for good measure. Feeling quite ridiculous in this getup, I found my way to the beach where, in the early dawn, locals waded out into the ocean to harvest the sea worms. In Sumba, the spawning signals the opening of the Pasola season, when the tribes come together, gathering in open fields for ritual warfare. The first battle took place on an open space behind the beach. Two sides formed, one at each end of the field, teams of men dressed in traditional cloth, each astride a local pony. The tension and energy built with drumming and chanting. A signal was given and the battle began, young men charging at one another, hurling wooden spears at the enemy. Occasionally someone would be knocked off their horse, or a horse would slip and fall in the mud. Someone would let out a battle cry and, breaking away from the group, lead a little gang of horsemen into the fray, racing at the opposition in a wide circle before hurling spears and retreating to the safety of the team. The battle raged for an hour or so as the day began to heat up.

The sea worms in Sumba tell of the end of the wet season and the time for planting. The spilling of blood, though rare, apparently ensures a good harvest. In recent years, the human and horse blood which used to drench the field has been replaced with the blood of sacrificial pigs, dogs and chickens. Traditional leaders, village elders and local police are on hand to make sure the battle doesn't get out of hand.

It was hard to see who had won the event. Perhaps no one had. Eventually, tiring of the game, I was led to a high-roofed local house. I sat cross-legged on a raised wooden veranda under a thatched roof with the Governor of East Nusa Tenggara and two or three of his mates – all dressed in similar traditional garb. Breakfast was served, consisting initially of strong, sweet coffee and cigars. It was about six in the morning. I asked if there are any rules for the Pasola.

'Oh yes!' replied one of the men. 'If you kill someone, you don't go to jail. If you get hurt, you go to hospital.' As an afterthought, he added, 'Oh, and everyone has to behave in a chivalrous fashion.'

***

The nyale sea worms are associated with fertility. Some are eaten raw, fresh from the sea, some are steamed, some fried, and some are ground into a paste, mixed with coconut and spices then wrapped in a banana leaf, roasted over a fire and served in little green packets called *pepes nyale*. In Lombok, some farmers grind them up and sprinkle them in the irrigation channels around their paddy fields to ensure a good harvest. But the communal flirting that Peter and I had observed in Lombok that afternoon suggested to me that the Bau Nyale festival might be as much about human fertility as it is about spawning sea worms, rice harvests and old legends.

The festival offered a brief respite, a temporary truce, in the ongoing civil unrest. Amphibi's ground troops continued to strut about in West Lombok, setting up bamboo security posts, flaunting their orange shirts, demanding money from passing motorists and generally making their presence felt. There was no recurrence of the big January riots, but disputes between rival gangs over land and authority continued sporadically. A soccer field at a crossroads in west Mataram became the scene of a daily battle as Lombok gradually settled into normal routines and balance was restored.

It took the island a few years to recover, and all of this is history now. Our school, Sekolah Nusa Alam, grew quickly and is now thriving – and Laras and I have made Lombok our home in Indonesia.

Two

Lombok is a gem of a place. A little rough around the edges, like an uncut diamond, an unpolished stone, it sits on the fringe of the Indian Ocean, just east of Bali and somewhere near the centre of the sprawling archipelago that is Indonesia. Far enough away to be out of the mainstream, but close enough that you come and go, the island is essentially one massive volcano in the north and wide floodplains to the south.

With a young family, it was not long after settling on the island that Laras and I started looking into buying land and thinking about building a home. Early on we settled on the idea of living on a hill rather than in the city or on the beach. The beachfront land is beautiful, yes. But it was becoming scarce and expensive and we didn't really want to live in a tourist enclave. Something about the idea of living up on the hill with its fresh air, clean space and wide views appealed. We began exploring the beautiful green hills behind the resort area of Senggigi and along the coast.

The Hill was Andrew's idea. Halfway through our first year in Lombok he took me for a walk. It was the middle of the dry season. Twenty minutes of huffing and puffing up a ridge path brought us out onto a broad expanse of grass which sloped away to the west. Behind us the land dropped precipitously into a valley to the east.

We stood together in that airy space. I caught my breath. It was hot. A light breeze blew up the valley. Rising high above the coast, the hill offered huge views – three hundred and sixty degrees from along the ridge. To the north we looked up to wooded foothills and toward the peak of Rinjani, hidden for most of the time in cloud. To the east we looked back across a deep green valley and a second ridge to the provincial city of Mataram and the hazy central plains of Lombok beyond. To the south the view was across the southern beaches and to the distant islands and bays of Sekotong and South Lombok. And to the west, the most stunning view of all took in the lower hills, coconut groves and coastal bays along the west coast. The little Balinese temple of Batu Bolong jutted out into the sea in the foreground, white water rising where the swell hit black rocks, and across the Senggigi surf break and the Lombok Strait, the neighbouring island of Bali was prominent in the distance.

Andrew pointed out the land he was in the process of acquiring. Two large sloping fields split by a seasonal creek, a dark line of scrub which dropped away to the south, wild mangos, scrubby banten and the occasional remnant forest tree. The banten are used in Lombok as living fences. Plant a row of sticks and, soon after the rains, you will have a hedge.

And then he came to the reason he had brought me along for the walk. 'There's another piece that I'm thinking about,' he gestured with a sweep of his hand to the north. About a hundred metres up the ridge from where we stood was a smaller strip of land, with perhaps the best views of all. 'Are you interested? I think it's available.'

Interested? I was more than interested. I was in love! The hill was an extraordinary place. We had been talking to Andrew for some time about the idea of building on a hill. We had even gone so far as acquiring a property on the ridge to the east and had discussed the idea of splitting it with Andrew. But this was something else.

'We might be,' I replied with what I hoped sounded like sensible caution. But I don't have much flare for poker and I'm sure my attempt at a poker face was a complete failure.

It did take some imagination to see the potential. There was the question of access. We had walked for nearly two kilometres up a steep hill across private land. No road, just a narrow village walking track. Once the initial flush of enthusiasm had faded and my ever-sensible wife had been given a chance to join the conversation over the following days, more questions arose. What about water? Electricity? There were just a handful of cottages in the area. Hovels might be a more accurate term, one-room shelters constructed of bamboo and *alang-alang* grass cut on the site. Each with an outdoor bathroom – a tiny space walled off with banten bushes and rotting blue tarp or woven palm leaf, a traditional, baked-clay water container wedged in a fork in the banten. But no road, no water source, no electricity supply, no toilets or sanitation.

Fortunately, Laras could also see what I saw. Having grown up in a Javanese village she was not too fazed by the lack of amenities. And Andrew had a plan, of sorts. 'Don't worry, I've thought about all that,' he said airily.

'We'll figure out as we go,' it was agreed.

So it began. We set out to individually acquire blocks of land up the hill which is now known as, simply, 'The Hill' or, on local maps, as Bukit Batu Layar. The land was mainly in local hands, almost none of it certificated by the government. Purchasing meant learning the local land laws, along with local customs and local ways of doing things. Some was owned by Sasak farmers, some by the local Balinese community group or *banjar*, and one or two blocks by local Chinese businessmen from the city. As each block was purchased, we went through the lengthy process of legally establishing ownership and obtaining a freehold title under Indonesian law.

The inhabitants scratched a living from the dry, sandy soil, grazing goats and pretty little Balinese cows, harvesting coconuts, tending cassava plots on the slopes, and trying to keep their chickens out of the clutches of predatory monitor lizards and the odd silvery python. But they did not own the land. They did not own the coconut palms, or the cows. This was a feudal society and they were tenant farmers, sharecroppers. Under the traditional system, the owners – also Sasak villagers or absent landlords, living up in town and one rung up the social ladder – took half the value of each harvest. Acquiring the land meant first identifying the owner, or sometimes owners if several siblings had an interest in a plot. Proof of ownership sometimes meant a tax certificate, and sometimes was a matter of communal memory. Then the boundaries and dimensions had to be established. All of this was often open to dispute – especially with the scent of money in the air.

Once over these hurdles, the real fun began. The West Lombok branch of the National Land Body seemed to have been carefully constructed in order to extract the maximum amount of money in the form of informal payments out of both sellers and purchasers of land. When, some years later, the National Corruption Commission started sniffing around West Lombok, an unexplained fire mysteriously destroyed all the computers and records in the office. When Laras visited, tired-looking bureaucrats sat and smoked in the lazy heat, shuffling piles of papers from desk to desk, each level in the organisation beholden to those above and below in a complex system of loyalties and payments. Acquiring a property meant first getting it certificated. And then getting the certificate listed in the name of the new owner. This meant payments for villagers who provided information on the land ownership or made introductions, payments for government surveyors and their hangers-on, payments to village-level officials who had to sign off on the ownership papers, payments to notaries, and basically payments to everyone in the Land Office – along with some official fees and taxes that were due.

'You stay away,' I was instructed. And, for once, I was happy to comply, happy to let Laras do the running. This was her domain and my presence would only complicate matters. The whole business depended not only on money, but on relationships – on gradually building trust, getting to know people, figuring out who was a crook and who was not – or, perhaps, which were the honest crooks. This needed time – and a lot of it. Endless days spent sitting on little *barugaq* pavilions chatting to Balinese and Sasak villagers. Getting to know the way things are done, the local politics, and, literally as well as figuratively, the lie of the land. Endless delays, false starts, lost payments and dead ends. Meetings that didn't take place, hours spent sitting in office waiting rooms, disappointing outcomes. Learning to interpret the local language: when 'I'm sorry, can't do' means 'You haven't offered me enough money yet' when 'Tomorrow, I promise!' means 'Forget it, it'll never happen ...'

Somehow, Laras found she had a talent for this game. Somehow, she managed to navigate this ambiguous and fraught new territory. Somehow, she made friends. And somehow, we became landowners.

Our first piece was a prize: the block that Andrew had first suggested, it was right at the top with big views up the forested valley and to the west. I immediately started envisaging our new home and sketching out ideas. At the time we couldn't afford to purchase much land or to match Andrew's contribution to finance the construction of the road and infrastructure required to open it up – so we turned to friends from around the world and invited them to join us. Initially six decided to take the risk – all Australians who had some connection with Lombok and were now living and working elsewhere. For each one we arranged the purchase of a block from the local owners.

In those early days, I was not allowed to be seen on the hill. Fearing that the sight of foreigners pacing about and looking for land borders would drive the price up, Laras had strictly forbidden it. Unfortunately, like most Indonesians, my wife was unaccustomed to reading maps. Not that there were any maps available. Knowledge of borders, rights of way, and ownership was locked in the collective memory of the villagers. In order to get a sense of the layout of the land, and to verify the rough dimensions and locations of blocks, from time to time I was sent up the hill after dark – preferably in the rain and wearing a hooded jacket as disguise in case I should bump into a curious local. Stumbling about on the dark scrubby slopes I paced the lengths of imagined borders and located the corners – 'Look for the big tree by the creek, keep going up about a hundred and fifty metres until you reach the hedge by the ridge track ...' – before reporting back, piecing together the information, and sketching progressively more meaningful 'mud maps' of the area.

***

Long before all this, before we even knew about Lombok, Laras and I had begun dreaming and scheming about owning a block and building a home. I had something in mind. I didn't want a square plot of flat land on a straight road. I didn't want to be hemmed in by urban sprawl, surrounded by people. I wanted something with character, something with space. Ideally on a romantic bend in the road, bordering a small stream – and with views. Some big trees would be good too. Forever the optimist, this was not too much to ask, I thought to myself. Life is what you make of it.

Before moving to Lombok, we had looked at a few blocks in the hills north of Yogyakarta, where Laras grew up. Nothing caught the imagination. We had also bought a traditional Javanese joglo from a village near the famous Prambanan temple complex in Laras's hometown. The idea was to dismantle the dilapidated old timber house and reconstruct it wherever we ended up buying. And we had begun to acquire the teak pillars and antique carved panels with which to assemble a traditional Javanese *limasan* house. The two architectural forms are part of the same Javanese tradition. The joglo is built around a simple four-pillar frame, the pillars creating a central space and load-bearing structure upon which the house rests. The limasan is essentially the same thing but with eight pillars, creating a rectangular rather than square building. The roof line reflects the importance of this structure, with a high central high-pitched, hipped roof denoting status in the village. Like the brim of a wide-brimmed hat, the surrounding roof slopes at less of an angle to low outer walls which surround the house. The entire structure is built of teak and is held together with joinery, rather than bolts, meaning that it can be dismantled, like a giant piece of knock-down furniture.

The structure of the traditional joglo is rich in meaning. For those who can read the symbolic language, our house will tell a story. The basic structure is said to derive from old temple forms. The architecture tells a story of the human body, of the soul and the balance of male and female. Traditional Javanese homes are fronted with an open-sided *pendopo* pavilion, a spiritual mountain, representing the male – the phallus – and the inside of the house, a cave, the *dalem*, is regarded as sacred, female – the central space beneath the high roof form is the vulva. The high roof is the head and the stone base of the central wooden pillars, the feet. Detailed carvings on the wooden panels tell another story, flowers representing fertility, dragons over the doors, providing protection against evil, and stylised suns symbolizing life.

When we visited Lombok to discuss plans for the new school in early 1999, we knew immediately that we wanted to live on the island; that this is where we wanted to build and settle down. And thus it was that we had the joglo dismantled, labelled piece by piece, packed onto the back of a truck and driven to Lombok, where it was stored in the back yard of our newly rented home in Ampenan. Rory, our son, took his first steps. I was about to embark on a new career as a development consultant. We had opened the doors of our new school and we were starting out on a new life on a new island.

This was a time of changes. It was a time of portents. On the last day of the year 1999, Laras and I sat by the beach in Mangsit on Lombok's west coast. We held hands and watched the sun quietly set behind Bali's Gunung Agung across the Lombok Strait. The sea glittered gold, clouds piled high, reflecting the brief sunset. The end of a millennium. A new beginning. Two weeks later, the riots broke out. Ten years later we built our new home.

* * *

Over the years since we moved to Lombok, the dismantled joglo has several times been shifted, first from Ampenan in the Arab quarter – our first home after moving from temporary quarters at the back of the school – then to a rented cottage in the little Balinese village of Baruna Shanti in the valley to the east of The Hill. Then, when we later moved to Flores, the joglo was packed up and carried across the lane to another cottage in the same village. Meanwhile, in Yogya, Central Java, a collection of panels and timbers of various dimensions, the recycled remains of a limasan house from Seleman, waited, stacked in the workshop of Pak Tarno. There they gathered dust among ornate carved *gebyok* panels from Klaten on the north coast and rustic pieces of antique furniture from Tuban and Blitar in East Java.

Pak Tarno has become a friend. A specialist in traditional Javanese architecture, he showed us around a number of old joglo and limasan buildings in Yogya. An old-style Javanese merchant, he values tradition and authenticity over the bottom line, he cares as much for good relations with suppliers and customers as he does for profit.

A year or so after we had acquired the limasan pieces and moved to Lombok, Pak Tarno came to visit with his friend Pak Tono, an architect. Tono was in town for a conference of interior designers. Tarno decided to join him to see where we planned to build and, no doubt, to shore up his position as a supplier and builder of antique Javanese homes.

Although it was still early days, I was now allowed to be seen on the hill. In case of questions I was to say I was going for a stroll, taking in the air, getting some exercise, or some such. Strictly no mention was to be made of land or development. This was a flimsy ruse. Without doubt, the word was out. But no one let on. The polite thing to do when meeting anyone on the track – stranger or acquaintance, friend or foe – is to stop for a chat. With big smiles and a welcome excuse to put down one's load for a few minutes, the first question is always: '*Mau ke mana?*' – 'Where are you going?' – which could be interpreted as 'What are you up to?' but is, more often than not, simply a way of acknowledging the other. Just as Westerners who ask 'How are you?' don't really want to know the answer, no one expects you to respond with a detailed explanation of the purpose and object of the journey. The polite response is thus *'Jalan-jalan!'* or, literally, 'Walking-walking!' – just out for a stroll. These protocols made it easy to avoid the risk of giving away too much information. We could all happily overlook what was by now, no doubt, common knowledge; that foreigners were investing on the hill.

Incidentally, the second question, following quickly on the heels of the first, is usually *'Dari mana?'* – 'Where are you from?' – to which the appropriate response is either *'Dari bawah'* – 'From below' – or, perhaps, in my case, 'Australia'. But it doesn't really matter, the purpose is not to exchange information, it is to establish a brief relationship between fellow human beings.

We set off to walk up the hill with Tono and Tarno. It was mid-morning, a lovely day for a walk. But it soon became apparent that our guests were unaccustomed to such strenuous exercise. Poor Tono, after only ten minutes or so, and just at the point where the hill begins to slope towards the ridge, collapsed in a panting heap on the grassy ground.

'I don't think I can do this,' he managed to say between gasps. And, noting the pallor of his face, I was inclined to agree.

Tarno was doing rather better – but was also glad to have a rest before heading on. Eventually, after a series of short stints and long rests, we made it to our block at the top of the hill. But it was a reminder of the value of good health – and of the terrible condition in which some middle-class men manage to get themselves. A lethal combination of strong *kretek* cigarettes, a fatty, sugary diet and a total lack of exercise will do it to you.

Tono and Tarno were somewhat puzzled by our choice of a house site. Having struggled up the hill to the block we had bought, the two of them stood there, admiring the view, puffing on unfiltered cigarettes and quietly shaking their heads.

'We normally build Javanese houses on flat land,' said Tono eventually. 'That is the tradition.' He spoke slowly as if to a child. Only poor people live on the hills. People who can afford it live on the plains.

'A proper Javanese house should be oriented on a north-south axis,' added Tarno. 'Why not find a block in the valley?'

We were in the wrong world for Tono and Tarno. In their Javanese world, north pointed towards the smoking cone of Gunung Merapi and south to Parangtritis and the Indian Ocean. Somewhere in the middle, lay the old city of Yogyakarta, in the centre of which was the Sultan's palace, aligned on that north-south axis. There was spiritual power in this arrangement, but also practical value. The gentle morning winds blew in from the ocean, returning from the mountain in the evening. Aligning one's house to this axis ensured both spiritual harmony and cool breezes. But what to do on the west coast of this strange island, what to do with these strange people who wanted to site their house high on a steep-sloping, west-facing block?

'It's okay,' eventually Tarno relented, perhaps recalling the business imperative and his reason for being there, 'You can build here. The house can be oriented towards the sea and the view.'

Three

It was not long after the visit of Tarno and Tono that we moved east to the Catholic island of Flores. Twelve-hundred metres above sea level and surrounded by peaks and chasms, this was my kind of place. The climate in Bajawa, on Flores, is about as good as it gets – crisp mornings, mild days and balmy evenings. The morning skies were so clear that you could see forever, or so it seemed, the island's volcanic peaks arrayed in a long line that disappeared into a bright blue distance.

I had landed a new job running an Australian-funded aid project. Somehow, we needed to pay for our plans, and this seemed like an interesting and worthwhile way to do it. At that stage we had not managed to sell any land, and there were no buyers in sight – but I was confident we'd figure it out. We had appointed a British teacher and long-term Lombok resident, to run the school. Peter and Ace would be around to keep an eye on things. And Andrew was in charge of The Hill. Plans to build our house would have to be put on hold for a couple of years.

My bright green Toyota hardtop, a somewhat irascible but sturdy thirty-year-old member of the family, was ideal for the rough roads of eastern Indonesia. We had acquired the four-wheel-drive from a Dutchman who had a bamboo furniture business with Ibu Ace, which folded after the riots. Rory was turning three when we packed up the old hardtop and had it driven across Lombok, Sumbawa and Flores. Laras was pregnant with our second child. We stored our joglo, a great pile of teak panels and pillars, in the rented cottage in Baruna Shanti. Then we packed up and moved to the remote town of Bajawa in the mountains of Flores.

We set up house in what we knew to be one of the classiest places in town – for it had tiles on the floor, painted walls, glazed windows, a ceiling, and, wonder-of-wonders, running water. Well, in order to get the last bit sorted we had to find a plumber who serviced the little Sanyo pump that drew water from the tank below the kitchen. He asked if we wanted normal pipes or 'AusAID quality' – presumably filched from a previous Australian project. We opted for the latter, noted the irony, and enjoyed hot and cold running water in the bathroom, though not in the kitchen which operated on a traditional bucket system, with slops and scraps thrown out the back window to the chickens that scrabbled about below.

* * *

Work on The Hill had begun in the months before we moved to Flores. Andrew's Sasak partner, Pak Wir, had negotiated with the Balinese banjar community to acquire their land. At the same time, Andrew found an engineer and got busy designing the road. Laras played her role: she and Wir forged an alliance with the village head. The road would not only provide access to our land but would benefit a much larger community. It would give the village head considerable political kudos. Past the land we had purchased, the walking track continued on up the hill for a further two or three kilometres, eventually meeting a ridge at the top, where it linked to a network of paths. One day Andrew and I walked up that way, passing through a community of scattered homes, emerging about four hours later on the other side of the ridge, at Pusuk on the old Dutch road near the monkey forest. We were in the foothills of Gunung Rinjani. A sizeable community of Sasak villagers was hidden away in those hills. There was even a mosque and a school – but no road, no electricity or phone lines, not even a motorbike track.

Eventually the two plans, the technical and political, came together. Pak Pujo, our Javanese engineer, produced a wonderful fold-out map of the proposed road, illustrating the route and the borders of all the land it would pass through. The map looked very official with a stamp and signature from the village head. Each block was named – and each owner signed off as an agreement to cede the land for the road. Nearly half of these 'signatures' were actually the thumbprints of villagers. Illiterate, they may have been. Stupid, they were not. They knew a good deal when they saw one. The value of their land would be greatly enhanced by the road.

Laras and Wir arranged a *padat karya* to reinforce the community nature of the project and get things started in a traditional way – a way that would be understood and appreciated by the locals. The idea was that everyone – man, woman and child – would pitch in to open the route for the road. To encourage a little goodwill and to ensure that the villagers would not be out of pocket, we provided a modest payment in the form of rice. Our contribution of five million rupiah was equivalent to around a thousand dollars at the time. There was plenty of rice to go around. The day arrived and a crowd of people turned up to help. The aim was to mark the route – not to actually do anything much towards building a road. The atmosphere was festive as the villagers hacked and hoed, scratched and scythed, lifted and carried. Dense clouds of smoke rose from piles of green refuse; packets of steamed rice, fried chicken and veggies were washed down with cold sweet tea; and by the end of the day a six-metre wide route snaked up from the main road towards The Hill. But it wasn't yet a road, more of a would-be road.

***

By the time the real construction of the road began, we were well ensconced on Flores. I became a silent partner in the enterprise, collecting and contributing funds for the road. Andrew adapted his daily exercise routine to the needs of The Hill. He was up there most mornings and most afternoons, inspecting, demanding, complaining, cajoling and generally ensuring that the work was done to his satisfaction. Andrew's jutting jaw, sweating, furrowed brow and belligerent manner must have been a source of amusement to the generally mild-mannered and slow-paced Indonesians. While everyone showed appropriate deference when in his fearsome presence, they no doubt mimicked his strange, foreign ways when his back was turned. But this rather colonial style of management served its purpose. The road was an engineering marvel.

Every trip home to Lombok for Laras and me – for 'home' it had become – became an opportunity to check on progress. And the progress was startling. Rusty-looking excavators shunted about, their orange heads waggling up and down, swinging from side to side, as they grunted and chuffed, cut and filled, dug and tamped, graded and levelled. Heavy yellow dump trucks roared up and down, shifting loads of rock from one place to another. Lines of wiry men with picks and shovels laboured in the sun, while their supervisors smoked and looked on with sleepy eyes. Nets of reinforcing steel were created. Retaining walls were constructed. Teams of women shuffled back and forth with buckets of wet concrete on their heads. And gradually a fine gravel road took shape.

'We are building the drains first,' explained Andrew. 'Water flow is everything. If we don't get that right, the road will wash away with the first big rains.'

I knew this to be true from the state of the road on the next ridge, where we had first bought, to the south-east. So, while the surface of the road was rough, it was edged with beautifully crafted concrete drains, large enough for the storms that would come, and fitted with deep culverts at agreed intervals to slow the flow and prevent erosion.

All of this was new to me and more than a little unnerving. I was more familiar with the science of child development, of classrooms and community, than of storm water flows, concrete and camber. Fortunately, Andrew was in charge and Pak Pujo was always ready with a smile and reassurance that the project was on track. There was much shaking of heads and muttering about the incline of the steepest section, though. Fifteen degrees was as steep as a road should be according to Pujo. An extra S-bend was required to reduce the pitch. But we were unable to obtain permission from the owner of the critical piece of land. The work went ahead anyway. Lombok would have to learn to cope with steep roads.

Life continued in Flores. Rory was enrolled in kindergarten – there was a choice of three: the yellow uniforms, the blue and the green. Yellow was for the children of civil servants, blue for the police, and green for the small Muslim community. Rory joined the greens. And I got on with the job of running an international aid project.

***

Laras returned to Lombok in preparation for the birth of our second child. This was a somewhat fraught business. Communications between Lombok and Flores were not so easy, and it was difficult to arrange flights at short notice, the nearest airport being at Ende, a three-hour drive from Bajawa. Flight schedules and manifests were a mysterious business. Laras's phone call came through at around two in the morning. She was calling from a *wartel* telephone booth outside the doctor's surgery. The doctor had advised Laras that she was ready to give birth and that he would perform a caesarean section the following morning.

'Why?' asked my wife, a question not normally asked of Indonesian doctors.

'Because it will save you and the baby!' replied the doctor in a haughty tone.

'I'm not sure,' said Laras, 'I need to speak to my husband. Can I use your phone?' There was no phone in the office, or so she was informed, and thus it was that at two o'clock in the morning I was woken from a dead sleep by my distraught but ever-sensible wife, who was alone in a public telephone booth, at least a day's travel away, two islands to the west.

Laras was furious. 'I'm going home!' she exclaimed. 'I don't need a caesarean. The baby's not ready. It's not even due for another fortnight. I want a natural birth.'

'I'm on the way,' I said. 'I'll be there as soon as I can.'

By the end of the next day I was there. Laras had abandoned her doctor and registered at a different birthing centre. There was still no sign of the birth and, according to our calculations, everything was on schedule. A week later we checked into the new centre. The birth canal was dilating and it seemed like there was some movement. In fact, there was a great deal of movement: Harry was a lively character in the womb, just as he proved to be in later life. We spent a day resting in a well-appointed room, watching movies on my office laptop while Rory played around at the end of the bed. Laras asked to see the doctor, a different one.

'Nothing's happening,' she said. 'What should we do?'

'I'll put you on a drip,' he said. 'That'll do the trick.'

But it didn't. After two nights and two bottles of whatever it was that was supposed to do the trick, there was no further dilation, no contractions and no sign of the baby.

'I can do a caesarean,' suggested the doctor, hopefully. It seemed to be standard practice for middle-class ladies in birthing centres and was regarded as much more modern and convenient for everyone involved, as opposed to the messy and unpredictable business of natural birth, such as would be normal for village women.

'No,' said my wife firmly. 'I'll go home and come back when the baby is ready.'

Three days later Harry decided that the time had come. It was late in the evening. We rushed back to the birthing centre only to be told that all the rooms were full. 'You can wait in the doctor's office,' suggested the duty nurse helpfully. And Harry was born on the doctor's inspection bench a few hours later.

There are no words really adequate to describe the birth of one's child. Harry was my fourth, so I knew what to expect – but the experience was just as intense as the others. It is a messy, scary, noisy and emotionally exhausting experience. The pain, exhaustion and ultimate victory belong, of course, to the mother. But sharing in that experience is, in equal parts, a joy and a torment for the father. And once it's done you feel like a king.

Harry's older brother, Rory, was born three years earlier in Jakarta, with the colourful chaos of an Indonesian election as a backdrop. I had arranged for birthing music. 'Turn that bloody thing off!' screamed Laras, sweat streaming off her face. Pachelbel's Canon in D has never sounded quite the same since.

So, there was no music for Harry. In the early stages of labour, while Laras collapsed between contractions on the doctor's inspection bench, I sat at his desk tapping away at the keys on my laptop, putting together a report for the Australian Government International Aid Agency. It was the small hours of morning – the darkest time of night. At some point, as the tempo picked up, and Harry's arrival became imminent, the doctor turned up. I hovered about in an agitated state, not really sure what to do, not being particularly helpful, but being there for Laras. In the end, after much commotion, Harry appeared, a slippery little character with a puzzled expression, he looked a bit angry about it all. But once cleaned up, weighed and checked for vitals, he was in Laras's arms and looking for the sustenance of her breast. Harry nuzzled. Laras smiled the most beautiful of smiles. And once again I was in that rather dazed and overwhelmed state. Defeated by love.

We had decided on Harry's name some time ago. We wanted the boys to have names that would work in Australia and in Indonesia, names that would sound familiar in both contexts, reflecting their dual cultural heritage. Rory's full name is Asrory, while Harry's is Asharry; Indonesianised Islamic names that sound familiar enough when shortened. I tried to find the meaning of both, but it's still a bit unclear. Asrory (or Asrori), common enough in Indonesia, may stem from the Arabic for 'night traveller' or 'sacred secret' – both of which sound a little mysterious. Asharry (more commonly transliterated as Asari or Asyari) might mean 'wise' or it might mean 'brave'. Either will do. Both would be good. At any rate, the boys will be known by their short names; Rory, a good red-blooded Celtic name, and Harry, a solid English name and, as his Australian grandfather later noted, '...a nod to his paternal great-grandfather, Harold.'

Harry's afterbirth was rinsed and put aside. It is an old custom in Java – one of those that is fading away with modern attitudes and changing habits – to save and bury the placenta following a birth. Tradition would have it that everyone, male and female, is born with two brothers: the first, Kakang Kawah, the older brother, is the waters that break as the birth commences. The second and younger brother, Adi Ariari, is the placenta that follows. These two are regarded as guardian spirits who look after the child as he or she grows – and throughout life. The placenta should be treated with respect, given a proper burial. While this tradition would have seen Harry's placenta buried in a clay pot beside the entrance to the family home, we had to adapt to our current situation. Laras wasn't too sure of the procedure.

'What should I do?' I asked. 'Are there some words to say? Some kind of ritual we should follow? Where should I bury it?'

'I don't know,' she replied. 'Just bury it somewhere on the block where we will build our home. You choose a spot.'

So, Rory and I headed up to the block we had first bought, the one Andrew had showed me on that first walk up the hill. It was there that we intended to build, though the plan subsequently changed, and Harry's younger brother is buried in a lonely place, an empty plot high on the hill. I figured that it would be smart to choose a spot near the fence at the rear of the block so as to lessen the chances of it later being dug up during construction. Not really knowing what to do, I dug a small hole in the dry clay and, while Rory scampered about, I emptied the contents of a plastic bag – and Harry's little brother slithered into his final resting place without ceremony.

Pak Dullah, a villager who was taking care of the land, appeared as he often did when we visited in those days, and shimmied up one of the lanky palms that stood watch over the land, returning with a couple of fresh green coconuts, which he proceeded to open with a big bush knife and a broad, toothy grin. The subtly flavoured and mildly sweet young coconut water always feels like a blessing on a hot day. Rory and I drank our fill, scraped out some slippery shavings of coconut flesh, thanked Dullah, and headed back down to the valley on a motorbike.

A week or so after this we held a traditional Islamic barbecue to welcome Harry into the world. Actually, it wasn't really traditional or Islamic, though there was an Islamic element, the sacrifice of a goat. Laras found a village haji who knew the trade. The goat, who had been happily munching on grass and leaves in the backyard of our cottage for a few days, suddenly found himself hobbled and held firmly facing Mecca, while the old man muttered verses from the Qur'an and then slit his throat with a splendid sharp blade. There was a bloody, gurgling sort of bleat, the goat slumped, and it was over. The next part followed standard procedure. The carcass was strung up from a mango tree in the corner of the garden. The head was removed – that prize goes to the slaughterer along with the hide and several other choice parts – the goat was gutted, all the gloopy bits collected in bowls to be turned into sate, soup and various local delicacies, and the skin was removed. Three-year-old Rory watched all of this – close-up and with wide intelligent eyes. Now in his twenties, he no longer eats red meat.

At this point, we departed from tradition. Rather than immediately butcher the animal and distribute it in bits to family and community, I had decided to hang it in a coolroom for a couple of days to age the meat. As I had never done anything quite like this before I wasn't too sure how to proceed but, having grown up in rural Tasmania, I had a fair idea. The only coolroom available was the bathroom. Over the next few days, ablutions were performed in the company of a hanging carcass. The traditional Indonesian *mandi* became a macabre dance with a dead goat. This was also a chance to give the meat a good sniff, in case it was starting to turn.

The next part of the process was borrowed from Andrew, who had recently hosted a churrasco barbecue. Andrew had learned about the churrasco from visiting Brazilian tobacco growers. We, in turn, learned from Andrew. After two days of hanging, the meat was deemed ready. With a large bush knife, I managed to quarter it rather cleanly (or so I thought to myself), after which I scored it, rubbed it with salt and garlic, and plunged the lot into a large plastic basin full of vinegar, fresh lime juice, garlic and water. Wine was unavailable – or prohibitively expensive – in Lombok at the time.

The next morning, we lit a fire in a cut-off twenty-four-gallon drum that had been prepared for the purpose. Once the fire had died down and produced a good bed of coals, the marinated goat quarters were skewered and slow-roasted high above the glowing embers. It was a good four hours before we began to think about carving and eating the meat. By this time the guests had arrived, a motley collection of friends from the expatriate community – Italian, Australian, British, Irish, Canadian – our neighbours, who were all Balinese (Baruna Shanti being a Hindu village), and a mix of Sasaks, Javanese and others from the school and surrounds. Harry was passed around, a perfect little bundle of swaddling with a worried face. The drinks flowed freely, and Andrew, who was the acknowledged local expert on churrasco, pronounced the meat to be very good. We all tucked in and, in this way, thanked God and the fates for their providence, welcomed our second child into the family, and introduced Harry to his community.

Then one day, after the excitement had died down, Laras had recovered from the birth and I was collecting my wits and mentally preparing to return to Flores, we decided to drive up our new road. It was Laras's first time. Turning off the bitumen, we headed up the rough gravel road on a step-through motorbike. It took a few attempts to get past the slippery bit at the top of the steep section. But we did it. The feeling is hard to put into words. I had never imagined that I'd be part of a team building roads and infrastructure, a property developer. But there it was. Around two kilometres of road, which wound up into the hills, high above the valley. And now we were driving on it! The Hill looked, and felt, completely different from the seat of a motorbike than it did from the perspective of a walker. I may have been a silent partner, but this road was part mine, and I was proud of it.

* * *

It was sometime after this that we talked to Andrew about nomenclature. Our roads needed naming. The area had already been christened by popular usage among the expatriate community: 'The Hill'. Batu Layar, which translates as 'Sail Rock', is the name of the Sasak village in the valley. At the foot of the hill, on the beach below the Islamic graveyard, is a small Balinese Hindu shrine erected on a rock which, if you exercise a little imagination, looks like a sail. Our main access road became Jalan Bukit Batu Layar. The two side roads were christened Jalan Lembah – Valley Road, and Jalan Semilir. Laras had suggested the poetic Indonesian term, *semilir*, which means 'refreshing breeze' in the old Sanskrit. Not inappropriate.

One morning, armed with the map that Pujo had produced for us, now marked off with blocks and street numbers, Andrew and I walked up the new road. With us we carried a pile of numbered bamboo stakes, which we drove into the ground at appropriate points, to physically indicate the numbering system we had settled on. Following standard convention, heading up the hill, blocks on the left were given odd numbers and those on the right, even numbers. Every now and then we had to skip a few so that the numbering continued to make sense and those on the left didn't get too far ahead of their neighbours on the right. The site, where we would eventually build our home, and where Laras performed that little ceremony, now has an address: Jalan Lembah, number twelve.

All of this was fine, until Andrew insisted that the block on which he intended to build should be Jalan Semilir, number nine. Apparently, the number nine has a special significance in the Feng Shui system, which Andrew must have picked up from his Chinese employers. It signifies high attainment, accomplishment, and is likely to bring good luck and prosperity to the household. Not a bad thing, I thought.

There didn't seem to be much to argue about. And so it is that, as you head up Jalan Semilir, the numbering on the left of the street proceeds in an idiosyncratic manner: one, three, nine, five, seven, eleven ... and so on.

'I do think we have some privileges as the pioneers of The Hill, don't you, Mark?' he said, his jaw jutting out, ready for a fight. 'If I want to have the number nine, I'll jolly well have it!'

Four

Our plans to build a house remained on hold while I got busy with my paid work and we attended to our small family. The years passed by without further contact with Tarno, the Javanese joglo expert and timber merchant who was still storing our teak panels and pillars. We got on with our lives in Flores and then Tasmania and Sulawesi. Lombok remained the anchor point.

Occasionally I would mention this to Laras. 'Shouldn't we have some sort of written contract with Pak Tarno for storing our stuff?' I would ask. 'What if he forgets about us? What if he sells it to another customer? We haven't been in touch for ages.'

'Don't worry about it,' Laras would laugh, dismissing my concerns as those of a foreigner, one who doesn't fully appreciate the Javanese way of doing things. 'He's fine, our stuff is fine. Don't worry.' And she was right – up to a point.

In 2006 a major earthquake flattened the southern part of Yogya, levelling schools, hotels and government offices – and destroying the old home of Laras's grandfather. By this time, we were living in Makassar. Some pieces from our carefully inventoried but loosely stored pieces of limasan were damaged. I visited Yogya for work and called in to see Pak Tarno.

'Yes, there is some damage,' he explained, showing me around the jumbled collection of furniture, carved panels, window frames and stacked timber. 'But your pieces are mainly still intact.'

Another couple of years passed. Then, as we started to formalise our plans with Agus and Rani, the local engineer-architect team, we renewed our contact with Tarno. Once again, I visited the businessman in his Yogya home and showroom.

'It's time to get serious,' I said, as we sat together over cups of thick coffee and kretek cigarettes in his little anteroom. 'We need all the pieces measured up so our architect can design the home around them. Then we need to figure out what else we need.'

Laras and I picked out a beautiful old three-piece panel for the front of the house. The *gebyok*, a formal house frontage, stood about two and a half metres tall and about six metres wide. It was old carved teak from Tuban and included wide folding doors in the centre and matching carved windows to each side. It was solid; thick, broad timber pieces, marked with an adze, rubbed smooth with age. Carved wooden latticework, the designs echoed a pre-Islamic culture.

'I can make matching pieces to make it wider', explained Pak Tarno. 'We will use old recycled teak. The carving will be identical. This way you can make it fit your design for the house.' We had already settled on a standard limasan design, a rectangular shape, fourteen by ten metres.

The old timbers spoke to me there in that dusty workshop. They spoke of age and tradition, of layered love, of memories lost and of lives now passed. The rough silky feel of the dry timber, the raw smell of sawdust and resin, the intricate designs of the carved panels, all of this combined to seduce me. It was impossible not to smile.

A fortnight later the scale drawings arrived in Lombok.

Altogether, there were about thirty individual pieces. We looked at them together with Agus and Rani, and over the weeks that followed, the design took shape. I have harboured a love of architecture since childhood. As a boy I would amuse myself making maps and designs, sketching dream houses, or – with my brothers – building cities of sand, or forts, cubbies and treehouses of discarded timber, construction equipment and bush materials. Architecture is a marriage of art and functionality, of dreams and reality. Unfortunately, my maths education was a mess and, without decent scores, I decided I would have to put aside my aspirations.

My early sketches got a major makeover. My initial thinking was simple. Take the internal pillars and roof structure of the limasan form and put them on the second floor, leaving the external cladding, the old carved gebyok panels, on the ground floor. This way we get the traditional forms, but adapted for modern living. The top floor could be like an open-sided *pendopo* pavilion. This would let in light and fresh air, while not easily letting in burglars or uninvited guests, who would need to enter in the normal way through lockable doors on the ground floor. This way, I reasoned, we get reasonable security, at the same time as a breezy, open-to-sky lifestyle.

All good, but when Rani appeared sometime later with the designs – including front elevations – there was one major difference. In my version, the ground floor was exactly the same height as the second floor: I had simply transposed the internal structure to the second storey. In Rani's version, the ground floor was substantially taller than the second storey – leaving out the elaborate roof structure, which sits on top of it all. What she had done, I now realise, was apply the 'golden ratio', making the height of the second story approximately sixty per cent that for the ground floor. What a marvellous thing! The golden ratio, the divine proportion, formulated by Euclid nearly two and half thousand years ago in Greece, used in the design of sculptures in the Parthenon, and described by the German mathematician, Kepler, in the early seventeenth century as 'a precious jewel', present throughout nature, related to phi, to the Fibonacci sequence, and now appearing in the design of our house in Lombok. No doubt Rani learned this in first-year architecture, I think to myself. And this is the very reason we hired a professional.

Five

The day begins early. It is the first day of the Islamic month of Ramadan. We wake at around four o'clock for the pre-dawn meal of *sahur*. This is a family time. After a light meal, plenty of water to drink, and having performed the ritual washing known as *wudhu*, we prepare for the first round of prayers. During Ramadan, Muslims fast each day from dawn until dusk, abstaining from food and drink, from smoking, from sex and from strong emotions or negative thoughts during the daylight hours.

Little prayer mats are spread out facing westwards toward Mecca. Rory, now nine years old, joins us, along with Harry who turned six last month. Laras dons her prayer gear, becoming a slightly different person in the process. Like the boys, I wear a simple, Javanese-style sarong. A loop of light checked cotton, I step into it, hitching it up and folding it tight around my waist in a practiced motion. Practical wear for the tropics. We stand in a row facing the dark, and Laras asks Rory to kick things off with the '*komat*'. He has been learning the words at school and in occasional Qur'anic lessons at home. The boys giggle self-consciously, elbowing one another, tousling and bickering quietly in an irritating, but good-natured, brotherly kind of way: whose turn is it, who gets the best prayer mat, who gets the prime position next to Mum? Eventually with a little gentle coaxing they settle down. Rory raises his hands after a brief silence, his palms facing inwards beside his head he begins to recite.

Allahuakbar Allahuakbar ... Ashaduanlailaahaillallah ...
Ashaduanlamuhammadarrasulullah ...
Hayya'alassholati Hayya'alalfallah ... Qod'komatissholati
Qod'komatissholah ...
Allahuakbar Allahuakbar ... Laailaahaillallah ...

God is great, God is great ... I bear witness that there is no
    god but God...
I bear witness that Muhammad is the Messenger of God ...
Come to pray. Come to success ... Stand for prayer. Stand
    for prayer ...
God is great. God is great ... There is no god but God ...

Laras takes the lead then, acting as imam, and begins to recite the Qur'anic verses that follow. It should, perhaps, be my job as the senior male, but I am happy that she does it. I haven't learned enough of the tongue-twisting liturgical Arabic to do it myself anyway. And maybe our practice can serve as a modest, private protest against the hegemony of men in this harsh, dry desert religion, translated as it is here into the routines of an ethnically mixed family in the moist and fecund tropics. There is a larger irony in this, too: like Jesus before him, the Prophet Muhammad was a revolutionary, a social reformer. And a big part of his mission was to improve the lot of women. The way in which the oppression of women that characterised the medieval cultures of the Arab Peninsular has become calcified, enshrined in Islamic law, Islamic practice, and Islamic politics is a cruel irony, a testimony to the power of misogyny – and the misuse of religion for political ends.

Twice we stand, bow, stand, kneel, prostrate, and stand again. Laras recites the verses, and we join in with a choral *'Amin!'* at appropriate times, silently mouthing the prayers at others. For me this is a form of yoga, of meditation in movement. My mind drifts in and out, a cock crows and a distant dog barks in the dawning darkness. I centre on the little ritual, pushing worldly cares aside, surrendering to something greater, something ineffable and beyond, surrendering the ego in some way to my part in a community, in a history, and in this gentle little congregation of four.

The brief ritual concludes with the four of us sitting on our floor mats, exchanging the traditional blessing in Arabic, *Assalamu'alaikum warahmatullahi wabarakatuh*, 'Peace be upon you,' 'And with you.' Hands are clasped and raised to the forehead in a chaste familial kiss. Harry rolls onto the floor and hugs his mum. 'I'm tired!' he says.

As usual, we all retire for a couple more hours of fitful sleep before waking again and getting on with the normal business of the day. Life goes on in the fasting month – albeit at a slower pace than usual. Each year I ask myself why. Why do I fast? Why do I deny myself the regular nutrition – and especially the hydration – necessary for healthy functioning? Why do I mess with my sleep routines for an adopted religious duty? Why do I bother with these occasional prayers to a silent God? With a medieval practice that sits at odds with a rational worldview? Why? And each year

I find the same answer. The change of pace, a sort of gear shift brought about by fasting, creates space in a busy life for reflection. It is both a private and an intensely communal activity. It brings the family together. Even without all the prayer and ritual, for a time it shifts the focus away from the mundane; reorienting life, tilting the axis just a little. Like the Christian month of Lent, the Catholic absolution, Ramadan offers a spiritual cleansing. The physical abstinence, the fasting and change of pace, leave the skin feeling dry and brittle, the mind empty, and the heart open.

**

The Islamic calendar follows a lunar cycle and each year its festivals and events move forward around eleven days on the regular calendar. This year, the month of Ramadan falls in September. In Lombok it is hot and dry, the peak season for tourism. The industry has crept back since those riots eight years ago. In July and August, Senggigi's scruffy main drag fills with German backpackers and Dutch package tourists, Australian retirees and Malaysian students – all scouting for bargains, sniffing out a decent restaurant, looking for some action. The hawkers hawk, the beggars smile, and the beach boys are at the top of their game. 'Souvenir, Mister?' 'Pearls, Mister?' 'Massage?' 'Transport?' 'Last price, Mister. Special for you!' 'Need a friend, Mister?' 'You look, just looking, looking …'

Meanwhile, Ramadan is a time for reflection, a time for spiritual concerns. Religious music, recorded sermons and live chanting are broadcast from loudspeakers, echoing around the valleys from around three in the morning and at intervals during the day. At night, young men let off fireworks and make a racket, mainly for fun, but ostensibly to remind the faithful to wake for prayer. The mosques and prayer houses fill with men in checked sarongs and black rimless *peci* or lacy white skull caps. The women cloak themselves in their white prayer robes. Together they sit on tiled floors and prayer mats, men at the front, women at the rear, rocking back and forth, rhythmically swaying, chanting long into the evening. There is a strange beauty in this. The *taraweeh* is a ritual, a repetitive trance-like prayer, meditative in a communal way.

The melancholic *adzan* calls the faithful to prayer five times a day. *'Allahuakbar, Allahuakbar!'* 'God is great, God is great!' Sung in a wailing minor key, like an echo of the Arabian deserts, for pious Muslims this is the most beautiful sound in the world. For the less pious, including many non-Muslims and most of Lombok's expatriate community, it is an imposition, an expression of arrogance, insensitivity and intolerance. For a very small minority of radical Islamists it has become a war cry – and for many Westerners the sound has become associated with an alien terror, a foreign evil that stalks their suburbs, entering their family homes accompanied by images of violence in the nightly news.

For me, the call to prayer is at once familiar and foreign, comforting and unsettling. It is an invitation to surrender.

Six

September is the tail end of the long dry season in Lombok; the turn of the seasons brings clear skies and dry cooling breezes. This month heralds the rains. The air is pregnant, heavy with promise. But the monsoon winds have not yet arrived. The nights are cool. The land is dry and parched, waiting, waiting for the rain. Grassfires sometimes blacken the hills, floating black sooty flakes into the air and turning the sun an evil red.

Six years have passed since Harry's birth. A new contract allows me to work in Lombok with routine trips to Jakarta. Now is the time to build our Indonesian home. Over recent years, as the hill began to take shape with terracing, vetiver grass and Singapore daisy to shore up the banks, we had decided to build not on the original block, where Harry's mythical little brother, Adi Ariari, is now buried, but on a different block nestled in a small valley on the lower slopes. The higher blocks along the top ridge, with their huge views, open aspects and wide airiness, are becoming quite valuable. Andrew has begun selling land. If we can sell our top blocks at a good price, I reason, we can recoup our costs for the road and put some aside for building a house. Earnings from the education consulting work can be used for future needs. And we have begun to feel that the lower site, while less spectacular, will make a better place for a home.

The site consists of two blocks, one on each side of a seasonal stream, the same one across which I looked with Andrew when he first introduced us to the hill on those high slopes. Halfway across our block, the stream cuts through a rocky shelf and curls around the base of a huge, tangled banyan fig tree. Beneath a screen of dangling aerial roots, an ancient-looking well is cradled in the tree's gnarled ground roots. A flat rock has been positioned above the well, a place for washing and perhaps prayer. The place smells of tradition, of mystery and hidden meanings: a little dank in the perpetual shade of the banyan tree, dim beneath the remnant forest giants that line the stream with their buttressed roots and attendant ferns.

* * *

On Saturday, I meet Ibu Rani and Pak Agus by the main road. It is about ten o'clock. The day is already heating up. The world is slowing down. I want to visit our proposed house site with Rani and Agus, our architect and project manager. And I want to do so before it gets too hot and I get too thirsty. Ibu Rani is very pregnant but seemed keen to come along when we discussed the plan at our cottage yesterday. As Hindus, they are not fasting. A friend joins us out of curiosity. Diane is an Australian teacher who works at Sekolah Nusa Alam, the school we established with Peter and Ace.

A sandy path takes us along a narrow lane between the buildings that line the main road, just wide enough for a motorbike between high walls. Emerging into sunlight from behind the concrete clad buildings, we walk across flat coastal land through dry fields dotted with coconut palms and scrubby cashew-nut trees to a palm roofed cottage about a kilometre back from the road. A collection of rough stilted structures sits comfortably beneath tall trees on a swept dirt area at the base of the hill. The little complex is bounded by the curve of a dry stream bend. We stop for a brief chat with the inhabitants. A wizened old woman sits on her *barugaq*, a wooden-framed, open-sided gazebo-like shelter with a thatched grass roof and split-bamboo flooring. A younger man looks up from the motorbike he is washing. We are met with a familiar Sasak attitude: a mix of reserved warmth and openness, friendly curiosity hedged with a wary caution, slightly standoffish. Is it fear or jealousy, I wonder? But we know the occupants. This is the cottage of Rawisa's mother. Rawisa, who has done some work for us in the past, leaves his motorbike, we shake hands and he invites us to sit on the barugaq, where his mother is sorting through a round woven tray of dried corn kernels. The black ones are cast aside, thrown to the chickens that scratch about below. On another occasion I might have stopped for a chat and rolled a smoke from Rawisa's sack of local tobacco. But not today. Not in the fasting month.

We take our leave and cross the dry creek bed, strewn with yellowed bamboo leaves and household rubbish, the marginal detritus of a modern world; little plastic sachets emptied of their single-use shampoo or washing powder, crushed cigarette packets, individual biscuit wrappers and empty plastic water bottles. Diane sniffs and raises an eyebrow; a silent question. 'Yep,' I nod in reply. A whiff of human shit sits heavy on the dry air, striking a dull off-key note in the harmony of this rustic idyll: a reminder of poverty and the day-to-day reality it represents for these people.

Across the creek, the track climbs through a grove of bamboo, massive towering clumps of green, a little menacing in appearance as if they harbour spiders and snakes, which they probably do, and perhaps evil spirits and mischievous *jinn* as suspected by the locals. From there it is a scramble up over knotted roots to a rocky outcrop and a ridge path which takes us several hundred metres further up to the site. Rani puffs and pants as we make the climb, Agus attentive by her side. We could have driven up the new road and walked down the path which extends into the valley where we have decided to build – but I wanted to explain our longer-term plans to develop the valley and ridge areas. I wanted Rani and Agus to share our larger vision. It is a hot climb, but Rani insisted on accompanying us.

After pushing past a living fence and onto a terrace we scramble through a mess of banten and wild acacia saplings up to a second, and wider, terrace. This is where we propose to build our family home. This is where the earth was opened in that little ceremony two months ago, the wound now lost amongst tangled lantana weeds, the chicken blood, water and flowers swallowed by the dry earth, scattered by the winds. Ibu Rani has stopped to sit and rest on the lower terrace. I stand with my friend, Diane, on the rim of the higher terrace. She has a sensible head on her shoulders. I value her thoughts. As we catch our breath and take in the view, I start to explain, to map out the vision I have in my head, as I did with my wife a few months earlier.

'We are standing on what will be the front room of our home,' I begin. 'Below us will be the pool.' Halfway up the slope from the lower terrace is a ledge about three meters wide. 'And maybe we'll put a tennis court on the bottom terrace.'

'You don't want much, do you, Mark?' laughs Diane.

'Well, we don't know if there's enough space for a tennis court yet,' I reply, a little chastened. 'We'll see.'

Agus joins us, leaving Rani to rest below. I begin again to explain what I have in mind, pointing out various features and where I think the house and cottages will be. Agus listens attentively, occasionally prompting me with questions. The two blocks form a combined space of a little over eighty *are* in the locally used metric measure. One are is a hundred square metres, so the block is nearly a hectare; a large, slightly irregular square shape intersected by the creek. The space is somewhat closed in, but expansive internally, with a row of large *duwet* trees at the top of the block along the northern border, the seasonal stream running through the middle with its remnant rainforest, planted trees and huge stands of bamboo, and the southern and western borders below us edged with a mix of palms, wild mangos and banten. In my mind, and on sketch maps, I have divided the space into a number of outdoor rooms to be defined with hedges, buildings, paths and natural features. The land has a beautiful aspect and retains the ocean and valley views. While it lacks some of the drama of the high blocks, we have decided that it more than makes up for that with character; a private world, a little pocket of forest and terraced building sites held in the crook of the hill.

* * *

We have met several times with Rani and Agus over the year, usually sitting around the big table in our little garden in Baruna Shanti, sketches, photographs, concept designs, project workplans and contract documents strewn about. This is the third time we have visited the site together.

We plan to adopt sustainable housing principles; environmentally sustainable, economically sustainable, and sustainable in social and cultural terms. In sympathy with Laras's background we want a Javanese vernacular, rustic, village-style and at the same time modern and bright. Finally, we want green landscaping, a mix of productive and decorative planting that preserves existing trees and creates a strong link between the built and the natural environments.

These ideas have been garnered from afar, accumulating, gathering, gestating, for a long, long time – at least since the time we started acquiring the joglo and limasan materials in Yogyakarta, nearly ten years ago. Probably much longer. In the interim, I have been poring over glossy coffee table books and reading up on sustainable architecture and traditional Indonesian constructions. Laras and I have visited boutique hotels, contemporary villas and colonial mansions; Balinese hill resorts, Javanese palaces and village cottages; always observing, always taking photographs and sketching out progressively more meaningful concepts. I have been to floating villages and Bugis stilt homes in Sulawesi, fret-worked Malay bungalows in Aceh and North Sumatra, mossy Javanese compounds in Yogyakarta and Solo, rows of ornate high-roofed houses and rice barns in the mountains of Tana Toraja and Lake Toba, thatched villages in Lombok, Flores and Timor, timber mosques, shingled hovels, mansions and longhouses in Kalimantan, colonial pubs and Chinese temples in Singapore, planters' bungalows in the highlands of Java and Malaysia, teak palaces, gold-clad Buddhist temples and peaked Thai homes in

Bangkok and Chiang Mai. French villas and monasteries in Laos. Long days and late nights spent in conversation, exploring ideas, mapping out thoughts. This is to be a one-off, a family home that expresses everything we value and believe in. A home that belongs. It is to be an expression of who we are, a work of art, a work of the heart, a space for living and for loving.

* * *

Ibu Rani joins us on the rough terrace and together we look at the site maps and concept designs she has prepared over the last month or so. Pak Agus paces about with a tape measure, scanning the site with a practiced eye, while I talk him through the concept again.

'Yep, we can do this!' he says at one point and, once again, I get the feeling that we are in this together.

Just as we prepare to leave, a slightly built Sasak man of indeterminate age emerges from the scrub across the creek. Pak Mobin has lived his entire life on this land. As *penyakap*, or tenant farmer, he relies on our patronage to stay on with his family; his wife, *Inaq* Idah, two teenage sons, a disabled daughter who looks about fifteen and a younger daughter, maybe twelve years old. Having twice been relocated to different corners of the blocks, to make way for the machines which moved in to level and reshape the land on which he has spent his life, Pak Mobin now lives with his family in a two-room shack on the slopes above the creek just to the south of our site. Conversations with Pak Mobin are typically brief, consisting of congenial two- or three-word exchanges. Bahasa Indonesia is a second language for both of us. Mobin is a man of few words, but when he does speak it is usually in Sasak language – or Arabic for prayer.

'*Selamat siang, Pak!*' 'Good day, sir!' I call as I catch sight of his stooped figure loping up the hill towards us. He would no doubt doff his hat, if he had one. But, as things are, he bows a little to show deference and in the same slight movement nods to express approval and familiarity.

'*Sama-sama, Pak.*' 'Same to you, sir,' he responds with a well-weathered croak and a quizzical smile. For some reason, Mobin seems to find these conversations with me, a foreigner, a never-ending novelty, a source of great amusement.

'Will you be joining our work crew?' I ask. 'And the boys? Inaq Idah?'

'*Mudah-mudahan!*' 'With any luck!' he laughs.

Pak Mobin and his family are an asset. It is a very feudal arrangement, one with which I am not particularly comfortable. But it is what it is. The boys should surely be at school, completing their secondary education – but they are not. They are barely literate, and at home, members of the temporary labour force upon which we will rely to build our home. Both are in the process of getting married and will, no doubt, soon be producing another generation. Taking our leave of Pak Mobin, we retrace our steps. Heading back down the hill, I try to explain the broader plan to Pak Agus.

'Eventually,' I say, 'we plan to build a road up the valley here.' We walk together down the grassy slope, kicking through dusty banten leaves, and I try to paint the picture. 'One day there will be villas along this ridge, swimming pools, green lawns. The views are superb.'

'Let's just build your house first,' Agus smiles, exchanging a quick look, a look that might just be a wink, with Ibu Rani.

'Sure,' I agree, returning the smile. And this is what we do.

Seven

The construction begins. It is six or seven months since we met Agus and Rani, five months since we signed the contract, two months since that little ceremony to break the earth. The first task is to put together a work crew. First there is Eddy, a tall guy with a long face, a friendly smile and sleepy eyes, he wears his long black hair tied back in a ponytail. Eddy is to be the overseer, Agus' eyes and ears on site. He looks a bit too gentle for this role, I think. Then comes Pak Dewa. A heavy-set Balinese man from up the west coast, Dewa will take care of the electrical and plumbing installations.

Dedy, a tightly built and energetic Sasak lad from the village, is to have the job of keeping the records: workers' daily attendance, material deliveries, tools and equipment inventories. Dedy is the younger brother of Ibu Sri who helps us at home and was part of the buka bumi ceremony. Dedy will watch the clock, marking off the hours for starting work, lunch breaks and knock-off time, by tapping out a familiar tattoo on a hollowed bamboo log that will hang from the corner of the tool shed. Laras's brother, Mas Karno, will also keep an eye on things, checking that quantities are as stated on delivery slips and that prices are in line with the market. Karno is a soldier and commands some respect among the villagers. His wife, Bu Rina, will check the weekly accounts, matching receipts and attendance records with payments. At the end of the line in this low-trust environment, it is safest to have a close family member checking the books.

'It's not so much that everyone is a crook, that people are dodgy,' I said to Laras when we were setting this up. 'It's that the entire system is dodgy, isn't it? Trust is established in societies with strong governance, with consistent laws and independent courts, with credible media, with checks and balances. Indonesia has a way to go to achieve that.'

'Yep,' she replied, in a sad and resigned tone, 'and meanwhile, we'll keep a close eye on the books.'

There are basically two kinds of tradesmen, *tukang batu,* or stone masons, stringy-looking middle-aged men who will handle the concreting, bricklaying, masonry, plastering and tiling, and *tukang kayu,* or carpenters, who will handle all the woodwork. With the exception of the timberwork from Yogya, everything will be constructed on site – and nearly everything from local materials. Then come the unskilled workers, lots of them, local Sasak villagers, men and women. Everything is done by hand. Pak Mobin and his family will join.

As the crew is assembled and roles are assigned, the work begins.

* * *

A couple of weeks pass, and I arrive back from a work trip to Jakarta. The hill looks dry, the earth is bare. The terraces have been cleared and raked level. Foundations are pegged out and marked with plastic raffia twine to the south of the shed for the joglo, and across the valley on the western terrace for the main house. In the corner of the site, an essential but frequently overlooked item, a drop toilet, has been constructed. A simple squat design surrounded by a low plaited bamboo wall for the sake of modesty.

Agus looks business-like as he greets me with a wave, walking across from the western terrace. Eddy hovers in the background. Agus joins me in front of the shed, spreading his arms in an all-encompassing sort of way, 'Well, we've begun!' he smiles, somewhat superfluously.

I am unable to keep the smile from own face as I survey the scene. It is mid-afternoon. Hot. We sit together on the bench. The crew is split into two groups, one on the western terrace and one here on the eastern side. About twenty workers are busy with picks and shovels, sledgehammers to break up the larger rocks, crowbars to pry them out of the hard earth, buckets and barrows to cart the dirt away. Women trudge back and forth in an orderly row, carrying broken rocks and buckets of dirt on their towelled heads, as if bearing offerings to the temples. Piles of rocks rise on the side. A series of trenches is taking shape where foundations known as *cakar ayam* (chicken feet) are to be constructed. In this way, the outlines of the buildings are beginning to take shape.

'The work is a bit slow in the fasting month,' says Agus. 'They get a bit sluggish in the afternoons, so we don't insist on a full day.'

'Well, it looks good to me,' I respond, still smiling.

'The rocks will be used in the walls,' he explains, 'the soil as landfill.'

'Don't let them touch the rocks and boulders from the creek,' I remind him, pointing below. 'We want to keep the creek as a natural feature. And we don't want to create erosion.'

'Don't worry!' Agus assures me. 'I haven't forgotten.'

'We've started on the ground tanks,' he continues. 'I've pegged them out as we agreed.' The rectangular pits are only just beginning to take shape, one in the centre of each house. The plan is to create underground water storage tanks beneath the joglo and the main house. Like dark, subterranean swimming pools hidden beneath the floor, each will hold about seventy-five cubic metres of water, for domestic use.

'You have to sort out your water,' Andrew was fond of reminding me. 'Water is everything!'

Water is an issue on The Hill. It is an issue everywhere. Our plan is to harvest rainwater. From various sources I gathered that we should allocate between two and three cubic metres a day for usage. With smart fittings, low pressure, and the addition of a system for recycling wastewater, I figured we could budget on an average of two and a half cubic metres per day for the entire complex.

The problem is that most of the rain falls in a six-month period between October and March. Months can pass in the dry season without a drop. A good rainfall could fill the tanks in a day or two, while in the dry season, at an average of two and a half cubic metres usage a day, we will run dry in a couple of months. Storage of around a hundred and fifty cubic metres will go a long way to ensuring a self-sufficient supply, but we will need a bore to supplement the rainwater supply. Building the huge tanks underground will hopefully ensure that the water doesn't go bad in storage, keeping it away from light and heat. It might also help cool the houses above.

Standing there and watching as sweaty men swing picks and shovel dirt, I reflect on what could go wrong. Among the many potential disasters, what if an earthquake cracks the tanks and the water leaks away? What if my calculations are out and there is not enough storage – or too much? What if the water is too warm and it turns green in storage? What if we don't strike water in the valley? What if?

But it is not so hard to push these thoughts aside in the afternoon sun. Pak Agus looks confident and we are committed now. We will just have to make it work!

**

This evening we host a communal fast-breaking event on the site. This is the last week of the fast. The full moon has long passed. The Night of Power must be soon – or is it tonight? To the faithful, this is the most powerful, the most holy, of all nights. It commemorates the night when the first verses of the Qu'ran were revealed to a fearful Prophet. When, camped out in a lonely mountain cave near seventh-century Mecca, Muhammad heard those words: 'Read, read, read!' and the whole thing began. The moon is waning, a thin crescent already visible with early stars over the ocean. Little bats swoop about chasing insects, and the sun drops low in the west and begins to colour the sky, briefly painting the clouds in pale brassy tints and spreading a sparkling sheen across the ocean.

According to the calendar, the sun will set at two minutes to six, signalling the time for the faithful to break their fast. Big blue tarpaulins have been spread out on the grassy terrace above the house site. The guests begin to arrive at around five thirty, all scrubbed up and dressed in fine clothes, the men in long-sleeved batik shirts and sarongs, the women in colourful headscarves and gowns. In addition to the work crew, we have invited a number of tenant farmers from the valley along with teachers and staff from the village school that we have been supporting up the hill at Duduk Atas. Together with family members and our own house staff, I count about sixty gathered in time for the sunset.

The guests sit cross-legged on the ground, forming a wide semi-circle around the fringes of the terrace. Young and old, men and women, adults and children, all sit quietly, chatting about the mundane, or silently waiting for the sun to set behind Bali's Gunung Agung. The sun drops below the island and a minute or two later we hear the call to prayer drifting up from the valley on clean, cooling air. Cups of water are handed out, together with dates and sweet treats. The mood shifts a little as thirsts are quenched and appetites appeased. Smiles appear on weathered faces and cigarettes are passed between the men, filling the air with fragrant clove scented smoke.

Then, without any signal I can see, people begin to assemble in rows on the tarpaulin. They face west towards the dying embers of the setting sun, west to a distant imagined Mecca. Sandals are left at the edge, men stand at the front, women at the rear. A young man introduces the prayer, calling the faithful in formal Arabic, half-sung, half-spoken. People shuffle forward, filling the spaces, the elderly and more senior take their places at the front, the younger boys at the rear. One of the older men of the village acts as imam. Standing in front of the group facing west, a prayer mat spread before him, he begins the recitation. The congregation follows, half a heartbeat behind; three rounds of standing, bowing, prostrating as prescribed for the sunset prayers. At the conclusion, all sit cross-legged, palms faced upwards in supplication. A meditative communal chant gathers momentum, the worshippers swaying slightly in unison:

La ilalla, illallah, La ilalla, illallah, La ilalla, illallah, La ilalla, illallah, La ilalla, illallah ...
There is no god, but God, no god but God ...

Time passes, perhaps five minutes, perhaps more, and eventually the chanting comes to an end. A few more verses are recited to wrap up proceedings and then, one by one, the worshippers rise, reclaim their sandals, and move off. Boxed meals are handed out with bottled water. People sit about in groups on the grass, eating the steamed rice, fried chicken, spiced water spinach, soy-bean cake and sweet meats. Fingers move from food to mouth, the meal consumed with a quiet joy, an act of communal reverence, relaxed but serious. Food is a serious matter.

The men smoke and Pak Karno stands to make a brief speech. His experience commanding a squad of soldiers has given him confidence and an easy authority to call on when required.

'We gather today,' he says, 'to break our fast together, to pray together, and to strengthen our bonds as a community.'

'*Amin!*' – 'So be it!' – a number of the guests respond.

The gist of the speech that follows is that all have a role to play as members of a community. Those with greater wealth share with others. Loyalty and honesty are expected in return. Karno looks at me. 'Do you want to say something?' he asks. Rising hesitantly, I launch into a half-prepared speech; words I have used on other occasions and in other places, adapted to each context, but carrying the same basic message.

'*Assalamu'alaikum warahmatullahi wabarakatuh,*' I begin. 'May the peace, mercy, and blessings of Allah be with us all.'

'I look a little different. I come from a different place. I speak a different language,' I continue in Indonesian, 'but I am not so different from you all. We are all the same before God. We all want the same things: peace, health and prosperity for our families. I hope you will accept me and my family as members of your community.'

At this there are grunts and nods of approval. Laras has arranged packages of basic foodstuffs for all the guests – rice, sugar, noodles, salt, biscuits, cooking oil – and envelopes containing money for workers. With a few words to explain the purpose of the gifts, who gets what and why – one package per family – she hands over to her sister, Aisyah, and brother, Karno, to give out the offerings. As each receives his or her gift, with smiles and muttered thank-yous, we shake hands and the guests take their leave, prayer shawls hitched up, cigarettes alight, some clamber aboard motorbikes and putter off up the hill, others walk. Within a few minutes we are left with the silence, left to

clean up the debris, fold up the tarpaulins and make our own way
back down the valley.

THE SEASON
OF THE WIND

One

As the land heats up in the morning, so the air heats up with it – and rises, drawing cooler air in from the seas to the south and west, creating an onshore sea breeze. In the early evening the reverse occurs. Cool, dry air from the hills funnels down the valleys, drawn back out to the sea as the land cools down. This is the wind that takes the fishing fleet out for the night. Little dugout outrigger canoes, each with a lonely fisherman and a single triangular sail, the boats sail each night to the offshore sandbanks and fishing grounds that lie far out in the wide bay south of Senggigi. There they spend the night, between the west coast of Lombok, the southern arc of Sekotong, and the Balinese islands of Nusa Penida. Their pressure lamps attract the fish and ward off the darkness, creating a picture in the night, clusters of bright stars on the surface of the dark sea. In the calm, dawning light the fleet returns with a light onshore breeze, the colourful sails a flock of butterflies spread across the early blue.

The festival of Idul Fitri marks the end of the month of Ramadan, the end of the fast, and the start of a new month. This year, for no particular reason, the solar and lunar calendars align: the final day of Ramadan is, coincidentally, the final day of September. Idul Fitri falls on October 1st. The last night of the fast is alive with the sounds of chanting from the mosques, and the whoop and whistle and crash of fireworks.

Like the old Balinese and Javanese calendars, the Islamic calendar, its months and festivals, are determined by the phases of the moon. This is fine, except for the fact that the two major Islamic organisations in Indonesia differ in their methods to determine the appearance of the new moon, signalling the start of a new month and, importantly, the day on which Idul Fitri is to be celebrated. The reformist Muhammadiyah uses a scientific method to calculate the date years in advance. The traditionalist Nahdlatul Ulama uses, of course, a traditional method. This involves sending wise men out to various vantage points to stare into the night sky and report back on the state of the moon. This method remains mysterious, but I am told that a thread of cotton is sometimes involved. As a result, Nahdlatul Ulama followers don't quite know when the festival is to be celebrated until a day or two before. In some years the two groups celebrate on different days, which can give rise to tensions with one lot still fasting, while the other holds a great feast. Fortunately, this year the two have agreed on the same date.

Early in the morning, the cottage is already busy. Laras rouses the boys, readying herself for the day and making sure that everyone is scrubbed up, squeaky clean and dressed for the morning prayers – me included. Idul Fitri is a big day. Something like an Islamic Christmas. It begins with communal prayers. This year we have decided not to make the annual trip home to celebrate with Laras's family in Yogyakarta. Instead we head down to the mosque in Montong, near our school. Like most mosques in Lombok, this one is not quite finished. The construction seems to go on and on for ever, one brick, one tile, one pot of paint at a time, as the funds – mostly collected from congregations and passers-by – trickle in. Notwithstanding this, the main, central area is smart, a large square of shiny, tiled floor, this morning scattered with prayer mats all facing towards the western wall. The dominant colours are white and lime green – for some reason the latter is symbolic of Muslim piety – broken here and there by gold and blue trim.

By the time we get there, the place is already filling with worshippers. I take the boys with me, little *peci* caps and prayer mats slung over their shoulders. We weave our way through the throng of men, at various stages of standing, bowing, or sitting quietly, cross-legged and waiting for the main event. Laras has taken the bare concrete stairs at the side to a mezzanine floor where the women and girls gather like a flock of geese in their lacy-white, head-to-toe prayer shawls. Towards the front of the ground floor I spot Peter. We find a space to sit beside him. The atmosphere is cool and pleasant. A subdued sense of joy is in the air, the celebratory mood tempered by reverence but evident in the quiet smiles, handshakes and nodded greetings that wash around us.

After the worship – communal prayers followed by a lengthy sermon and a report from the committee on funds collected for the mosque – we navigate the crowds, reclaim our sandals from by the front door, and leave, tipping a lad who has been keeping an eye on them for us. I spot Laras, already out front on the street chatting to some local women. Peter takes me aside.

'Would you like to join us?' he asks. 'We have some interesting guests for breakfast.'

Peter and Ace's house, located a couple of hundred metres

away, is one of the inspirations for my own house design. Set back from the beach, and its line of fishermen's shanty shacks, the two-storey house sits on a grassy expanse. Beneath this thin green skin lie extended sand dunes, causing the house to shudder when big seas thump against the steeply shelving beach in front. The high-ceilinged ground floor is cool and breezy, its large, unglazed windows carefully positioned to make the best of sea breezes and prevailing air flows.

The house is a hybrid English-country-home-cum-tropical-planter's-bungalow. But, aside from the eclectic style, it is the lack of glazing that impresses me. Like the great Geoffrey Bawa, father of modern architecture in Sri Lanka, Peter is insistent that tropical houses should be open to encourage cross-ventilation. And it works. The house is comfortable and cool. Peter, a mining engineer who has spent a lifetime considering such things, has positioned his home perfectly to draw the air, funnel the breezes and limit overheating from the sun. There will be no glass in the windows of our new home.

Peter is in fine form, in holiday mood. An old-style Englishman who grew up on a citrus plantation in the Indus Valley of Pakistan, he sometimes seems more Asian than the Asians and sometimes more British than the British. Peter ushers us in and introduces his house guests, a couple of fellow Brits, members of the international yachting fraternity. Peter and Ace's newest venture, a marina in a quiet bay on Lombok's north-west coast, is open for business and they are taking care of some of their first customers. Lombok is well positioned on the east-west route for cruising yachts. An easy day's sail from Bali, the new marina offers a much cheaper, laid-back alternative to berthing at the more commercialised island to the west. The visitors look the part – tall, worldly, and weathered in a salty sort of way. Sporting carefully casual and slightly rumpled clothing, the pair contrasts nicely with the groomed and Indonesian 'Sunday-best' appearance of the rest of us; the men in pressed batik shirts and the women in colourful head scarves.

Breakfast over, we join Peter and Ace with their guests to call on the province's new governor. Idul Fitri is as much about confirming allegiances, about showing respect to elders, about shoring up alliances, declaring loyalties and reaffirming the strength of family and community, as it is about religion. In the village, that means formally seeking forgiveness and blessings from parents and elders, visiting uncles, aunts, cousins and village notables. The unwritten rule is that the juniors with lower status in a relationship call on the seniors with higher status. Within the family this is a powerful cultural tradition: forgiveness and blessings are bestowed in an intense and emotionally charged, private ritual. Once immediate family are done, elders get to stay home while the youngsters run around town calling on them one by one. Here in Lombok, we are free of all that and tag along with our friends to visit the most senior of all, the governor.

We are not the only ones with this intention. The governor's formal residence in Mataram is busy. A large, open-sided *pendopo* pavilion is extended into the garden with marquees to cope with the influx of visitors and well-wishers. We get a fleeting chance to shake hands and chat with the recently installed, young governor of West Nusa Tenggara, a local man, a Sasak with good Islamic credentials – and his glamorous wife. After this there is more to eat and we wander about making small talk for a few minutes, before taking our leave and driving back home to catch up with Laras's brother, Karno, and his family in the village. After calling in on a friend who has been running our school for some years, we are at the beach for a picnic and a less conventional celebration of the Eid.

Lombok's coast is blessed with a great many picturesque bays and sandy beaches, each lined with coconut palms and *ketapang* shade trees, and punctuated every so often by rocky headlands. The west coast, north of Senggigi, is especially beautiful, and unlike much of Indonesia, where it would be quite impossible to find a quiet corner on which to lay out a picnic lunch – undisturbed by litter, insects or inquisitive locals – at Malimbu we know of a shady spot where we can do just that. The rest of the day is spent with Karno and his family. The kids caper about, woven *tikar* mats are spread out, and coolers full of good stuff appear: roast chicken, fresh bread, rice, green salads and all kinds of Indonesian snack foods, sweet and savoury, along with a few cold beers and soft drinks. And, rather more reminiscent of an Australian Christmas than an Indonesian Idul Fitri, lunch is followed by a game of beach cricket, a dip and a snooze. The beach is clean, the water sparkles, nobody bothers us (the locals are all, presumably, busy with their own traditional Eid activity), God's in His heaven, wherever that may be, and, for once, all's right with the world.

***

The following day, Laras and I head off up the hill to see what progress has been made. We leave the car on the field where last week's fast-breaking event took place and walk the few metres down the strip road, past where we are constructing a dam with Andrew. The slopes are largely bare dirt now. Concrete drains have been engineered, the storm water is to be channelled into the dam, which is beginning to take shape in a triangular hollow sitting in the palm of the little valley.

The foundations for the joglo have already been constructed, creating a concrete map of the room layout. Where last week a gravelly hole indicated the site for the below-ground water storage, now concrete cinderblock walls descend to a rectangular dirt base about three metres beneath where the floor of the joglo will be.

There is pleasure to be found in this quiet scene: a mess of bare dirt, piles of cinderblocks, rocks, sand and gravel. Lengthy noodles of reinforcing steel are stacked to the side, some welded together to form square webs of rusty-looking metal. And the whole thing is bathed in the soft glow of a late afternoon sun. A little industrial magic set amongst the greens and browns of the valley.

* * *

One week after Idul Fitri, locals celebrate the annual Sasak festival of Lebaran Topat. It seems that half of Lombok descends on a small stretch of coast at the foot of our hill for this purpose. For a long period, the Sasak peoples of Lombok followed a syncretic Hindu-Buddhist religion which had spread from Java, mixed up no doubt with healthy doses of indigenous animism and ancestor worship. Islam arrived in two waves, the first from Java – possibly as early as the thirteenth century in the north-west of the island, though the evidence is thin – and the second in the sixteenth century, brought by Arabs from Makassar and Java. This is a matter of pride for the Sasak, who like to think of themselves as having acquired Islam directly from the source.

As well as this religious legacy, the Arabs also left behind a community of traders and small businesspeople, whose cultural identity and links back to Yemen and the Middle East remain strong. They compete for space in the local economy with the more recent Chinese immigrants. I once attended the wedding of a neighbour in Ampenan, where the young man, born and raised in Lombok, was marrying a girl from Yemen. The whole affair was redolent of that Arabic tradition. The men were seated in an outdoor pavilion amongst the dusty apparatus of a tile manufacturing industry, the family business. The women were visible only in glimpses. They peeked from behind a curtained screen that separated the front veranda, where the formal ceremony was to take place, from the back-stage interior of the family home. There they giggled and fussed over one another in their finery. This transplanted Arab culture, which has survived for centuries on Indonesian soil, has, in recent years, been supplemented by an influx of new Saudi money to support mosque construction and the spread of Wahhabi Islam through boarding schools, madrasah and Friday sermons.

The Islamic faith was introduced by locally revered saints, including Sunan Prapan, the son of Sunan Giri, one of the nine Arabs who are credited with bringing Islam to Java. But more important to our story is one Sheikh Muhammad Al Bagdadi Syayid from Baghdad. Some say the sixteenth-century missionary was a descendent of the Prophet. Reportedly, he planned to return to Arabia when his work was done and Islam was firmly established on the island. As he prepared to leave, his disciples took him to the beach at Batu Layar, just down the hill from our new house site. The sheikh apparently sat out on the rocky point by the sea waiting for his boat to arrive. Before long a tropical storm blew in, bringing heavy rain, strong winds and lightning. Sheikh Sayid disappeared, leaving behind only a pile of stones, his cap and turban. The sheikh's tomb sits on a bend in the road just above the beach. It is said to contain not the saint's body but the cap and turban.

The rocky area surrounding the tomb also serves as a community burial ground. I once attended the funeral of a still-born baby there, the child of a young woman who had married Pak Mobin's older son and lived nearby. This was a sad day. There, under the thin midday shade of gnarled old frangipani trees, the tiny shrouded body was laid to rest in the dusty earth. The men of the family and village elders sat about as an Imam muttered prayers in Arabic. Dust to dust. We all have our allotted time.

The family, like most on the hill, live in a parallel world: a world inhabited by spirits, both good and evil. A world without doctors or medicine. On one occasion, Mobin's youngest son, Roni, was suffering from a fever. The illness was attributed not to malaria or dengue but to devils. His prescribed treatment was a mix of rest, prayer, Qur'anic recitation, and local herbal remedies. Sleeping with the Holy Qur'an nearby was also thought to assist. Roni recovered over time. But it was too late for the baby, dead before alive. He could have been born at the local clinic, but for the insistence of the girl's father that she give birth in the cottage, attended not by a trained midwife but by a local *dukun* – a traditional faith healer. What's good enough for me is good enough for you, he had declared. Had it not been for Karno's assistance, driving the girl to the hospital for treatment they could not afford, we would probably have been burying her too.

It was after this that we realised Pak Mobin and his family had never been to the community health clinic, just a five-minute drive down the coast. The clinic provides free health care. Under Indonesian regulations, doctors, who spend their afternoons and evenings earning a decent living in private practice, are required to serve the public in state hospitals or clinics in the mornings. But this service is unavailable to the poorest of the poor, the undocumented. In order to access it, patients require an identity card. In order to have a card issued by the village administration, fees are required. None in the family had ever had the money – or had ever seen the necessity of spending the little they had – for a card. Consequently, not only could they not access basic health care, but they could not vote and were effectively non-existent as far as the state was concerned. This is something we were subsequently able to assist with.

'How are you, Pak?' I would ask, when I came across Mobin on this hill, as I often did. 'How's your health? Inaq Idah? The children?'

'Mudah-mudahan!' he would laugh in response. 'All good. God willing!'

On Sundays and holy days, the Batu Layar graveyard fills with local people, families picnicking and looking for a little divine intervention – blessings and good fortune. The tomb is especially busy in the months leading up to the Hajj, as pilgrims and their families pray for safe passage; and before Ramadan, as the faithful settle old debts and seek forgiveness ahead of the holy month. But for this one day each year on the festival of Lebaran Topat, it is mayhem.

**

Early in the morning, before the hordes arrive for Lebaran Topat, holy water is drawn from a sacred well in the foothills of Batu Layar located somewhere in the valley near our house site. The water is brought to the tomb in a ritual procession. Apparently rinsing a child's face with this water ensures that he or she will grow up to be virtuous. Votive offerings such as flowers, yellow rice and baby's hair clippings can help. As the day warms up, more and more folk arrive. The religious festival is an excuse for a great party. The roads jam up with bikes, buses and pickup trucks from the east, all overloaded with village passengers; through-traffic becomes impossible as crowds converge on the site.

At around two in the afternoon, quite unexpectedly, the rains arrive. It begins with the usual build-up of heavy skies, raggedy looking clouds march across the hills from the north-west, transforming the morning's light haze into a thick blanket, obscuring the sun, turning the world a little darker. But this time the clouds do more than tease the thirsty earth. One or two miraculously large drops splatter onto the dust. Folks stop what they are doing. Everyone looks upwards, not quite ready to believe. But within minutes those scattered droplets have become a deluge.

Like a wall of water, the sky is obliterated, and a roaring, thundering cascade of joyous rain envelopes everyone and everything. After four months of hard dry weather, this feels like a blessing. Huge puddles form shallow lakes in the fields, plastic rubbish sloshes about, and the dry slopes are transformed into a network of muddy little streams, the water scouring the hills as it finds its way to the sea. Drains overflow. Dry creeks become bubbling brown torrents. And while the people duck for cover, crowding beneath whatever shelter is available, plastic bags and shiny green banana leaves appropriated as makeshift umbrellas, a little girl dances madly, her cheap cotton dress clinging, water dripping from her loose hair, streaming from her ears, from her nose, she blinks away the rain, a bright tongue darts in and out, lapping like a cat. The monsoon rains have arrived!

A makeshift carnival has been established by the beach across the road; rickety-looking amusement rides, games of chance, cheap toys, medicine shows, tricksters, fairy floss, a ghost house and local food stalls line the beach. After an hour or so, the rain subsides, the clouds now spent, a late blue sky emerges from behind. The earth is steaming. Crowds mill around; excited kids splash in the puddles, running in and out and getting into harmless mischief in the mud.

Laras and I take our boys down to join in the fun. We wander down a sideshow alley and try our luck at a game of hoopla. Attractive-looking prizes, mainly little bundles of cash and electronic gadgetry, are arranged on a makeshift table, each tied to a bottle resting on a wooden block. It looks easy enough to win a prize by casting the small hoop over the block. But inevitably every attempt is a failure, there is no way the hoop can encircle the block; an early lesson for the boys in how the odds are stacked against the punter. In the end they are content with a cloud of pink fairy floss, sticky faces, and a couple of hand-made bamboo popguns to take home.

In the evening, cool after the rain, free entertainment is provided in a nearby field by a local band: manicured and modestly sexy singers gyrate on a temporary stage to the *dangdut* beat of an Arab-Hindi influenced Indonesian pop song, in this case given a spicy Sasak flavour. The thump-thump-thump of the rhythm section carries on the night air, reaching our cottage in the Balinese village up the valley. Eventually the boys nod off to sleep, worn out by the excitement of a small-town fair. A good time was had by all.

***

In the quiet of night, I reflect on the day and what it means. The festival of Lebaran Topat is part of a uniquely Sasak form of Islam. As in Java, Islam was introduced through familiar cultural and religious forms. Mosques were built to resemble Hindu temples; the Qur'an was transcribed using Chinese ink, and sacred texts were translated from the original Arabic into old Javanese; gamelan music and wayang puppet theatre were used to spread the word and enhance worship; lakes, wells, mountains – the sacred sites of an animist tradition – were co-opted first by Hinduism and then by Islam; and the tombs of holy men like Sheikh Syayid from Baghdad became local pilgrimage sites where devotees can pray to Muslim saints for intercession.

All of this interwoven history and mythology found expression in a Sufi-influenced tradition that came to be known in Lombok as *Wetu Telu*, meaning 'three times.' There is some dispute about what this means. It is commonly said that the adherents of Wetu Telu don't follow the standard Islamic practice of praying five times a day, preferring three daily prayers. But I also heard that the 'three times' is not a reference to prayer sessions, but to three elements – the sun, the moon and the stars, symbolic of heaven, earth and water. Like many things on the island, it's hard to get at a single truth about this. The Qur'an is interpreted in classical Javanese and important prayer sessions are conducted by priests, known as *kiai* or *pemangku* on behalf of the congregation. Old practices such as prayer meals consisting of white and red rice porridge persist. All of this, of course, greatly irks Indonesia's puritanical reformers and the Wetu Telu faith has all but died out today, but it lives on in and around the village of Bayan in North West Lombok, and at a deeper level in many local traditions such as Lebaran Topat.

Lombok was dominated by Java in medieval times, long before being colonised by the Balinese, who introduced their own brand of Hinduism over a one-hundred-and-fifty-year reign, and then by the Dutch, who added a thin veneer of European colonialism during the next fifty years. Then followed a brief period of Japanese occupation during World War II, after which, in the mid-twentieth century, the island was absorbed into the new nation of Indonesia. The last seventy years have brought first nationalism and then globalisation, and with both a more standardised and increasingly puritanical form of Sunni Islam.

Lombok is now known as the island of a thousand mosques. This Islam is replete with white robes, checked headscarves and religious leaders known as *Tuan Guru*. While the religion is mostly benign, local Amphibi militia still sometimes strut about in silly quasi-military uniforms, armed with sticks and bravado, and occasionally more serious extremism erupts like a boil on the island's smooth face. Once, not long after the riots, when I mentioned to a taxi driver that I had embraced Islam in order to marry my Muslim wife, he smiled a brotherly sort of smile and gleefully boasted about how he and his mates had eradicated all traces of the Chinese Christian community from his home town in East Lombok. Proof of piety, apparently.

Meanwhile, the Balinese Hindus remain as a significant minority, especially in the west. And the village of Pemenang on the west coast, which until recently practiced the old syncretic Hindu-Buddhist animism of pre-Islamic Java, has, under the influence of contemporary Buddhist preachers, now adopted a more orthodox version of Indonesian Buddhism. With the exception of this tiny Buddhist community, the population of West Lombok is today divided into Balinese Hindus and Sasak Muslims. For the most part the two groups seem to live together in harmony, although occasional spats over land ownership do erupt into conflict as Indonesia's Dutch-derived national land laws gradually replace customary local law, and the short-term greed and business imperatives that accompany development and tourism edge out more traditional concerns.

* * *

One such dispute came to a head in the valley below our building site. The land in the valley, some twenty-seven hectares of it, was owned by the Balinese community, the banjar. Unusual in

Indonesia, where freehold title is usually only given to individuals, the banjar held a certificate for this land on behalf of their community. Their history tells of how the land was gifted to the banjar by the local Sasak ruler of the time, a reward for loyalty and service. Most of the land was level flood plain, good fertile farming land with a seasonal creek running through the middle. Some of it stretched up the steep valley sides, including the land that Andrew's driver and fix-it man, Wir, had acquired. This was no easy feat, as the legal purchase required the agreement and signature of every adult member of the community.

The problem was that a Sasak community had settled beyond the banjar land, where the valley narrows into a gorge. Cramped around their village mosque and hemmed in by steep forested slopes on either side and a decent waterfall at the northern end of the valley, the Sasaks had begun to farm the adjacent banjar land. Things went along without much fuss for some years, until the village head decided to take it a step further, claiming that the land was rightfully theirs. He began selling plots of banjar land to his villagers, and people began to build permanent houses and establish substantial farms. Then the lawyers got involved. By this time the value of the land had become apparent, foreigners were settling down the valley near the coast, and a number of European-style villas had sprung up.

The Sasak community mounted a legal challenge to establish ownership of the disputed land. The Balinese kept their cool, and quietly built a war chest to fight their legal battle, selling off some of the land which was not in dispute, nearer the coast. After a protracted case, the judges ruled in favour of the Balinese in the district court. The Sasaks appealed. A bigshot lawyer from Jakarta took over and set about raising funds from potential investors, and lobbying politicians and judges. The Balinese sold off a bit more land. The case went to the provincial high court and, after a decent legal stoush, the appeal was dismissed, and the court ruled in favour of the Balinese.

Of course, the Sasaks refused to vacate the land they still believed was rightfully theirs. Not only that, they had built homes and farms there, their livelihoods were tied to the land. Banners were strung up on the fence in front of the sub-district office and across the main road – 'Sasak land for the Sasaks!', 'Defend the rights of the little people!'. A local non-government organisation got involved, media reports about how foreign investors were pillaging the land of local people appeared.

Then the police arrived – in force. Their task was to execute the court ruling, by shifting the Sasaks off the land. Truckloads of uniformed police with blue berets headed up the valley. The Sasak villagers made themselves scarce, the police erected signs and ribbons of yellow tape, to clarify the court decision to the locals, and left. The villagers removed the signs and tape, moved back into their homes, and continued to farm the land. There was talk of taking the legal battle to Jakarta, but before that could happen, a larger police force was assembled to execute the court decision. The villagers were informed that their houses would be demolished if they weren't vacated before the due date. The village head rallied his troops and wrote to neighbourhood leaders and other village heads.

'This is a test of our faith!' he declared. 'A jihad! Help us to defend our property and our religion against the Hindus!' No one responded. Fortunately, the fellow's reputation was well known.

No one wanted trouble.

The big day arrived, a large contingent of military police turned up, this time accompanied by an excavator and a bulldozer. The operation began, but the Sasak villagers had decided to fight it out. One of the good things about Indonesia is that there are basically no guns in the hands of civilians, so the villagers' armoury consisted of sticks and farming implements. The police fired a few warning shots over the heads of the villagers, and a pitch battle ensued. The police outnumbered the villagers, and used their discipline, training and batons to good advantage. The village head and his loyal supporters, bruised and battered, were herded into a truck and taken into custody – there to cool their heels and lick their wounds, while their homes were razed. The Balinese kept their distance throughout.

* * *

While land disputes are not unheard of, they are not the norm. For the most part, the Balinese Hindus and Sasak Muslims get along just fine. In these western districts especially, the two cultures have blended. Over the years, intermarriage has been common. The Sasak expression of Islam is seasoned with local flavours. At times it looks like an import from the Middle East. At a reception that Peter and Ace held for their yachtie friends last month, a group of young men in white robes and headscarves chanted in Arabic to the beat of tambours and the twang of electric guitars. At other times, it is more influenced by the colourful traditions of Bali and Java – wide-eyed beauties dressed in silk, and lacy, gold-braided *kebayas*, dance the sinuous dances of a pre-Islamic world.

Sasak wedding celebrations begin with a procession – the bride is escorted by the entire village to the groom's home, to the accompaniment of live music and dance. The main attraction in a traditional *kecimol* procession are the big drums, called *kendang beleq*. Half a dozen fit looking young men, bare-chested and wearing black-and-white checked sarongs, march with bent knees and a swaying gait at the head of the procession, beating away at the huge drums strung across their chests. Behind them, rows of men with Balinese-style cymbals create a clashing rhythmic din, and behind this, the villagers stretch out down the road in a long raggedy line of happiness. Traffic delays are common, especially on Sundays in the harvest season, when weddings usually take place. Somewhere in amongst all of this, the bride can be spotted, heavily made-up and looking a little terrified, with a tasselled, regal looking umbrella waggling about above her to mark her as the star of the show. Modern versions of the kecimol sometimes substitute the big drums and clashing cymbals with a pick-up truck on which an entire band is perched, drum kit, electric guitar, keyboard, bass and singer. Speakers mounted on the top of the cab are cranked up to full volume and the band produces a distorted cross-over *dangdut* ethnic fusion. Kampung rock.

Weddings are plentiful in Lombok. Village girls marry early and often. Compared to the more staid Javanese Muslims and Balinese Hindus to the west, and to the Catholics and Protestants in the east, the Sasaks are rather flexible when it comes to marriage. Divorce and remarriage are common. Children are often raised in blended families and in amongst the extended familial village community. Elopement (known as *kawin lari*, literally marriage-on-the-run) is also common, as is forced marriage. Polygamy, while rather frowned upon in polite society, is permitted under Islamic law and is not uncommon. The dashing young governor of Lombok and Sumbawa raised eyebrows when he took a second wife. Pak Mobin's fourteen-year-old daughter, Bayan, dropped out of school before completing grade four. Bayan was needed at home to babysit her nieces, so that the girls who had married her older teenage brothers could go out to work. Our efforts to get her back into school were unsuccessful, and then one day Bayan disappeared without explanation. A frantic search was mounted. Karno got involved. When eventually the girl was found, she was already 'married' to a much older man who had taken a fancy to her. No chance of completing her schooling now.

'How is Bayan?' I asked Pak Mobin, sometime later.

'Ya, mudah-mudahan,' he frowned. 'Hopefully, fine.'

In a rather different set of circumstances, a young Balinese woman who worked as a secretary in our home office, failed to turn up for work one day. It turned out she had run off to marry her boyfriend, a Catholic from Flores who lived in Bali. The family would never have agreed to the marriage, or to Dewi renouncing her Hindu faith in order to marry a Catholic (marriage is still legally possible in Indonesia only between members of the same faith). But Dewi knew that in time they would forgive the transgression, and would welcome the couple into the family. And so they did.

As to our office administration, once over the shock of Dewi's sudden unexpected and unexplained resignation, we hired another young Balinese woman who was quite good in the job, until she, too, ran off – this time with a Belgian fellow. Dewi remains a friend, although we lost contact for a while. Her aged grandmother was a masseuse; a tall woman with a gnarly face and strong hands who often called around to the cottage to give massages on a slow Sunday. She would rub an oily herbal mix into my back, before picking out little tufts of grit and declaring it was bad stuff that the massage had somehow released from the body. One day Dewi called to say her grandmother had passed away. We were expected to show our respects, which we did, visiting the family home in the Balinese end of town, where the old lady was laid out in the front room and we chatted over cups of sweet tea.

Seasonal temporary marriages are also common in Sasak Lombok. Couples tie the knot in the harvest season and then, if things don't go as expected, untie it before the next harvest. These 'trial marriages' are not uncommon and can work for both parties. Less appealing is the practice of short-term customary marriage arranged for foreigners, usually visiting Arabs, who, in return for a donation to the village (a few goats may do it) can take a young wife for the duration of their annual holiday, before divorcing the girl and heading back to their real wives and families in the Middle East. Unsurprisingly, family connections and blood ties get somewhat convoluted in this tangled setting. Some say that the results of unions between family members, unwitting or otherwise, are evident in the frequency of birth deformities such as cleft lip and cleft palate. Others say it's more to do with malnutrition and low folate levels in the Lombok vegetation and hence diet, particularly in the east.

* * *

Adding to the cultural mix of the island, and in a small way to the gene pool, recent years have seen an influx of foreigners and business folk from overseas and other parts of Indonesia.

The new breed of Western expatriates is having an impact on Lombok. Bringing wads of cash and strange habits, snapping up land, buying offshore islands and beachfronts, and building boutique hotels, the newcomers, of which I am one, are a mixed blessing. The land grab has been going on in Lombok for about twenty-five years now, interrupted only by a period of about five years during the time when I first lived on the island. Following the end of the Suharto regime, investment slowed to a standstill as a result of the riots and civil unrest. Now it is back in full swing.

All of this development provides jobs and opportunities for locals, but it also creates jealousies, feeds corruption in local government and upsets the delicate cultural balances that have been achieved over the last couple of centuries. Land in prime tourist areas has increased in value by as much as a thousand per cent in the last ten years. Everyone has become a real estate agent, everyone has an angle, a plan, land for sale, a friend who knows a friend; everyone is a salesman; taxi drivers, porters, waiters, beach-sellers, farmers and local officials. Government employees get rich in the middle, especially those in the Land Office. And along the beautiful west and south coasts, locals rub shoulders with Belgians, Dutch, French, Australians, Germans, Japanese and foreigners from all corners of the earth, together with Javanese, Balinese, ethnic-Chinese and Malays from across the archipelago. It is a mixed lot that have washed up on the shores of Lombok, attracted by this smorgasbord of opportunity and loose regulations. As many fingers have been burnt as fortunes have been made. Meanwhile, small businesses and contemporary accommodations have sprung up along the west coast, ranging from grass-roofed backpackers to luxury villas and the exclusive Sheraton, Tugu and Oberoi resorts. Scantily dressed foreign tourists sip cocktails by the pool, mixed marriages are common, and ageing Westerners prop up beachside bars and see out their days in an alcoholic haze. .

Two

The morning after Lebaran Topat is bright and blue following the cleansing rains. Rory and Harry, scrubbed up for school, head off on a horse-drawn *cidomo*, their regular morning ride.

The early air is dry as I take the bike out from the village and past the field where last night's event took place. The aftermath is shocking. A group of men is busy dismantling the stage where the band performed, loading scaffolding and hoardings onto the back of a pickup truck. The entire field, a couple of hectares of dry grass matted and muddied with yesterday's rain, is blanketed in a layer of plastic and paper rubbish: bottles, wrappers, waxed paper, bags and detritus of every description. Barely a square metre of land is left uncovered. Across the main road, the fair ground is much the same. Stallholders are packing up and moving on, the litter is thick on the ground and remaining patches of earth are sticky, bare and trampled. The beach is in a similar state; the rain has swept the accumulated rubbish from drains and streams – plastic washes along the tideline past the little Balinese Hindu shrine that sits on a rocky outcrop in the shadow of the sheik's Islamic tomb. Across the creek a large field of coconut palms fronts the beach and serves as a picnic spot for locals. Work is already underway to clean up the mess here. Three small teams of women methodically work their way across the area, picking up the rubbish and collecting it into central piles for removal.

I subsequently discover that this clean-up is the work of Husein Abdullah, a colourful character who lives in a homestay a short distance down the coast. Husein was at the Arab wedding in Ampenan. Depending on who you choose to talk to, he is either a saint, a crackpot or a pest – sometimes all three.

'The world needs eccentrics!' Andrew once opined with a smile, but even he has grown weary of this one. Known to locals as *Bule Gila* or Crazy White Man, Husein Abdullah is a New Zealander. He first came to Lombok in the eighties and became concerned that the island's natural beauty was being despoiled, littered with garbage. Ten years later he returned, married a local lady, adopted an Islamic name, and started cleaning up Senggigi Beach. Since then he has devoted his life to the cause – cleaning the Batu Layar area, recycling, composting and improving sanitation, building toilets for villagers, and doing whatever he can to preserve the environment. When not in the field or sitting by the beach in front of his homestay, he is busy either lobbying local government officials or haranguing people like me, whom he regards as a potential source of funds or influence with funding agencies.

'Mark!' he shouts, his voice roughened with age, agitated; his eyes are wild, his face inches from mine, spittle flies from the corners of his mouth. 'Mark! You've got to do something! Look at me, look at me! I work my bloody guts out to do what I do. All I am asking for is a little support!'

He has a point. The government does nothing to educate the people about the problems of litter and sanitation, and even less to solve the problem. There is no rubbish collection in the village.

Household waste is managed as it always has been; bash, burn and bury. The problem is that much of that rubbish is now plastic. Burning it is not such a good idea. And many have no space to bury rubbish. It thus collects in informal tips – empty blocks, corners of crossroads, creek beds and riversides are favourite sites – or it is just discarded wherever one happens to be at the time. The creeks carry rubbish out to the sea, where it sloshes around between the islands and washes up along shorelines across the archipelago. When the rains arrive, and the dry creek beds are flushed out, the beaches become a filthy mess.

Yes, Husein has a point. But there is only so much one can do. The challenges in this country are so great, the problems so overwhelming. In the end, you do what you can and learn to be content with that. Over the last few months I have been working with Andrew and a few others to create a document which we hope will set the tone for our development on The Hill, establishing some rules and expectations around management of the environment and rubbish; a covenant that we hope, perhaps naively, everyone will sign onto.

***

It is Saturday morning, and I drive up to meet Agus and inspect the building site. It is a week since Laras and I were up there and the progress is marked. There must be fifty workers on site. Three crews are at work on separate projects. Pak Pujo, the Javanese engineer who designed and built the roads and drains for The Hill is supervising construction of the dam. Pak Agus is supervising the house construction. And a small team is installing a fence. Eddy sits in the shade of the duwet tree with Karno and Dedy, poring over lists of materials and worker attendance sheets. We need the dam completed, along with a bridge, which will allow materials to be delivered to the site for the main house construction on the western terrace.

Wearing sneakers, a pair of jeans, a t-shirt and his signature floppy hat, Pujo is squatting on a half-built central pier in the cleft of the little valley that defines our block. This pier will support the bridge and form part of the structure of the dam. From this position he surveys the scene. A slightly built man in his early forties, Pak Pujo's sharp eyes and ready smile are familiar to everyone.

'Since we started designing the road and drainage back in 2001, I have worked without stop on The Hill,' he told me recently. 'The Hill has given me my independence.'

Pujo doesn't say more than he needs to. He walks along the top of the dam wall, an unfinished concrete and rock construction, to where I am navigating piles of sand and gravel at the bottom of the road. The path is wet and slippery with loose gravel. We shake hands. A couple of men are working a cement-mixer at the edge of the terrace at the top of the western slope. The grey slurry they produce is shovelled down a shoot to the base of the dam, now floored with concrete, the sharp smell of fresh concrete in the air. The eastern slope of the dam is finished, an incline of concrete and rock. The western slope is under construction. A line of women carry rocks on their towelled heads to the men who are at work on the dam.

'Looks good,' I say. 'When do you expect to finish?'

'Give me another few weeks,' he replies. 'It should be done

before the rain really sets in.'

We hope the dam will serve a number of purposes. It will create a large pond, which can filter the creek water, water released from houses and runoff from storms on its way to the sea. The dam may provide a source that we can draw on in the dry season. We also hope the pond will make an attractive feature as our access road winds around it. The plan is to plant it out with flowering lotus and stock it with fish to keep the water healthy and prevent mosquitoes breeding. It will be beautiful, I tell myself. Right now, it is an ugly mess of soggy concrete.

Standing precariously on that half-built dam wall affords me a view down what will become an entrance driveway to the main house on the western terrace. A team of women walks back and forth in a long line along that green path, each bearing a wide red bucket on her head, as if on the way to a Balinese temple ceremony. Until the bridge is completed, this is the only way of getting materials to the building site on the western terrace. As far as possible, we will make use of the materials we can quarry on site, but inevitably truckloads of rock, sand and gravel will be needed, along with sacks of cement, stacks of reinforcing steel, timber, tiles and more. The buckets are filled with sand or gravel as required and carried back down to the site. Work is underway to hack out a hole which will house the underground water storage for the main house. Progress is slow here on the ridge; the earth is hard and stony, unlike the loose dark earth on the eastern slope.

Agus wanders up to where we stand, observing all this activity with a practiced eye. A great stack of galvanised steel fence panels sits up against the hut below us to the east – and the perimeter fence is already taking shape. Foundations have been built and a gleaming line of galvanised cyclone fencing winds around the border of the block behind the shed and above the joglo site. About four-hundred metres of fencing will eventually mark the border, each panel held in place by a steel pole embedded in concrete footing.

Agus explains the progress on the joglo and main house. Work has also begun on the foundations for a cottage to be built by the creek between the joglo and the main house. The cottage is to be set into the hillside. A team of young men, including Mobin's lanky eighteen-year-old son, Lali, is busy hacking a basement and ground floor for the cottage out of mud and solid rock.

Over the next week or two, in between trips to Jakarta, work in my home office, and occasional school meetings and activities, I am up and down the hill most days. Progress is rapid. The rain has settled in, too. Since that first downpour we expect to get wet at least every two or three days. The mornings are bright and sunny, humidity builds during the day, and around mid-afternoon the tension is broken with an hour or so of heavy rain. The late afternoons are lovely, the sunsets spectacular in the clear air, dramatic storm clouds boil up over Bali in the distance – and the evenings are cool and pleasant.

***

A curious thing happened this morning. It is a Monday, mid-October. A young man called Gunawan came to my workspace in our cottage in the village to fix the computer. The internet was down again. He promised a brand new gadget that would put things to right. But Gunawan is not only a tech-savvy and personable young man, able to put computers right. He is also a seer, a clairvoyant of sorts. So, after the hardware was sorted and the internet traffic was once again flowing, Laras asked him if he would check around the cottage for ghosts.

To those who can see, or hear, or in some other way sense, the spirits – which is pretty well every Indonesian – the country seems to be full of them. Old homes, offices, hotels, gardens, office toilets and, of course, graveyards; the restless souls are apparently everywhere. One well-educated and senior member of the cultural elite in Jakarta reportedly hangs his many paintings on a slight angle to prevent the ghosts from perching on them at night. (I think I'd rather put up with the ghosts than my pictures all hung on an angle.) Why we Westerners seem incapable of sensing the ghostly presences, when the average Indonesian has no trouble at all, is a mystery. But, for whatever reason, my ever-logical wife thought it wise to ask Gunawan to give the place the once over. I have no reason to suspect any ghostly presence, the closest thing to a supernatural experience being our landlord, Pak Nengah's serious request when we first moved in.

'You can do what you like to the place, really,' he said. 'It's all up to you. I just ask one thing. Please don't disturb the bees. They are sacred. Oh, and we'd be grateful if you could permit me and my family to come on occasions for ceremonies in the little Hindu shrine in the corner of the compound.'

'Sure, no problem,' I replied, rather pleased to have the colour and cultural curiosity of the occasional household temple ceremony to look forward to. And perhaps the bees might attract good luck and ward off evil.

Gunawan took only five minutes or so to check the place out.

The cottage is not very big after all.

'There are two of them,' he reported in a matter-of-fact tone, 'a mother and her child, a boy, perhaps nine years old.'

'Should we be worried?' I asked.

'Nah,' Gunawan replied. 'They're no trouble. They won't bother you. Just let them be.'

And that was that. I'm not quite sure how it helps to have the ghostly residents identified in this way. But for what it's worth, we now know with whom we share the cottage. And I am once again able to email my colleagues.

Gunawan's experience with ghosts contrasts with that of Alfred Russel Wallace, the British naturalist, who passed this way a hundred and fifty years ago. Bent over the task of skinning and drying the beautifully plumed birds he had shot near Lembar in the south of the island in 1856, the intrepid explorer was chatting with Manuel, his Portuguese servant from Malacca, and a Malay from Borneo who was helping out.

'One thing is strange in this country,' observed the Malay, who had been living for many years in Lombok, '...the scarcity of ghosts.'

'How so?' asked Manuel.

'Why, you know,' he went on to explain, 'that in our countries to the westward, if a man dies or is killed, we dare not pass near the place at night, for all sorts of noises are heard which show that ghosts are about. But here there are numbers of men killed, and their bodies lie unburied in the fields and by the roadside, and yet you can walk by them at night and never hear or see anything at all, which is not the case in our country as you know very well.'

While Wallace was inclined to accept this as a provisional

fact, and '...a contribution to the natural history of the island,' he commented dryly that, 'as the evidence is purely negative, we would be wanting in scientific caution if we accepted this fact as sufficiently well established.'

* * *

The following Saturday is a blustery brawl of a day, electricity crackles in the air and you can smell the ozone. The change of seasons has brought on a head cold which dulls my senses somewhat, a reflection of the darkening sky above. But this morning my skin feels raw and tight, an uneasy prickling in the gut tells me we are in for a big one. A bank of clouds rolls in from the north-west. From this vantage point on the hill, sheets of rain are visible as the storm sweeps across the Lombok Strait from Bali, stirring the sea ahead of it. A hard, eastern light paints the ocean with a battle-grey sheen – flecks of foam glint even at this distance, white horses and watery skirmishes visible as the front steadily advances.

Ahead of the rain, Agus and I take a walk around the building site. Gone are the dusty bare terraced slopes. The earth is dark and damp, the foliage bright and green. The joglo's below-ground water storage is now walled with cinderblocks and the base has been concreted over. A mesh of reinforcing steel lies over this floor, ready for another layer of concrete. Three men toil away at the base of the pit, tying the steel bars together to complete the mesh. To all intents and purposes, it looks as if we are constructing a swimming pool under the house.

Below the joglo site, down by the creek to the south, a new

home has been built for Mobin and his family. Woven bamboo walls, known as *bedeg*, hang on a coconut wood frame that has been erected over a concrete slab. Corrugated fibro-cement roofing and a couple of twenty-four-gallon drums for water supply complete the picture. While basic, the accommodation is a step up from their former home. As well as a decent shelter, they now have water and electricity.

Across the creek, a steady bubbling flow now that the first brown rush has past, Lali and his friends are still hacking away. Standing about in a mess of muddy clay, the young men are busy with crowbars and long-handled hoes, the centre of their attention a large boulder embedded in the wet soil. It is probably too early to tell, but I fancy that I can see the outline of our second cottage starting to take shape in the hillside.

On the western terrace above, pegs and string define the shape of our main house, a fourteen-by-ten metre rectangle. Work continues on the underground water tank, similar in dimensions to that on the eastern terrace, it will sit directly under the house. At this stage, though, it is no more than a hole in the rocky ground.

By the time the rains arrive, about twenty minutes later, I am gone. Laras, who has been busy measuring another block with a surveyor, joins me and we pick up the boys and head off for a late lunch by the beach in Senggigi. Thunder smashes the quiet. Water pours in great sheets from the eaves of an open-sided pavilion, wind whips off the ocean spraying us with occasional watery blasts, and we relax as best we can over drinks, steamed rice and spicy squid while the storm rages about. I hope our new dam, still under construction, survives the onslaught.

Three

On Monday I take the early flight to Jakarta. A familiar routine – to be repeated several times this month. Up before dawn, a taxi to the airport, where I get a charge of coffee while waiting for the departure call in the lounge. Allowing for a two-hour flight, a one-hour time difference and half an hour in traffic, by eight-thirty I am in the lift, clutching a fresh coffee, and heading to the twenty-ninth floor of the office tower where the American-Government-funded education project which currently employs me conducts its business.

Jakarta is not only the centre of government but also of commerce, business and entertainment. Slowly sinking into the mud, disappearing into the wide Jakarta Bay, and sometimes cheekily referred to as 'The Big Durian', Jakarta is where it all happens. The head offices are all located there. To get anything done in this country you need to be familiar with Jakarta. But like all big cities, she is a complex and contradictory companion. The relationship is never easy. A crazy, crowded village of nearly thirty million souls, this is not an easy or a natural way for people to live. The city is moody. And its moods bleed into your soul in a way that is hard to fight. That heaving mass of glitz and grime, of wealth and poverty, energy and lethargy can probably be found in any big city. But Jakarta has its own vibe, its own story and its own character. And it is hard to untangle the mood of the city from one's own. There is a darkness behind the glitter.

My office in Jakarta is about five minutes' walk from an apartment where I usually stay. Sometimes it takes longer to get up the lift to the twenty-ninth floor than it does to walk from the apartment. The walk takes me across a footbridge which spans a ten-lane road in downtown Jakarta. To the south of the bridge is the Flaming Pizza Man, one of President Sukarno's Soviet-style monuments. An outrageously kitsch statue honouring the struggle of nationalist youth, it stands twenty-five metres tall in the middle of a roundabout at the end of Jalan Sudirman. (The penultimate monument to Sukarno's hubris is known as 'Monas', the national monument. Constructed just before he was deposed in the 1960s, Monas is a huge tower in the centre of the old Dutch park previously known as Koningsplein, the King's square, and now known as Freedom Square. It is sometimes irreverently referred to as Sukarno's last erection.)

North of the overpass the road snakes away to a hazy distance, an oversized corridor between tall office buildings; the broad tree-lined boulevard is choked with traffic. A constant stream of pedestrians moves purposefully across the footbridge, weaving around the hawkers, stepping over displays of pirate DVDs, lurid covers promising sex and violence, little stands of street food, steamed snacks, sellers of copy-watches, umbrellas and tissues, the occasional busker playing a violin or bamboo *kulintang,* and, in the evenings, a giant bubbling wok which produces deep-fried snacks for hungry office workers. Halfway across, a fresh stream of commuters enters from the city busway station below.

Sitting strategically at the end of the span is a beggar, an elderly woman. Like other beggars on the bridge, she sits patiently on the paving every day, clutching a small paper cup to collect her donations. Like the others she looks up at the stream of pedestrians, trying to engage individuals as they surge past, to elicit some response which might result in a few coins or a couple of grubby, folded notes dropped into her hands. Unlike the others, she smiles. The beggar smiles with her whole face, a real smile. Her smile is arresting. And, as a result, I sometimes give her some money. I feel like she has earned it. Not through peddling misery, the common currency of Jakarta's beggars. But through selling a smile.

And so it is that I now find myself commuting back and forth from Lombok to Jakarta, living in two places, two worlds, two lives. A few days later I am back in Lombok, catching up on progress with the build. The culture shock has become so familiar as to be unnoticeable – or perhaps it has mutated into a permanent cognitive dissonance.

***

Lombok is always a relief after Jakarta, the green earth and blue skies a salvation. Today the sky wears a gauzy white veil and the air feels heavy. But the sun is hot, the air is bright. And progress on The Hill is evident.

The hill has responded to the rains. Bright little leaves appear on the woody banten trees along the western border, and the high branches of a deciduous giant rise above the mangos to the south, trimmed in a fresh coat of green. In the valley by the creek and beyond the house site to the west, pale and slender branches are hung with a mass of rusty red-brown seed pods, creating a picture in the green. The change of seasons is a kind of tropical spring. Brownish toads appear, their rhythmic croaking a constant accompaniment, huge snails slither about with their spiralled shells, and the air begins to crowd with insects. On the flood plains below, the irrigation channels are full, crops of corn are ripening, water runs into the rice fields, and rows of farmers – men and women – their backs bowed and their feet caked in grey mud, plant bright little rice seedlings, one by one, in orderly grids.

It's Sunday and I make my way down the side road to the worksite. Pujo is not around, but the lining of the dam looks more-or-less complete, the formwork for the bridge construction is up, grids of reinforcing steel have been laid and wet concrete is churning in a small mixer. The petrol-driven motor coughs up a cloud of white smoke and creates a din in the valley, from where it now sits by the piles of sand and gravel at the end of the road. Workers are busy finishing the planter boxes in the corners of the dam. Work on the dam seems not to have been hindered by the rains.

A crew of bent-backed women is busy planting. The slopes above, to the east, and beyond the dam, reaching down steep slopes to the creek below, have all been planted out with Singapore daisy, course lawn grass, and long rows of vetiver grass, all intended to stabilise the banks of loose earth created by land-shaping – another lesson learned from Andrew. The vetiver grass, a type of citronella, grows in clumps like its cousin, lemon grass. Plant it in rows and it will form a barrier, protecting the fragile earth. Once established it multiplies, creating a massive root system which tangles together forming a continuous matt of long fine roots. These roots shore up loose banks, the plants forming little terraces, a much cheaper, greener and more attractive solution than building expensive retaining walls which create an eyesore and interrupt the ground water flow, sometimes collapsing under the weight of trapped water. When we run out of vetiver, we use lemon grass. Both make an attractive feature, and both not only provide a structural element, but serve to deter mosquitoes. And, as an added bonus, the lemon grass is useful in the kitchen. The Singapore daisy is regarded as a weed in Australia, where it doesn't belong. And for good reason. Once established it spreads, supresses other plants, and is difficult to remove. This is what makes it useful on the hill. After a couple of rains, it is already getting established here and will prevent erosion, while creating beautiful banks of green.

The rains have also brought up a fresh crop of giant *suweg*, an extraordinary seasonal plant known locally as *'bunga bankai'* or 'carrion flower' – closely related to the giant Rafflesia. The broad-leaved fleshy-stemmed plants are already dotted about the landscape, each about a metre in height, none yet flowering. When some of the female plants do flower, the stink they create around sunset will no doubt cause consternation among the workers.

Across the creek, on the western terrace, foundations are in place for the main house. Agus appears from where he has been supervising excavation by the creek for the second cottage. The underground water storage has been walled with cinder blocks – in the end not as deep as planned. The rocky ground was just too stubborn. By extending out beyond the house to the west, the same capacity will be achieved, about seventy-five cubic metres, with less effort. I walk about, trying to get a feel for how the house will be, stepping from imagined room to imagined room. The bedrooms at the eastern end feel very small.

'It will feel different when the place is built,' Agus reassures me. 'The rooms will be plenty big enough.'

* * *

The week soon passes by and Friday evening comes around again. Laras and I take the motorbike to Senggigi. The boys are staying over with friends. The offshore breeze is light but creates pockets of surprisingly cool air as we pass through the fertile valleys that lie between Rinjani's foothills, long ridges that disappear into the sea in a series of dark rocky headlands. It is another cool, balmy evening in Lombok.

Friday night is, according to local custom and family tradition, a night out. In the small resort town of Senggigi that usually means catching up with a few friends over a beer at a local restaurant. I am hoping we will bump into Andrew or Iwan to discuss our plans for the covenant and rubbish collection – and to talk to Andrew about progress with the dam construction.

By the time Laras and I get down to Asmara Restaurant on the motorbike it is nearly eight. The regular crowd is gathered around a long table beneath strings of hanging thunbergia, delicate white bell-like flowers, a few lights, and the open sky. Friday night is *Stammtisch*. The restaurant's German owner, Christine, is known to all as Sakinah. She came to Lombok in the early days and, like many young women, she was smitten with the laid-back lifestyle, the easy friendliness of the locals, the empty beaches and warm evenings – and the opportunity all of this represented. And like many others, before long she was in love – and then married and starting a family. Her husband, from one of the old Taliwang families of Rempung in East Lombok, is gone, but he left Sakinah with an Arabic name and twin boys – tall and with striking mixed features – and the family business, Asmara.

Asmara is a local landmark, Sakinah is a stalwart, and the Friday night Stammtisch is an institution among the small international community, a Bavarian tradition transplanted to Lombok – an open table at which regulars and newcomers alike are welcome. Pay your own way and enjoy a few cold beers, a hearty meal, a laugh or two and the company of a curious group of locals, expatriate and Indonesian. Stammtisch guarantees a good night.

The lights are low. The heavy scent of frangipani mingles with motorbike fumes and the smoke of a fish grill from over the road. The other tables are starting to fill – a few tourists, Indonesians and a smattering of expatriates. The usual suspects are seated around the Stammtisch table. Hand-shakes, smiles and cheek kisses as we reconnect, one by one. There's Sakinah, of course, tall, blonde and with a distinctly German poise that may have been softened by her years in the tropics. Gert, another German, is there with his partner, a young woman with a sweet smile who seems a little out of her depth in the older company. Gert is a stocky roguish fellow who runs a dive business with his former wife. Always good company. Peter and Ibu Ace are there. Then there's Derek, a gentle giant of a man with twinkling eyes and a wry smile, an Australian teacher, who will later end up running our school for a couple of years. Derek is there with his Bandung wife, who is deep in conversation with a mixed Makassar-Bali woman – a law student with an attractive, professional look. The conversation is lively, laughter ricochets around the table. We find our seats, order drinks and food, and ease into the group. Neither Andrew nor Iwan is there – but it is still early.

Ary Juliant is playing at Asmara tonight. I wander over to where he is setting up. He ties his long hair back and tunes a guitar before plugging in and doing a quick sound check.

'*Mau main?*' he asks with a smile. 'Feel like playing a few songs tonight?'

'Not tonight,' I reply. 'Maybe next week.' Over the years, Ary has become a good friend. Another Bandung connection, a long-term resident of Lombok and a senior figure in the local music scene, Ary is treated with respect by the younger players. And he is generous with his musicality – encouraging part-time musicians like me to join in. When the mood takes me, I do like to play a few songs, simple ballads about love and life in Indonesia that I have put together over the years. But not tonight, I am out of practice, my fingers a little slow, my singing a little rusty.

I return to my seat at the table. Ary begins to play. A motorbike rattles noisily past. The table chatter and the occasional jangling harness bells of a horse-drawn cidomo add a pleasant distraction. But the music quickly draws me in. The clink of glasses fades, and the clean sound of finger-style acoustic guitar sets the mood. Taut strings and polished wood. Gradually, quietly, a musical pattern emerges, Ipang's acoustic bass kicks in, and then Icink on drums – just a snare and a single cymbal. The volume grows steadily, though is never allowed to become intrusive. The bass player and drummer work together to create a rhythmic foundation on which Ary's guitar builds its architecture. But it is the singer that paints the pictures, Ary's high tenor giving the musical structure colour and meaning.

And so it is. There is a warmth in this scene, an easy sense of community around that long table, beneath that tropical sky. Differences are put aside. It is Friday night. Stammtisch! As the evening wears on, news is shared, the latest gossip traded, and bottles of local beer are emptied. Andrew turns up at some point. All smiles and 'Hail-fellow-well-met!' he looks like he's had a few drinks. He's probably been down at Richard's bar or maybe at The Office, a cheekily named pub on the beach behind the Art Market. It's good to see him. We have a few laughs and talk briefly about developments on the hill and progress with the dam. And then, just when Laras and I are beginning to think it might be time to head home, Sakinah's new husband, Iwan, arrives, making a blustery grinning entrance.

'Hi! Try this, try this!' he insists, uncorking a bottle of liquor. It might be whisky. 'This is the feckin' good one. Believe me! You know what I mean!' He calls for shot glasses and pours a round. 'Come on, man, it's on me!'

Sakinah rolls her eyes and smiles an indulgent smile. Iwan's face is flushed, untamed dreadlocks loosely tied back, he lights a cigarette, his eyes sparkle in the night lights. He plays the bad boy, fixing me with a slightly blurry gaze and then, with a big smile and a prodding finger, launches into a tale of Senggigi intrigue, betrayal and skulduggery.

Iwan tells the story of a local leader, head of the village up the hill from our building site, a man with whom Laras has dealt over land matters. The fellow was well known as a small-town thug, a gambler, a drunkard and a womaniser. But he was apparently admired by the locals for his strong-arm tactics, his tough defence of their community and their interests. Last week he was found dead in the early morning, over the road from a large karaoke bar south of Senggigi. The body was reportedly uninjured, but he was foaming at the mouth. Did he die of an overdose of crystal meth? Was it a heart attack, the result of a lifetime of heavy smoking and poor diet? Or was he poisoned? We will never know. Following Islamic custom, the body was interred before the end of the day. No autopsy.

As usual, I listen with interest. Iwan is a clever man, insightful and connected. His friends include gangsters and politicians, locals and foreigners, high and low. He knows people. He knows stuff. But I struggle to make sense of the mélange of Indonesian and English, all liberally punctuated with obscenities acquired on the building sites of London and the timber camps of Norway. Originally from the conservative Islamic stronghold of Aceh at Indonesia's far western reach, and the product of an elite East Javanese Islamic boarding school education at Gontor Pesantren, Iwan is an anomaly – and the perfect foil for Sakinah's poise and Germanic good sense. For whatever reason, this colourful language, when coming out of Iwan's mouth, does not seem so offensive. It is what it is...

Ary and his friends have already packed up, but the party seems to be in full swing. Someone produces an acoustic guitar. More rounds of liquor are downed with more beer chasers. A couple of Iwan's mates, crusty kampung fellows from Ampenan, join the table and the guitar is passed hand to hand as we trade songs; old Javanese *keroncong* tunes, cheeky courting songs from Ambon in the east, sing-along country standards, beery crooning and laughter, and a few reflective ballads. This is my chance to play a little. The mood is fine. The instrument is impossible to tune, but no one seems to mind. I play a couple of my own songs. But, in the end, it is an old Ambonese folk song, led by one of Iwan's mates, a curly-haired fellow from the east, with a boyish grin, that gets everyone singing.

Ayam hitam, telurnya putih, cari makan dipinggir kali,
Nona hitam giginya putih, kalau tertawa manis sekali
Ayo mama, jangan mama marah beta, Ia cuma-cuma
    pegang beta
Ayo Mama, jangan marah beta, orang mudah sudah biasa

A black chicken, her eggs are white, she looks for food
    beside the stream,
A black girl, her teeth are white, when she laughs, she's very
    sweet
Come on Mama, don't be mad at me, Mama, she's only
    holding onto me
Come on Mama, don't be mad at me, Mama, its normal for
    young folks, see.

'Ahhhhh,' smiles Sakinah, when we eventually call it a night, the streets now quiet, the guests drifting away into the dark. 'Just like the old times. Just like the kampung days...'

Four

Saturday is a slow day. Unsurprisingly. In the afternoon, Laras and I drive up to town to check out some furniture and fittings. It will be a long time before we need to think about all this, but it doesn't hurt to make a start.

Mataram is a pleasant Indonesian city and the seat of government for the province of Nusa Tenggara Barat, which encompasses the islands of Lombok and Sumbawa. The small city has the comfortable air of a sleepy rural town, albeit a largish one. From our cottage in Baruna Shanti, the drive takes us south along the coast road through Montong and past the mosque, our school, and Peter and Ace's seaside home. A little further on we pass by the traditional market, where Laras likes to shop. (I am strictly barred from this activity, so as not to drive the prices up, destroying Laras's credibility as a local shopper with my pale face and foreign features.)

The two-track road is busy with motorbikes, open-sided minibuses, small trucks and pickups, horse-drawn cidomo, bicycles, cars, taxis and the occasional large bus, which bores down the centre of the road scattering all others in its path. The bikes weave in and out, some bearing uniformed children on their way home from Saturday school, some head-scarved village women with huge baskets of produce on their laps on their way to or from the market, some slim Balinese girls sitting side-saddle and clad in beautiful lacy kebayas and colourful batik sarongs on their way to the temple, and some village officials and businessmen or school teachers about their business. The occasional teenage dare-devil roars past in a cloud of fumes, head bare, hair streaming, hips swinging, as the bike sways from side to side, dodging the traffic. But for the most part, the traffic moves slowly in an orderly if seemingly chaotic fashion.

Over the Meninting River with its wooden fishing boats, its carpets of *kangkung* water spinach and glimpses of sand, open ocean and the distant Gunung Agung, we drive south through coconut groves, past a large Chinese graveyard on the right, rice fields and plant nurseries on the left, and into the old port city of Ampenan. Here we pass by our old home, where Rory took his first steps, and I attended that Arab wedding with Pak Husein in the grounds of the dusty tile factory next door. The Arab quarter stretches away through crowded kampungs to the beach.

At one time Ampenan was an entrepôt, part of a trading network, a long line of ports and safe harbours stretching the length of the Malay Archipelago from Penang, Malacca and Singapore on the Malay Peninsula to Batavia, Semarang and Surabaya on Java – and east to Ampenan on Lombok, Makassar on Sulawesi, Ende on Flores, and Kupang on Timor. This is the oldest part of the city, with a mix of Arab, Chinese, Bugis, Javanese and Sasak communities. Many businesses in this area were defaced or burnt out in the riots of 2000. The five-way crossroads at the centre of the old city define that history, that ethnic mix. In the centre stands a quirky old building wedged between two roads that lead away to the east; it could be an office or a salon, and was for a while put to use as a restaurant, but now it stands idle apart from housing a minimarket on the ground floor, a good spot to drape banners advertising events, political campaigns and sales. To the south-east is another crumbling piece of three-storey art deco, a grimy concrete wedding cake; to the north-east an ornate stucco-fronted colonial building is obscured by an ugly addition built in the style of the Sasak rice barn, known as *lumbung*. And to the west an impressive archway is erected between a clutter of open-fronted hardware stores. The archway, decorated with graffiti and advertising posters, marks the entrance to a road leading down to the beach and the old harbour.

This road divides Kampung Arab to the north from Kampung Melayu to the south, where a community of Javanese and Bugis from Makassar live. The street is lined with mossy, arched Chinese shophouses; a warren of narrow lanes leads in behind the shops on both sides to where tiny homes with concrete walls, green with mould, share the space, cheek-by-jowl, with oily mechanics' workshops, tyre-repair shops, prayer houses, warungs and cottage industries of various sorts. A fleet of smart red- and yellow-painted trucks is parked near the end of the road, each draped with a bright blue tarpaulin; tethered horses stand patiently with their cidomo, heads bowed, sweating in the sun, and a row of motorbikes is parked beneath the trees. Just around the corner, a grubby Chinese noodle house called 'Mie Ayam Jakarta' serves splendid bowls of mushroom and chicken noodle soup, dished up by giggling girls from huge vats of steaming broth on stands beside the road – a favourite stop. And in the late afternoons, when the temperature drops, the wide sandy beach at the end of the road becomes a sports field for kampung dwellers – games of soccer and volleyball are fiercely contested as the sun sets across the straits.

On the corner near the beach is an orange-painted Amphibi security post, behind which a Pertamina oil complex has been carved out of the coastal kampung; huge shining oil tanks and smart offices, where the business of distributing fuel is coordinated. On the southern side of the old harbour is a mess of warehouses and small factories, where Ibu Ace at one time ran a business fabricating pressed bamboo furniture – until the riots put an end to it. Beside the beach on the northern side sits a solid Dutch colonial building; an old bank, now empty, that may once have been the customs house or harbour master's office – in the days when the harbour was busy with freighters, steaming passenger ferries, inter-island ships and local vessels. For a while it was a pub where expatriate miners, on leave from the big mine in Sumbawa, could get a cold beer and mingle with the local lowlife. But the harbour is no longer a port, the only reminder of its glory days a line of rotting wooden pillars, which march out into the ocean, providing a perch for visiting terns where a jetty once stood.

Back up the street a little way, a colourful Chinese temple stands behind a bright red steel fence. Nearby, set back from the road, is an airy old brick warehouse in which Peter and Ace operated their pottery and freight business for many years before moving to a larger space in the east of Ampenan. When I visited, the beautiful, mottled brown pots were on display, stacked to the ceiling on wide shelves and piled up in various corners of the warehouse, some packed for freight to Europe, America or Australia – wide bowls, nests of plates, traditional water coolers, jugs, and huge, big-bellied vessels. Crafted in the old way by village women, and fired at low temperatures, under a pile of dry grass and kindling in the open, the unique Sasak pottery is prone to breakages. Peter had figured out a clever way to export the fragile pots in open-sided crates – cubes constructed from timber battens, inside which the large pots are suspended by tightly-tied raffia. This open-crate system apparently results in far few breakages than packing the pots in in the usual way in closed boxes filled with shredded paper.

* * *

Word has it that this warehouse was Ampenan's killing ground, the place where crowds of Chinese Indonesians and alleged communist sympathisers were herded together and slaughtered in the dark days following the attempted coup of 1965. Every Indonesian town has its killing fields, its memories, its ghosts and taboos; unhealed wounds that date back a generation; its unspoken accusations and untold stories an un-mended tear in the fragile fabric of this communal society. Indonesian history is punctuated with these catastrophic events, as if, once in every generation, blood must be spilled, throats must be cut, to appease the gods of social harmony on these crowded islands.

In the mid-eighteenth century, the Balinese conquered Sasak Lombok, exploiting a lack of unity and constant warring among the island's petty chieftains. But internal conflicts between Balinese kingdoms and shifting alliances with the Sasaks provided plenty of opportunity for blood to be spilled in the years that followed. When Alfred Russel Wallace arrived in Ampenan in the 1850s, he found a divided country of Muslim Sasak peasants and

Balinese Hindu merchants and overlords. The English naturalist spent a couple of months on the island. While waiting for a boat to Makassar, he took the time to collect specimens of birds, plants and insects and to acquaint himself with the locals, recording his observations in his marvellous book, *The Malay Archipelago*.

'Every man without exception carries a kris, stuck behind the large waist-cloth which all wear,' Wallace observed, 'and it is generally the most valuable piece of property he owns.' The ceremonial daggers are often beautifully carved and ornamented with inlaid silver and jewels, but they served a deadly purpose when required. Theft was punishable by death – along with infidelity and a range of other misdemeanours. 'It is an established rule,' he wrote, 'that anyone found in a house after dark unless with the owner's knowledge, may be stabbed, his body thrown out into the street or upon the beach, and no questions will be asked.'

Wallace went on to describe the case of a local man running amok in Ampenan. Apparently, the practice of running amok, thought to be peculiar to the Malay peoples and particularly the Bugis, was not uncommon in Lombok. Typically a group activity, a form of mob violence triggered by some affront or perceived attack on the group, and sometimes racially based, the practice is familiar enough to anyone living in Indonesia today – though the term 'running amok' is no longer much used, with terms like 'communal riots' or 'civil unrest' more common. Wallace also describes how individuals frequently ran amok, and explains this as a form of suicide – one that was acceptable, even honourable, within the culture. The desperate man, who has run out of options, who 'thinks himself wronged by society ...will be revenged on mankind and die like a hero,' he writes. 'He grasps his kris handle, and the next moment draws out the weapon and stabs a man to the heart. He runs on, with the bloody kris in his hand, stabbing at everyone he meets. 'Amok! Amok!' then resounds through the streets ... It is a delirious intoxication, a temporary madness that absorbs every thought and every energy.'

Fortunately for science, Wallace did not fall foul of any kris-bearing locals, and having spent a pleasant enough time in Lombok he boarded a ship for Makassar, where over the coming years he collected butterflies, observed birds, and formulated the theory of natural selection, eventually writing a paper in Ternate, which he sent to Charles Darwin, thus prompting the more famous scientist to publish.

Forty years later, in the dying days of the nineteenth century, the Dutch finally took charge in Lombok. The people were suffering the combined effects of war and famine. Many were homeless. Invited by a Sasak prince to support his rebellion against the Balinese, the blue-coated troops arrived in 1894, sailing into Ampenan harbour and marching through Mataram to Cakranegara, where the old Balinese raja, looking for a political solution, agreed to talks with the Dutch and Sasaks. The hot-headed Balinese princes, however, were not ready to capitulate and ambushed the Dutch where they were camped in the beautiful, park-like Mayura water palace. There, from the protection of the surrounding clay walls, they turned their guns on the exposed invaders – and then they advanced with their bayonets. It was a moonless night, and the soldiers, together with their camp followers, found themselves caught in a hail of crossfire. Over a hundred died, including the commanding officer, General Van

Ham. Bullet holes can still be found in the walls. Under fire, the survivors retreated west to a second camp in Karang Jangkong at the crossroads near today's Mataram Mall. While holding out within the walls of the Balinese temple there, the general breathed his last and was buried nearby.

Locals have been known to boast that the only Dutch general killed was killed in Lombok. A neglected monument now stands in a little courtyard beside the temple – beneath the tall trees and strangling vines of the overgrown park. I met the Sasak caretaker when I visited recently. The old man makes a living collecting parking fees and selling the trunks of bananas to the Balinese for their cremations. The green logs are used to contain the fires.

'It's my job to keep the monument tidy,' he explained, with a worried smile, his mouth stained red with betel nut. 'But someone took the key and I can't get in to clean it up.'

The Dutch responded to the attack by sending a much larger contingent, employing their big guns to bombard Cakranegara, and thoroughly routing the defenders, turning both Balinese and Sasaks into serfs and subjects of the Dutch East Indies. But it was a hard-fought war. Over nearly two months of bitter fighting in and around Mataram, the Dutch inched their way east – blow by blow, man by man, kampung by kampung – until they finally took the Balinese stronghold of Cakranegara. A mix of cannon fire, rifle volleys, sniping and hand-to-hand combat, this was a bloody war. Around two thousand are thought to have perished. From their hard-won position in Pura Meru Temple across the road from the water palace, the Dutch launched their last attack, broaching the walls of the royal palace, Ukir Kawi. The final battle took place in the palace grounds. The royal families and Brahmin priestly caste committed *puputan,* a ritual suicide in which the defeated nobility donned white clothing and advanced, wielding spears, into the guns of the bewildered Dutch. Fifty women and twelve men reportedly died in this way. Meanwhile the aging raja and his eight-year-old son escaped to Saksari in the north-east of the town. The last king of Lombok finally conceded, and was exiled to Batavia, where he died a few months later and was buried in Karet cemetery near modern-day Jakarta's swish Shangri-La hotel and, across the road from the greenish Ciliwung River. The crown prince was executed by the Dutch.

Fifty years later, in 1942, the Japanese sailed from Surabaya into Ampenan harbour and, with little resistance from Dutch, Sasaks or Balinese, assumed command of the island. This was a hard time for the people, a time of hunger and terror. Between the cruelty of the Japanese military regime, the breakdown of the normal economy, and the indiscriminate violence of allied bombing, the locals suffered badly. In 1945, the war of independence provided another opportunity for the spilling of blood. Indonesians turned against the retreating Japanese, as well as the Dutch and their allies whose job it was to mop up after World War II; not only this, they turned against alleged collaborators and minority groups, against the ethnic Chinese and Ambonese, against the Eurasians who had enjoyed a privileged position in the Dutch apartheid system (though not as privileged as the Dutch) and had been detained in camps by the Japanese – and against Christians and eastern Indonesians with darker features, curly hair and a different religion. When guns and conventional weapons were unavailable, bush knives and sharpened bamboo spears did the gruesome job. An estimated one hundred and sixty thousand, from all sides of the conflict, died across the archipelago during the four years it took to convince the Dutch and the world at large to recognise Indonesian sovereignty, and for the founding President Sukarno to take up the reins of an independent nation. For two hundred years, the Sasaks had been ruled by the Balinese, the Dutch and then the Japanese. Now it was the turn of the Javanese again.

Then, in 1965, tensions between Islamists, secular nationalists, and reforming communists spilled over into the streets in the wake of a failed coup. Six of the country's top-ranking generals had been dragged from their homes and murdered overnight, their bodies thrown down a well in Jakarta. A splinter group of communists was blamed. A life-sized diorama in the old Menteng home of General Nasution, the only member of the top brass to survive, rather disingenuously depicts the rebels as dark-skinned eastern islanders. The economy was in tatters, poverty was rife, and the weary President Sukarno could no longer hold his fractured nation together. Wild stories circulated, mostly propagated by the nationalist military, law and order broke down, doors were barred as gangs of young men roamed the streets, and the young General Suharto saw his opportunity, seized power and embarked on a purge of the Left. Around a million Indonesians are thought to have perished. The rivers of Java and Sumatra were clogged with the bodies of the slain – and the old Chinese warehouse in Ampenan was awash with blood.

While the role of the CIA in all this violence is murky, this was the middle of the Cold War, and the United States and Great Britain had privately agreed that Sukarno had to go. Recently released historical records show that the CIA provided lists of known communists and sympathisers to the military, who delegated the job to local death squads, nationalist militia and the youth wings of Islamic organisations.

In the village south of Yogyakarta, my wife's father had made a name for himself as a *ketoprak* performer. Ketoprak is a traditional form of village drama, a kind of operatic pantomime in which heavily costumed and heavily made-up actors re-enact the old stories of mythical kingdoms in stylised performances. Laras's father liked to play the bad guys. A lot of laughter and innuendo is involved and, as a young man, he was apparently rather popular with the girls as a result of his lively performances. Many were also involved with the People's Culture Organisation, known as LEKRA, a coalition of leftist writers, artists, musicians and performers. Exploiting Indonesia's strong tradition of community-based arts – wayang shadow-puppet shows, trance dances, ketoprak dramas, broadsheet publications – LEKRA was able to help build support for a reform agenda in the villages.

Was Father a member of LEKRA? It's not clear and the old man is unable to coherently collect his thoughts these days, so we will probably never know. But what we do know is that he once attended a village meeting where agitators discussed land reform with local farmers. His brother, who would have been my wife's uncle had he not done so, made the mistake of signing the attendance register, and did not survive. For some reason, Father did not sign the list and survived to marry and produce a family – a little accident of history for which I am forever grateful. Years later, Laras was forced to cycle an hour and a half each way to school. Tainted by association, she was not welcome in the local junior-high school.

Thirty years on, tensions once again spilled over. Suharto was a strong leader; as the self-styled father of development, he built the economy and secured social stability over this period. But he did so at the expense of dissent, at the expense of freedom and human rights, and he finally outstayed his welcome. The greed and avarice of his children and business cronies became too much for the increasingly educated population to cope with. A monetary crisis tipped the balance, protesters filled the streets of Jakarta and major cities, and the old man eventually stepped down. But not before around five thousand people lost their lives across the country in a series of bloody riots.

It didn't end there. The dark days following Suharto's fall from power were catastrophic. A civil war between Muslim and Christian militia in Maluku killed five thousand between 1999 and 2002. Forced conversions and forced circumcisions were reported. Laras's brother, Karno, was stationed in the city of Ambon. The security forces took sides, the Javanese army siding with the Muslims, and the local police siding with the Christians. About the same time, indigenous Dayaks and local Malays turned on transmigrant Madurese in Kalimantan, killing over three thousand; many were decapitated in a modern-day revival of the old practice of head hunting. In Ampenan, riots claimed an unknown number of lives in January 2000, when we had just arrived in Lombok. While the scale was much smaller, Arab businessmen reportedly took the opportunity to have Malay thugs pay out on their Chinese rivals.

In the eastern province of East Timor, fifteen hundred died after the referendum in 1999, mostly murdered by militia before the Australian-led UN forces intervened. 'Australia Attacks Indonesia!' read the front-page headline of the Lombok Post, which was a little unnerving at the time. There were stories of radicals conducting 'sweeping' operations to expel Australians from hotels in Java, Bali and Lombok. Around two hundred thousand locals are estimated to have died of violence or starvation during the twenty-five-year Indonesian occupation of Timor Leste – nearly a quarter of the population. No one really knows. Another Suharto effort to eradicate communism that got wildly out of hand. Another case of the West nodding in acquiescence while Indonesia runs amok. In West Papua, where an independence movement is still underway in the mountains, the number of deaths at the hands of the Indonesian military may be as high as half a million. In Aceh? Who knows?

Indonesia's emerald green rice fields are watered with blood. Sometimes I imagine that the islands of the archipelago are formed of a kind of opaque glass – just beneath that fragile crystal surface lie dark secrets, nightmares that some say are better left alone, undisturbed in the darkness. There are times when I think I can see beneath the surface, catch glimpses of unnamed creatures, of slithering forms, and shapeless horrors. But mostly there is nothing, just a raw emptiness, an uneasy feeling – like the echo of untold stories.

Calls have been made for the country to uncover this bloody past, to dig up its secrets and expose to the light those human rights abuses, those disappearances, massacres, systematic rapes and killings. But these calls have been resisted by the government, by the military and by the old guard. It is not the Javanese way, not the Indonesian way. Conflicts, uncomfortable truths, painful stories – all are managed with silence and denial. School history books are silent on the matter. And, while the old days of jailing dissidents, artists, novelists and playwrights, of supressing the stories, are gone – most are not ready to acknowledge the past, to acknowledge the lies. Why stir up painful memories, why rake up old conflicts? Better to let sleeping dogs lie. It may need another generation before Indonesia finds the confidence, the maturity as a nation, to face its dark history.

Five

From the five-way junction in Ampenan, we make our way inland past the shops and stalls that line the old streets: cluttered hardware stores, barbers, doctors, haberdasheries, notaries, minimarkets, and a beer wholesaler; around the corner an Arab bakery, purveyors of fake perfume, mobile phones, pirate videos, and electronics; a Chinese medicine dispensary, a doctor's surgery, a children's clothing outlet, fishing suppliers and boat chandlers, a gold shop, a tailor, a pool hall, rice stores, warungs, and, on the street, watch repairers, shoe repairmen, hawkers, buskers and beggars. In the mornings, Sasak women squat on the corner selling fresh fish from buckets, and, at night, a Madurese sate seller sets up by the archway and, fanning a tray of glowing coconut-husk coals, fills the air with clouds of aromatic white smoke as he grills the little sticks of chicken and goat meat sate.

Across another bridge and another river carpeted with crops of tethered water spinach, we enter the city of Mataram, with its broad tree-lined avenues, its rows of government buildings, commercial offices, schools, hospitals and occasional hotels. By the river, a large building is used to farm swiftlets; at dusk the little birds crowd the sky, emerging from holes in the walls in a cloud of wings to chase insects drawn to the streetlights. The nests they produce are the source of a valuable sticky spittle, highly prized in Chinese cuisine as the basis for birds-nest soup. We pass a huge Islamic centre, still under construction – the young governor's pet project. Billboards advertise cigarettes, motorbikes and mobile phone plans, and a huge sign promotes the national *Musabaqah Tilawatil Qur'an* event. The MTQ is an annual festival of Qur'anic recitation and Islamic culture. I once attended an MTQ in the hills of South Sulawesi. Something like a fair ground or a country show, kids played on stilts and giant, oversized swings; people milled around, and stalls sold coffee and fairy floss. The main event featured marching bands and Islamic-themed floats. Some rather sexy looking young women paraded in satiny split dresses and matching hot-pink pants and headscarves, and contestants from each district recited verses from the Qu'ran in taut voices and beautiful high-strained tones. It was a strange form of entertainment in those dreamlike mountains. A strange music.

Near the governor's office an archway with flashing lights and a stream of electronically generated messaging declares the city to be *'Maju, Religius dan Berbudaya'* – 'Progressive, Religious and Cultured'. It's all relative, I think to myself. To the north is the town jail, where I once or twice visited a friend, an Australian on the wrong side of the law. Visiting times were casual, chaotic and good natured; more like a kampung crossroad than a jail. To the south we pass by the town square, where I sometimes stop for a haircut under a tree. Each day an old man sets up, parking his rusty bicycle at the same spot, where he unpacks a little wooden stool and his kit: a mirror shard, scissors, a razor, sharpening stone, soap and a shaving brush with few wisps of horsehair remaining. Beyond the grand governor's office, the mayor's office and Bank Indonesia, we pass by a fountain, Mataram Mall and the park where the remains of General Van Ham lie unregarded. Here we enter Cakranegara, once a Balinese royal city, now a commercial hub. It is here that we have come to look for furniture and bathroom fittings.

In Cakra, we stop at a new store that boasts good deals on imported kitchen and bathroom fittings. Amongst the taps and showerheads, the toilets and washbasins, there are also piles of ceramic tiles – another set of choices to be made. Further east to Sweta and we stop near the traditional market at a big hardware store, not far from where I once watched a traditional cockfight. A Balinese policeman oversaw the illegal event in a dusty kampung square, ensuring that the bookmakers played by the rules and things didn't get out of hand. At the hardware store we are faced with a bewildering array of brass doorknobs, handles and window catches. Then it's back via the northern ring-road for a stop near the airport at a popup shop selling second-hand furniture out of refurbished hotels in Bali. We are building not one, but three, homes. The chance to acquire a set of twelve rattan chairs, cut glass mirrors, brass bedside lamps and a rocking chair is too good to pass. A lick of paint, new cushion covers, and they'll be as good as new.

But our best furniture, much of it stored at Peter and Ace's new warehouse and only recently shifted to a smaller storeroom in the village, is another story. When, as a newly married couple, Laras and I were setting up house in Bogor in the hills outside Jakarta, we took the chance to bid on a household full of furniture. A teacher at the international school where Laras taught was preparing to move back to America after a ten-year stint in Jakarta. We looked around the house – and liked what we saw.

'How much for the lot?' I asked.

'The lot!?' he replied. Bill was expecting to sell his precious things piece by piece over a period of time. But it didn't take long to negotiate a reasonable deal.

There was a wonderful oversized, squishy old lounge suite – the kind of quality they don't bother to make these days. There were woven baskets and wooden chairs and rattan shelves and coffee tables and office furniture and big colourful floor cushions. But, best of all, was a set of hand-crafted teak dining furniture – a beautiful polished oval table with a set of eight chairs, all made to order from recycled timber.

We shook on the deal, agreeing to call in and pick up the furniture when Bill was ready to leave at the end of term. But history intervened. In the violent days leading up to Suharto's fall, Jakarta was in chaos. Thick black smoke filled the air – buildings burned and piles of old tires were set alight at intersections. Mobs filled the streets. Rocks were hurled through windows. Looting was rife. Car jacks were reported. The military was out in force – but they were as much a part of the problem as a solution to it. Expatriates and wealthy Chinese were fleeing the country. The Jakarta International School, like many others, closed its doors and sent everyone home early. And the value of the rupiah tumbled.

'If you want the stuff,' said Bill, 'come and get it. I'm out of here!'

The fact that we had negotiated the price when the rupiah

was worth over ten times the current rate didn't seem to worry him. 'It's fine,' he said, 'just take it.'

And so it was that, while Jakarta burned, I was running back and forth in a pickup truck from South Jakarta to our little home in Bogor, ferrying a household of fine furniture. That furniture is now stacked in a room behind a cottage in the village of Baruna Shanti, ready to dust off and put to use in our new home on the hill.

* * *

On Tuesday, I fly to Singapore. Every so often, expatriates living in Indonesia need to leave the country in order to renew a multiple-entry visa, obtain a new limited-stay permit, or some such. Singapore does a brisk business hosting short-stay visits while agents make the necessary arrangements at the Indonesian embassy. The city is a marvel, an island of sanity, of good sense and good governance in the heart of corrupt, chaotic and steamy South-East Asia. The unique combination of Chinese business savvy, self-discipline and competitive notions of continuing improvement, together with the British legal, political and educational foundations – and large minorities of Indian Hindus and Malay Muslims – has positioned Singapore well to act as the business and financial hub for the region and, increasingly, as a centre for the arts, for fashion and food culture, for sports and intellectual life.

I learned early on that, for old Asia hands, Singapore is a bit of a wet blanket. Not the real Asia. Too clean, too organised, too well policed and well managed – and, therefore, somehow, lacking in authenticity, lacking in character; in short, dull and boring. I beg to differ. While I have grown to love the grubby chaos of Indonesia, Singapore is a wonderful break; refreshing in its orderliness, smart and modern, cosmopolitan while being thoroughly and proudly South-East Asian.

This time I stay for a couple of nights, enabling me to revisit some of my favourite haunts in the Lion City. First stop is a visit to the Asian Civilisations Museum, housed in a grand old public building down by Boat Quay in the colonial area near the historic Raffles Hotel, St Andrew's Cathedral and the Padang cricket ground. My focus is on details, I am looking for inspiration for our building project in Lombok. For an hour or two I lose myself in the high-ceilinged halls, happy amongst the echoes, artefacts and artwork gathered from the various corners of Asia: the first-century Chinese stamped bricks from Henan Province in Zhengzhou; the sixteenth-century game board, ivory, wood and metal from Gujarat; the Chinese scholar's porcelain brush rest; the piles of ceramic bowls, metalwork and artefacts recovered from a ninth-century shipwreck in the Java Sea; the superb terracotta statue of Garuda from Gupta; the fourth-century Greco-Roman Bodhisattva head from Gandhara, Afghanistan (his tight curls reminding me somewhat of Andrew's); the grave markers from Kalimantan, weavings from eastern Indonesia, illustrated copies of the Qur'an from Persia; the Dayak masks and Balinese shadow puppets, the Javanese silverwork; and the little silk painting of a European dandy in seventeenth century India, a rather foppish-looking gentleman sporting a fine, waxed moustache and a Chinese-Iranian jacket. The museum tells a story of goods, ideas, and culture exchanged across the region over the last two thousand years.

But it is over a quiet, late-afternoon drink in the graceful tea rooms that I find my inspiration. The museum's terrace overlooks a row of old 'godown' shophouses that line the river opposite, a colourful strip of history with the gleaming financial district behind. I find a shady table at which to sit and take in the view, a Joseph Conrad novel and a Tiger beer for company. A public statue of Sir Stamford Raffles stands by the river below the café. The fabled founder of Singapore looks suitably statesmanlike; until recently he was venerated as a sort of historic god-king on the island. But among all the colour and history of the place, the extraordinary collection of Malay, Chinese, Arab and Indian art and artefacts, the mix of Chinese and colonial architecture, the one element that strikes home is the lovely white-painted rattan furniture on the café terrace – an echo of an earlier colonial time that somehow retains its elegance in the modern world. A fresh coat of paint and the chairs we found on sale in Mataram will look the part, I think.

The next morning, I sneak off for a visit to some of the city's parks before the day gets too hot and humid, and I settle back into some more work in the air-conditioned comfort of a hotel room. A stroll over the hill behind the old Fort Canning and then a walk around the Botanical Gardens provide plenty of inspiration for landscaping in Lombok. The entire city is a garden – sidewalks are decorated with green planter-boxes and avenues of raintrees fill the air with a chorus of swallows in the early evenings; high-rise apartments are hung with creepers; flyovers and freeways are festooned with flowering bougainvillea; and, everywhere, lawns are neatly trimmed and sculpted green banks are carpeted with ferns and little Singapore daisies. Up behind Fort Canning, huge raintrees with tangled roots, birds-nest ferns and hanging orchids create a vast canopy.

A short drive away, the Botanical Gardens are designed around a series of lakes and small falls. The entrance is shaded by a massive raintree – it must be the size of a football field. Swans, geese and ducks dabble about in the ponds and wide sweeping lawns lead to shady groves, pergolas draped with bell-like thunbergia, and massed plantings of heliconia. The English landscape traditions of Capability Brown and his eighteenth-century mates translate well into the tropical gardens and parks of Singapore, creating an equatorial idyll that stands in contrast to the Dutch-influenced gardens of Indonesia, with their trimmed hedges, geometric designs and lagging maintenance, a seemingly futile attempt to impose order on South-East Asia's feisty and unruly natural environment.

I had long ago decided on a very plain colour scheme for the gardens in Lombok following a visit to the beautiful Oberoi resort on the coast of West Lombok. I noticed something which helped create the restful, relaxing atmosphere of the resort: sparse planting and the simple use of greens and whites as a colour palette. Avoiding the wild tropical colours, the shocking pinks and purples, the flaming reds and oranges, the bright yellows and blues – and sticking to whites and pale creams as occasional highlights in the green – creates a cool, calm and extraordinarily peaceful effect. At least, this is the conclusion I have drawn after a few visits. My brief wanderings around the gardens of Singapore do nothing to change my mind. Singapore in the height of the wet season is lush and green, it buzzes with activity, but it is also calming and refreshing.

Six

The following weekend provides another opportunity for gardening inspiration. My brother and his wife are in Bali for a short stay and we have arranged to meet at another favourite haunt: The Kingfisher Ecolodge established by old friends in the grounds of Udayana University in the dry coastal hills above Jimbaran. A retreat from Bali's out-of-control commercialism, the ecolodge became a home away from home in the years when I was frequently back and forth to Flores.

I drive the old hardtop, taking the slow ferry from Lembar to Padangbai on Bali, arriving on Saturday evening after a day's travel. Wallace is perched on his usual rattan chair by the bar, from where he can look, on a clear day, across the straits to Gunung Rinjani on our neighbouring island of Lombok. Wallace is a bird, a buffy fish owl to be precise. Due to an old injury he is unable to fly, or even to feed himself, and so has come to rely on the goodwill of Alan and Meryl, who take care of him at the ecolodge. Sadly, Wallace passed away some years after this visit, but, like his namesake, Alfred Russel Wallace, he is well remembered.

The couple, like Andrew, are refugees from Africa. And like Andrew they carry with them the values and habits of an older, colonial world. Meryl, who designed the ecolodge and the gardens, and has produced a beautiful hand-illustrated book on the lowland butterflies of Indonesia, tells of how, in 1975, they fled Ida Amin's Uganda in a single-engine Cessna and flew, in a series of short hops, to Australia with their two children.

The architecture of the ecolodge, with its passive cooling and open-to-the-sky second storey, was an inspiration when I was beginning to form my own ideas. Now the garden is an inspiration. Meryl and Alan's extensive gardens are loosely designed, using the existing trees and plants as a foundation, to attract the birds and butterflies. And in this they succeed admirably. My own planning for Lombok is taking shape. Earlier visits to the Botanical Gardens established by Raffles in Bogor and Cibodas in West Java, and to the extensive Botanical Gardens in mountainous Bedugul, Bali, have all helped. My mud maps are becoming progressively more refined sketches, and details are becoming clearer as I take note of the plants, the trees and ground covers, the flowering shrubs and lilies, that look right, that look like they will work in a certain context.

Monday is a public holiday, Idul Adha, the day of sacrifice for Muslims. A day when around a million unsuspecting goats will meet their end across the country. I make my way back to Lombok armed with a bag of thunbergia suckers from Meryl and Alan's garden, and a head full of ideas. After another trip to Jakarta I am back in Lombok for the following weekend and once again up the hill and checking on progress.

We meet with Pak Pujo on a Saturday morning and with Agus and Rani in the afternoon. The dam is completed – although the first attempt to fill it revealed a leak in the lining, the water seeping through risked not only emptying the pond but eroding the banks downstream and unseating the bridge foundations. Pujo promises to drain the dam and rectify the problem.

The discussion with Rani and Agus covers a lot of ground. We talk about how the work crew is shaping up and plans for the future, about budgets and cash flows, about materials and suppliers. We also talk about relationships on The Hill. Tensions between Pujo and Agus have been simmering since Pujo suspected Agus of undermining him by offering to pay his workers a higher daily rate – an accusation that Agus denies. The thing that really upset Pujo, though, was the time during Ramadan, when Agus made light of Pujo's religious practice, jokingly suggesting that he was not serious about the fasting. Coming from the younger man, and a Hindu at that, the slight on his faith was most unwelcome. Since that time, Pujo has taken the Javanese approach to conflict resolution by not speaking to Agus. He has also avoided offering any support or counsel to the younger engineer, something we hoped would be part of the deal as we have worked with Pujo for several years now during the design and building of roads and the terracing and shaping of land. There is nothing to be done. It will blow over in time – or not.

Over the last few months, since I met with Agus and Tarno in Yogya, back in August, correspondence back and forth with Tarno has brought us close to finalizing a deal for all the timberwork for the main house. Laras drives a hard bargain. Her brother-in-law has been in and out of Tarno's workshop checking on the timber and materials he is quoting.

'Better to have a shouting match now, at the beginning, than later when the job is done,' laughed Tarno at one point when the negotiations over prices were getting a bit heated.

Armed with the detailed drawings and dimensions of all the timber work to be supplied, Rani has prepared a series of wonderful technical drawings, drawings that Agus and his crew will turn into buildings, into homes and cottages. I find the drawings a delight, as if each is a work of art in its own right – rather than just a plan, a model for the real thing. There is genuine satisfaction to be had in pondering those lovely lines, the detailed sketches and maps, the north, south, east and west elevations, the cut-aways showing how the roots of the structure will penetrate deep into the earth – chicken-feet foundations, sloof beams, electrical and plumbing installations, and underground water storage. Rani has prepared the drawings in the old way; images of an idealised world, a clean, predictable and strangely beautiful world of straight lines, fine angles and elegant proportions.

On site, we find that the joglo water storage tank is now hidden beneath a smooth concrete lid, a slab which will form part of the floor of the cottage. Work continues on the excavation by the creek. Formwork is half constructed, and lengths of reinforcing steel are being tied together for the concrete beams which will support the second floor of the main house. Suweg plants dot the landscape. It is December, and a number of them are now flowering.

'Hey! Check this out!' Laras calls.

She is on the bank near the northern border, by the path that leads down from the dam to the western terrace. A couple of the fleshy plants stand a little over a metre tall, their pale green serrated leaves spread wide. Beside one of these, a single, crenelated, blood-red flower rises about forty centimetres from the ferny earth.

'I had to stop Pak Mobin from cutting them down,' says Agus. 'They can't stand the smell.'

At around sunset the flowers emit a truly dreadful odour, the putrid stench of rotting meat. The flowers are apparently pollinated not by bees, but by blowflies. The tuber which grows beneath the surface is supposedly good eating, a kind of yam. Pak Pujo told me once that he used to eat it as a child, but it made his throat itchy.

'Well, it might stink, but it's amazing,' I tell Agus. 'Make sure they don't cut them down. I think they're extraordinary!'

It is a wet day, a late morning downpour has eased off and become a drizzle, the type of rain that locals call *'gerimis'* and blame for causing the dreaded *'masuk angin'* – literally 'wind entering' – a type of head cold, sometimes involving fevers, bone aches, hiccups, bloating and flatulence, brought on by exposure to the cold and damp of such rain. Common during the change of seasons. But it is not so wet that I can't wander about and project my imagined landscape designs onto an innocent landscape. The plan is simple enough – as it mainly involves leaving everything where it is, the large duwet trees that line the borders above and below, the huge fig tree with its dangling aerial roots, the buttressed rainforest giants that cluster along the creek, the tall coconut palms, the sugar palm that Pak Mobin taps for palm wine and red sugar, the towering stands of bamboo, and the row of deciduous banten that marks the western border. Rather than designing a landscape, it is more a matter of filling in the details – a traditional statue here, a lawn and a bank of ferns here, a hedge of miniature bamboo there, perhaps a flowering frangipani or a fruit tree or two over there.

While the arrangement looks natural, as if plants have randomly self-seeded with no design, no intent, in fact the entire hill is a garden, a farm or a plantation. To those who know, among the weeds and saplings, every plant has a purpose; every tree has been planted by someone at some time with that purpose in mind. My purpose is to leave the landscape as it is, in broad outline, to preserve all the palms and large trees, and to enhance it a little by cutting and pruning, by creating open lawns, pathways and outdoor rooms, bordered by hedges, trees, changes in levels. The intention is to make the garden more productive and, at the same time, more beautiful by adding fragrant frangipani and kananga, and by planting or retaining existing fruit trees: avocado, mango, mangosteen, rambutan, tamarind, guava, jackfruit, and the Papuan *matoa*; and a modest grove of citrus: potent little dark-green limes, sweet mandarins, and huge grapefruit-like pomelo, known as *jeruk Bali*.

Terraces are being shored up with thick banks of smoky-green lemon grass. Access roads will become avenues of raintrees. Papaya and banana can be planted like giant vegetables where they will blend in with massed plantings of the birdlike flowering heliconia, hibiscus and stray acacia saplings. Broad-leaved monstera can be led to run up coconut palms. White flowering bougainvillea can climb along the fences. Pergola can be hung with thunbergia, passionfruit and *bangkwan* yam vines, banks can be filled with local ferns: maidenhairs, sword ferns, java ferns – and retaining walls can be painted with Balinese terracotta and softened with epiphytic ferns and creeping figs. The bones of the plan are in place, the big trees, the creek, the shape of the land and position of the buildings. Karno has begun planting the fruit trees.

Andrew has provided a dozen raintree seedlings. 'They are a legume,' he explained, 'a giant legume – and a nitrogen fixer. The leaves make excellent compost material.'

Little clumps of broad-leaved grass that have now been planted over the bare banks are growing fast in the moist conditions, reaching towards one another and beginning to cover the earth in a green lawn. It is not so hard to imagine the rest, like a watercolour sketch in the wash of drizzle and shining leaves, the trees dripping and the creek flowing.

THE RAINY SEASON

One

The air is still fresh, the western sky is clear and bright after a morning shower. The wild grasses, acacia saplings and lantana weeds are thick, green and dripping. We make our way up the hill. Everything is soggy. A dark blanket of cloud begins to creep in from the north-east. As the day heats up, the warm, moist air is drawn up by the mountain where it cools, condenses, and forms rain clouds. But a thin, high sun casts crisp shadows beneath the clouds in the midday light.

Last night I arrived back from a trip to visit my Australian family for Christmas. It is early January. Laras has decided to stay on in Tasmania where she plans to spend the year working on her doctoral studies. It looks like I will be in charge of both the build and the boys. Fortunately, I have a small army of locals to help with these responsibilities.

The dam is finally complete – along with a splendid-looking bridge. I drive the old hardtop down past where, on my last visit, piles of sand and gravel sat alongside the cement mixer. Somewhat tentatively I take the car across the bridge and onto the western terrace. The dam is full of muddy, brown water; the colour of a flat white coffee. After a quick exploration, the boys are off to walk up the hill and meet their school friends, a couple of lads who live on the ridge high above, sons of an off-beat entrepreneur from Belgium, and his estranged Indonesian wife.

I walk back across the bridge, to where Pak Pujo waits. We talk briefly, exchanging pleasantries, and verbally signing off on the work, now complete. It looks like a triangle of muddy water, bordered by lines of smooth concrete; not quite the ferny tropical pond I had envisaged. But it's a start. A little landscaping and planting will soften the edges. And the water seems to be staying put. We shake hands and I wander down to check out the eastern terrace.

The women with the red buckets are shuffling up and down the slope, carrying loads of grass tufts on their heads. Laras's brother, Karno, arranged for the grass to be dug up from an area in the valley floor. The women carry bucket loads from a pile on the terrace to where they are planting them out in a vast polka-dot pattern near the creek. Eddy is over by the cottage site, which now sports a solid slab – about ten by ten metres – ready to support the timber joglo structure. The water storage area is hidden beneath. Dedy strikes the wooden kentongan, which still hangs from the corner of the adjacent shed; tok-tok-tok, tok-tok-tok, the sound reverberates around the valley, signalling break time. The workers down tools and wander off to find a shady spot to eat, rest or pray. We walk back across the new bridge and down to the western terrace where Agus and Rani are pacing about, inspecting the structure.

Rani and Agus greet me with smiles and handshakes. Rani brandishes the design drawings. She looks confident and relaxed as if everything is as it should be. With the sun high and casting sharp shadows beneath encroaching dark clouds, it all looks remarkably attractive and well organised. I expect this is for my benefit, but nonetheless I am impressed.

'It looks great!' I tell Rani and Agus. 'Amazing.'

'Thanks,' Agus replies with a modest smile. 'We have worked hard over the last month. It's coming along nicely.'

It is quite a feeling, being able to walk about on the new floor, looking at Rani's familiar drawings, imagining the walls and the rooms they will enclose. It feels, if not quite comfortable or cosy, then at least pleasing, reassuring. The ideas, the concept, the imagined spaces, are becoming a reality. A raw, unfinished reality but a reality nonetheless. I am unable to keep the smile from my face as I walk from one imagined room to another.

A few steps away from the construction, with its spicy tang of raw concrete, the remnant forest smells dark and musky, of damp earth, of wet and rotting vegetation; the smells of sex and defecation, of growth and decay, of life and death. High above, a lone cicada strikes up, declaring his presence, calling for a mate with a single high-pitched, whirring, chirruping note that extends seemingly without end. Others join, one by one, creating a raucous, ringing chorus; the tuneless music emanates from nowhere in particular, from everywhere at once. It is the sound of the tropics.

We pick our way across the creek, through dappled shade beneath the giant fig tree. The creek trickles quietly over mud, stone, and roots – and I am able to step across a series of slippery rocks to the other side. The big fig tree has littered the area with little black berries. This kind of tree is sacred to the Sasak, Balinese and Javanese, along with many in South-East Asia. Known to the Sasak and Balinese as *beringin*, to the Javanese as *waringin*, and more generally as *banyan*, the trees are venerated in villages, at crossroads, in temples and at marketplaces, village commons and town squares across the islands. The Balinese build small shrines and place daily offerings among the knotted roots. Pairs of holy waringin guard both the northern and the southern gates to the sultan's palace in Yogyakarta, marking the pathway north to the sacred Mount Merapi and south to Parangtritis Beach and the Indian Ocean, where Ratu Kidul, the South-Sea Queen, resides beneath the waves. When one of the northern pair was destroyed by lightning, palace retainers redoubled their efforts to fend off ill-fortune through prayer and ritual. This was a very bad omen. The palace now faces a local crisis as the sultan, in defiance of tradition, has moved to name his daughter as successor, pleasing some and offending others – including his sons and conservative Muslims.

Our tree creates its own presence, with its huge canopy, its hanging aerial roots and its tangled ground roots, around which flows the creek. The tree is home to a crowded community of creatures: small mammals – little pointy-nosed shrews and bushy-tailed civets – along with snakes and lizards, frogs, spiders, insects, butterflies, bats, bees and birds. It was in the creek, some years later, that Lali caught an impressively large cobra, who lived with us for a few days in a large glass jar, before we released him up the valley. The poor creature, a symbol of fertility in Java, was not happy about his confinement and would rear up, flair his neck, and spit furiously at the glass every time the cover was lifted.

Fruiting season is a busy time. The tree also supports a range of plants, mosses, ferns, creepers and climbers. A little well, cradled in the roots and mossy rocks, provides refuge to frogs and toads; tadpoles huddle in the corners and tiny black fish flit about in the dark below; little shrimps dart in the shallows and pond skimmers sit lightly on the shadowed surface, drawing a tiny meniscus up around each spindly leg. And, for those who believe, the tree houses spirits, perhaps devils and the ghosts of ancestors.

Across the creek and beyond the giant beringin tree, the grass planting gradually extends across the entire eastern slope. Ferns fringe the creek and guavas stand with acacia saplings like ragged soldiers in a line. Karno has acquired a pair of gnarled old frangipani trees from an abandoned hotel on the coast. The trees have been replanted on the slope, propped up with bamboo, where they will enhance the view from the cottage on the terrace.

As we make our way up the bank, the view opens up. Bulbuls are busy in the crowns of the coconut palms and a bright blue kingfisher flashes across the valley, alighting in a tall tree on the southern border. The emergent giant is now dressed in green and strung with little seedpods like dull tinsel. The bird settles on its favourite perch, from where, silhouetted against a distant ocean, it surveys its domain, scanning for prey – for lizards, little snakes, worms, snails, and slippery tree frogs.

Drawn by the shouts and shrieks of boys at play, we make our way up to where I find them splashing about in the new dam. Four dark heads bob about in the muddy water; Rory hangs on to a piece of construction timber, which makes a fine boat.

* * *

Another week passes, and I am halfway up the hill on Saturday morning for a routine check on progress. Rory asks if they can ride on the outside of the hardtop. 'Not so sure about that,' I reply. 'It doesn't sound very safe!'

'We'll be fine, Dad,' he says. 'When I go to soccer, Abah always takes us in the back of his pickup. The whole team rides in the back. It's fun! Come on, Dad!'

'Yeah, come on, Dad!' chimes in Harry.

And so begins a tradition, the kind of tradition that may not have begun had I not been a single dad for this time – or if we were living in a more constrained environment. After a little more badgering from the boys, I concede, and let them stand on the running boards and hold on to the open windows.

'Hang on tight!' I say, rather unnecessarily. And we make our way for the last few hundred metres in this manner, with the two of them hanging on the side of the vehicle, whooping and hollering in delight as we bounce gently down the rough road to the building site.

Progress on construction of the cottage on the eastern terrace is rapid. Agus has ferried all the pieces for the joglo from our backyard in Baruna Shanti up to the site. The central structure is already up; four sturdy teak pillars known as *soko guru* support a central framework of interlocking timbers, known as the *tumpang sari*. Above this, roof beams reach high to form a steeply pitched, hipped roof over this central section. Traditionally, the higher the roof, the more intricately carved the tumpang sari, the higher the status of the owner. Our joglo is a simple, unadorned structure. The soko guru pillars rest on carved volcanic stone plinths. These, in turn sit loose on the concrete slab.

'There is beauty in simplicity,' I think to myself. It is extraordinary to see it going up so quickly, the timber becoming a dwelling after being stored in a pile in the backyard for nearly ten years. Agus appears with his usual modest smile and business-like manner. 'I found some references on the joglo structure,' he explains. 'I think we can figure it all out.'

'Great!' I say. All the major pieces – pillars, panels, large beams – are marked with white paint. Each has a coded number which corresponds to another piece where it should fit. In this way, the joglo can be put together, piece by piece, like a giant puzzle.

Meanwhile, Rory and Harry are looking for mischief. Their friends from up the hill have joined them and they are off exploring the site. After fresh rains, the black clay mud on the terrace below the joglo construction is pliable, ready to be employed as a weapon in a boyish war. Little piles of mud bombs are prepared, and the ammunition flies as the boys scuttle about among the trees, up and down the slopes, pelting one another – or at least attempting to – until eventually I call it off.

'That's enough, you'll make too much of a mess,' I tell them.

The boys surrender after a half-hearted protest, and head up to rinse themselves off in the dam while the workers stop for a break. A little fire burns, the men and women sit around, weary but chatty and companionable, a blackened billy sits over the flames; water is on the boil for coffee. A pleasant scene.

Two

Today is Imlek, Chinese New Year, a public holiday. Just a few years ago all things Chinese were outlawed in Indonesia. In the wake of the failed coup and the purge of the Left in the sixties, Suharto issued decrees banning the use of Chinese language – written or spoken – of Chinese names, and any expressions of Chinese culture. The days of Sukarno's flirting with the communist nation, with socialist ideology, were over. The Chinese Indonesian community provided a convenient scapegoat. Suharto's vision was for a unified, nationalist Indonesia; a country in which ethnic and regional differences were dissolved, a country independent but aligned with the West, in which Islamist political movements were suppressed and communism was totally eradicated. The term 'SARA' was introduced, an acronym for *'Suku, Agama, Ras dan Antar Golongan'* – 'Ethnicity, Religion, Race and Inter-Group'. All activities, publications or movements which threatened division on the basis of SARA were outlawed.

But the Chinese were singled out for special treatment. Under the Dutch, ethnic Chinese people were afforded a privileged status – somewhere beneath the Dutch but above the indigenous Indonesians, the *pribumi* or 'sons of the soil', as they are known. The colonial system classified residents as Europeans, *Inlanders* (Natives) or *Vreemde Oosterlingen* (Foreign Orientals). The

Chinese dominated business and some were appointed as local regents. This created an Indonesian identity out of the *Inlander* category but meant that the Eurasian and Chinese minorities did not fully belong to the nation. They have paid for it ever since. Arabs, Indians and indigenous peoples from the eastern islands were also left out – though the Arabs are now more integrated into government due, in large part, to sharing a religion with the majority.

The Dutch colonial authorities had adopted a pluralist legal system to enable local ethnic rulers to use their own traditional laws, to manage their own affairs under the colonial umbrella. In this system, native courts dealt with *pribumi* affairs in Java. Chinese citizens were required to carry a pass at all times. Their movements were somewhat restricted, and their legal affairs were dealt with by the *Kapitan Cina*, or the head of their community – as issues for Arab and Indian minorities were handled by their community leaders. When schooling was introduced in the early twentieth century, Chinese attended Chinese schools and spoke Chinese languages. Europeans attended European schools and spoke Dutch, and indigenous Javanese attended village schools in which Javanese was the medium of instruction. Eurasians were often included in the Dutch system, though with some disdain, and sometimes not. Although not apartheid, like the colonial education system in Indonesia, to my surprise when I visited Sarawak in Malaysian Borneo, I found a differentiated schooling system. There, the Chinese and Malays have the option of attending different schools and studying in different languages. There were parallels to the old Dutch apartheid in Australia, though, where Chinese immigrants and their descendants were treated with suspicion and were not afforded full citizenship until the mid-1960s.

In 1958, early in the life of the newly independent nation, Sukarno required all ethnic Chinese to declare their intention to become, or remain, Indonesian citizens. The passports and identity cards of Chinese subsequently indicated their ethnicity. Under Suharto, things went from bad to worse. For thirty years, while quietly developing the economy along with the nation's education, arts and professions, the ethnic Chinese, now known as *Tionghoa*, laid low. Any dealings with government were bound to be problematic as the pribumi-dominated bureaucracy discriminated against the Chinese – both officially and informally. Meanwhile, an elite group of favoured ethnic Chinese entrepreneurs – known as *cukong* – became extremely wealthy under Suharto's patronage – thereby further alienating the already jealous pribumi community.

All of this changed under the presidency of Gus Dur, a liberal Islamic cleric and leader of Nahdlatul Ulama, who was unexpectedly elected president by the national assembly after the first free elections, which were held at the end of B.J. Habibie's brief transitional presidency, following Suharto's fall from grace. Gus Dur was an unlikely president, half blind as a result of a stroke, and somewhat erratic, having been schooled in the Islamic pesantren system and brought up in Nahdlatul Ulama, with its traditional Javanese approach to decision-making and organisation. He was also very learned, very progressive and muttered about abolishing the Religious Affairs Ministry and lifting the ban on communism – neither of which happened. On a state visit to the United States, Gus Dur was reportedly asked by a junior aide whether they could trust the Americans: how could the Indonesians be sure that the food is halal?

'There are two answers to that question, son,' the great man reportedly replied. 'First, of course the Americans will serve us halal food! They know we are Muslims. They are not stupid and I'm sure they will be good hosts! Second, don't ask! What you don't know can't hurt you.'

When the aide subsequently did ask and was not satisfied with the answer he received about the nature of the food served, Gus Dur was apparently furious. 'I told you not to ask, damn it!' he snapped at the young man.

On another occasion, Gus Dur is reported to have quipped; 'Indonesia's first president was crazy about women. The second president was crazy about money. And the third president was just plain crazy.' What about the fourth president? he was asked. 'Me?' he replied with a laugh, 'I just make everyone else crazy!'

Gus Dur lasted just nine turbulent months before he was ousted and Sukarno's daughter, Megawati, became Indonesia's fifth president. But he is still revered, almost as a minor deity, by members of the Nahdlatul Ulama, that he once led. One time I attended an evening prayer event at an Islamic boarding school, or pesantren, in a dusty corner of central Lombok. I was there for work. A celebrity preacher had been brought in to provide a little Islamic entertainment and gee the students up after the trauma of an earthquake. There, I noticed, ten years after his presidency, and long after his death, Gus Dur was still president – his formal photograph remained on the wall beside that of Megawati, his then-vice-president.

Before he left office, Gus Dur declared that he himself had

some Chinese ancestry, an admission that surprised the Islamic majority who typically see ethnicity and religion as inseparable, and assume that Chinese are not Muslims. In fact, most Chinese Indonesians are Christian, Buddhist or Confucianist, but some are Muslim. Merchants from China have been trading in the archipelago since the First Millennium, and Chinese Muslims were among the early propagators of Islam in Indonesia. In the early fifteenth century the great Muslim mariner Zheng He visited Java. Zheng He was an explorer, diplomat, fleet admiral and court eunuch during China's early Ming dynasty. This was after Indian Sufi traders first introduced the new religion in the thirteenth century, but before the wave of Arab traders and missionaries in the sixteenth century.

Gus Dur officially ended bureaucratic discrimination against the Chinese, repealing the regulations that had been promulgated under Suharto – and no doubt, by doing so, antagonizing the many petty bureaucrats who made a tidy living extorting bribes from Chinese Indonesian citizens. He also declared Imlek, or Chinese New Year, as an official public holiday. This was a less controversial decree – Indonesians may not always be as tolerant as they should be of one another's faiths, but they are happy to enjoy the public holidays for Christian, Islamic, Buddhist and Hindu festivals – and now Tionghoa. As a result, within a year or two, Chinese culture is flowering in the country and Imlek is celebrated annually in a very festive and public way.

The Year of the Ox begins today. A decent fall of rain promises good fortune for the year to come. I take the boys down to Senggigi to see the *barongsai*. The lion dance is the central set piece in Chinese New Year celebrations in Indonesia and across the world. Imlek – also called the Lunar New Year or Spring Festival – begins today with the new moon, and ends in fifteen days' time with the Lantern Festival on the night of the full moon. Over the last few days, houses, businesses, graveyards and temples have been swept and scrubbed clean in preparation for the big day. Similar to the Christian celebration of Christmas and the Muslim Idul Fitri, the main event is a family feast. Tionghoa families, the descendants of merchants from Southern China, mostly Hakka and Hokkien from Guandong, gather to reconnect and celebrate together. This is a day to welcome the gods, to see in the New Year, to honour family elders and show respect for the ancestors. Everyone dresses in their finest, the colour red predominates – and the lions dance to bring good luck, to sweep away the past, to welcome in the new.

A small crowd gathers in Senggigi Square, an amiable mix of locals – Sasak, Balinese and Chinese – and a few stray tourists. It is early evening and the paving stones are wet from the afternoon's rain, glistening in the lights of surrounding shops, restaurants and salons. The atmosphere is heady, the warm air scented with incense. Paper lanterns and festive banners hang from many of the shophouses: *Gong xi fa cai!* Have a prosperous new year! A troupe of players from the Tionghoa community gathers – young men and women dressed in shiny red satin pyjamas. On a sign from the leader of the troupe, a series of violent thumps on the big black drum that rests between his knees, the players strike up in a cacophony of clashing cymbals and beating drums. The sudden energy is solid, tactile; it feels like a collision in the calm night air. Then the lions enter, two of them, bright red and gold, glittering tassels swish wildly as they dance into the arena, swaying rhythmically from side to side. Huge heads leap and swoop, dipping towards the circle of spectators; gaping white-frilled mouths snap in hungry grins – half-smile, half grimace.

The lions each consist of two red-legged dancers: young men who work their monster in a tightly coordinated but improvised set of movements, alternately rearing high, the front dancer leaping onto his friend's shoulders, bearing the great head aloft where it shakes its mane, arching at the new moon, before dropping, stooping in a sudden movement towards the audience like a massive puppy sniffing an unfamiliar visitor. A blend of fun, excitement and fear, the monsters' eyes goggle, long lashes flash, blinking with a snapping motion. A few Chinese kids, dressed in their best for the occasion, step tentatively forward – their mothers nudging them, standing protectively behind. Each child holds out a red envelope containing cash, hoping to get the attention of the lions. One of the dancers catches sight of a proffered envelope and in a moment the giant head is there, snapping at the child who starts in fear before regaining her composure and, stretching out her hand, she drops the envelope into the gaping jaws. A round of applause ripples around the circle as the monster dances away, looking for more prey, more envelopes, another child to terrify and delight.

The mythical lion and its larger relative, the dragon, have merged with local traditions across Indonesia, morphing into the *barong* in Bali, where the lion is king of the spirits and leader of the forces of good. The shaggy, elaborately costumed creature battles the evil Queen Rangda with her mop of hair, claw-like nails and hideous toothy grimace. A visit from the Barong is welcomed by villagers, happy to see the victory of good over evil re-enacted, the bad spirits banished and a good harvest ensured.

In his incarnation as the *Reog* of Ponorogo in East Java, the lion represents evil. The tradition is thought to have begun as a form of resistance, created by Ki Ageng Kutu, a local Javanese leader, and his Chinese advisor, as a way to build spiritual prowess and poke fun at the rulers of the late Majapahit Empire, who at that time ruled over a reluctant Ponorogo. The male dancers, known as *warok*, were trained in Kutu's hermitage, not only in the art of dance but in spiritual practice and armed combat. At its height, in the fourteenth and fifteenth centuries, the Majapahit Empire extended throughout most of the archipelago, but by the time Ki Ageng Kutu was devising his very Javanese form of resistance, the empire was well and truly in decline.

The warok dancers have a long history of resistance and rebellion. In 1825, around three hundred and fifty years after the tradition began, they joined forces with Diponegoro, the Javanese mystic, royal prince of Yogyakarta and pious Muslim, and supported his holy war and armed uprising against the Dutch. Apparently, after the Dutch finally supressed the rebellion in 1830, the warok and leaders of Ponorogo refused to submit. Over the following century, they continued to develop and practice their craft – a mix of dance, magic and insurgence, occasionally murdering a Dutch resident or burning down a coffee factory or colonial arsenal, before joining the struggle for independence in 1945. Then things went a little awry. Many of the warok joined the uprising in nearby Madiun in 1948, an effort by the Indonesian Communist Party to wrest local control from the fledgling nationalist government. The uprising was put down and its leaders executed by Indonesia's nationalists – and those involved were marked out as 'reds' and trouble-makers.

Trance dancers still perform the lion dance in Ponorogo on festivals and feast days, such as Idul Fitri. Here the tradition runs deep, and the fear associated with the lion is real as he channels the dark forces described in Kejawan, the old faith of Java, which still persists beneath the layers of a more recent Islam and contemporary understandings of reality. The warok traditionally follow the mystical tenants of Kejawan and practice celibacy, but take a boy as a protégé, fellow dancer, companion – and often as a lover. The boys, known as *gemblak*, are typically aged between twelve and fifteen. The practice is thought to increase the spiritual powers of both and was traditionally accepted within the community, though one wonders what the neglected wives of the warok and mothers of the gemblak thought of it. Occasional jealousies and disputes over gemblak apparently gave rise to fights and feuds between individuals and factions within the warok community, which at one time prompted the Dutch to try and abolish the practice.

Many of the warok dancers were killed by nationalists and Islamic reformers in the purge at the end of the Sukarno regime. Their reputation for belligerence, their involvement in black magic, their association with LEKRA and flirtation with the communists in Madiun were cause enough. The Reog was tainted and rarely performed during the oppressive Suharto period. But recent years have seen a revival. The dance is now seen as a valuable cultural heritage. As a result of changing attitudes, the young trance dancers of the Reog and the horse dance are now often girls, the dancing is taught in regular schools, and the sexual traditions associated with the warok have disappeared.

Three

Rory and Harry accompany me as usual on the drive to inspect progress on the building site. After the success of their first ride, I allow them to stand on the sideboards again. This time we stop at the top of the turnoff from the main road, Jalan Bukit Batu Layar, and they clamber on the outside of the old hardtop for the short drive down Jalan Lembah to the house site.

It is Saturday morning. Five days have passed since we watched the lions dance in Senggigi. I have been to Jakarta in this time – arriving back in Lombok on Friday night. This constant travel is becoming a little wearisome. A high, characterless cloud cover extends across the sky; the air is a dull white, close and muggy. It is the sort of day that casts no shadows and can wilt your soul – if you let it.

My mood lifts as soon as we arrive. A pair of beautiful little sunbirds potter about in the grass. And the progress is astonishing. The structure of the joglo is close to complete. Rafters slope gently from the central framework with its high-peaked roof to the outer walls, comprised of wooden panels, each wall with three sets of twin doors and shuttered windows. Light steel scaffolding provides a base for men to work on the roofing. Within a minute or two, Harry, barefoot and grinning, is up the scaffolding and peering down from what must feel like a great height, beneath the towering central roofline. Already it begins to feel like a house, and potentially a home.

Andrew turns up unexpectedly, to have a look around. He joins me on the terrace. 'It's wonderful!' he enthuses. 'Really! I'm chuffed!'

So am I. Together, we stand on what will be the balcony and admire the view. Bali is just visible in the pale distant haze; the greyish waters of the Lombok Straits look restless in the middle distance beyond Senggigi Point, and the crowd of big trees in the foreground offers a variety of shades of green, splashed with rusty reddish-brown where the leggy giants are hung with a mass of seed pods. But my eye is drawn to that little grotto, the corner in the creek where the dark well is nestled beneath the fig tree. There is something special, something a little magical, about this place. Beyond that, across the small valley and beside the creek, work is underway to lay a slab for the cottage. Three squares of smooth grey cement lie gleaming wet in a nine-square grid formed by the foundations where Lali and his mates have excavated the bank. The remaining six squares consist of raked and tamped dirt. It looks like a giant game of noughts and crosses. Work on the main house on the western terrace has been suspended while Agus and the crew concentrate their efforts on the joglo and wait for the timber to arrive from Yogya. Two trucks are reportedly on the way.

The big duwet trees on the terrace above are fruiting, covered with purple cherry-like fruits – a little like an olive or a grape in size and shape. The heavy seasonal rains have produced a good crop. Left to fall, the fruit makes a purple mess of whatever is beneath. Eaten raw, it is fleshy, sweet and rather acidic, plump and juicy after the rains, but leaving a furry taste on the tongue. A bit like a tart little plum. Collected, skinned and pipped, the fruit makes a wonderful jam – something Laras has discovered through experimentation. Mbak Rus has become expert at making jam from local fruits. Under Laras's tutelage she produces beautiful bitter marmalade from local citrus fruits and now a splendid duwet jam – it tastes a little like blackberry or blackcurrant preserve.

The duwet is also known to have medicinal properties. Sometimes known as the black plum and sometimes Java plum, *jamblang* or *jamun*, it has many names across the South and South-East Asian regions. Apparently, the leaves are good for treating diabetes, the pips can be dried and powdered for treatment of acne, and the fruit is good for stomach complaints. Today a tarpaulin has been spread beneath one of the trees and a couple of women are busy collecting the fruit they shake from the limbs.

Four

The generally calm sea is in an unruly early-February mood today. A huge swell pumps from the south-west. The beach shelves sharply and the big waves rear up as they approach the shore, before thumping into the sand. The boom, boom, boom as they slap the shore shakes the beach and drags away the sand, creating a cavern along the tideline. Every so often a bigger-than-usual wave washes up and over this sandy cliff, the foam reaching the feet of drinkers in Café Alberto before it retreats, drops out of sight and rejoins the ocean below. Of course, all of this rhythmic surging violence is an invitation to the boys – who run in and out, getting dragged out in the backwash before being thrown up again as the next set charges in. It's all a bit unnerving, but they seem to be managing the risk on their own terms – until Harry gets out of his depth and has to be rescued, panting and scared, by a young man on a banana boat.

These waves are no good for surfing – the better surf is just around a raggedy headland, or out on the point break at the end of the next beach to the north. On a good day, the ocean builds slowly; it curves and curls and rolls into the beach, a thing of beauty, perfect in its form, like a mythical creature. The white crests sparkle, blue water shifts in the sunlit wake, and the waves crowd with tourists on rented boards and village lads on their patched-up equipment. The Senggigi point break divides, curling away on each side of the point, surfers gather on either the northern or southern side, sometimes both, depending on conditions.

Afternoon eventually turns into evening, the sun sets across the straits beyond the Senggigi Point surf break and behind Bali's Gunung Agung, and it's time to think about heading home. Harry has recovered from his ordeal and I share a thin-crust pizza with the boys, an Alessandro Special, named after one of Giuseppe's sons – we take our leave, and clamber aboard the hardtop. The Sunday papers – one in Indonesian and one in English – are somehow waiting for me in the driver's seat. The papers arrive on the midday flight from Jakarta, and Leo, a good-natured, small-town Chinese entrepreneur, loads them onto his motorbike and every day, without fail – come rain, hail or shine (although hail is rather less likely in Lombok) – delivers them to his customers. If he spots the bright green hardtop in Senggigi or some other place, it's easier to drop the papers there than drive up the road to Baruna Shanti. What baffles me is not how he finds me – fair chance I'll be at Café Alberto on a Sunday, and the vehicle is hard to miss – no, it's how he manages to leave the papers on the driver's seat when the car is locked.

* * *

The trucks have arrived from Yogyakarta! Sometime between Sunday night and Monday morning the two trucks turned up – big, wooden-sided flat-trays, painted bright yellow and loaded high with the timberwork they have carried from Yogya, together with a team of carpenters from Pak Tarno's workshop.

Creamy morning clouds are scattered about in a blue sky, and I find the trucks parked among the coconut palms and ketapang trees in an open sandy area by the beach; the place where the Lebaran Topat fair took place a few months back. The area now looks clean and dry. The drivers are resting, sprawled about in the shade with Tarno's workers and craftsmen. The ten-man crew has spent the last three days perched on top of the piles of teak panels and timber; they have crossed three islands on the back of the trucks to get here.

Over the next few days, Agus arranges for the timber to be unloaded and shuttled up to the site in a smaller pickup truck. Karno and Agus carefully check off each item against the inventory prepared by Tarno and checked in Yogya by Laras's brother-in-law – over a thousand individual items, along with timber for flooring and ceilings. There are twenty large wall panels – or *gebyok*, each one an individual piece, ornately carved and including doors, windows and latticed ventilation panels – eighteen doors and twenty-seven individual window panels with matching shutters. There are sixteen sections of carved railing, a bunch of broad, heavy steps and a complete framework, banisters, posts and railings for the internal stairs. There is a stack of old *wuwung*, decorative terracotta tiles designed to fit on the roof ridges. Some have cracked and broken on the journey, but most are in good shape.

Another sixty substantial pieces of timber are each numbered and designated for a specific position and purpose in the construction: pillars and beams and joists and bearers and rafters and braces and purlins and plates and roof trusses and curved braces – and three massive old carved ridge beams called *dodok besi* to place with due respect in the high centre of the structure. There are twelve carved star-shaped pieces to fit at the top of the pillars and between the cross beams. There are sixty sections of fretted fascia boards to fit around the roof edges. There are eight carved window sections and twelve individual carved ventilation panels. And there is a massive pile of heavy timber for flooring and an even larger pile of light timber for lining the ceilings. Every piece has been reclaimed from a demolished building somewhere in central Java.

It is all teak, a plantation timber with lovely warm qualities, an oily hardwood that carpenters say is good to work with. Originally from the Indian sub-continent, the timber is grown and used throughout the region, valued for its strength and durability – and best of all, its resistance to water, to decay, rot and termites. The timber is equally valued for house construction, furniture making and boat building. The dry and sandy hills along Java's north coast are full of teak plantations; the tall trees dominate the landscape with their huge papery leaves.

Some of the prominent pieces for our house are old, with original carving and thick, wide timbers, the adze marks still visible. Most consist of old timber, freshly carved, cut and assembled to match the old pieces. The idea of 'antique' begins to lose its meaning here, where the carpenters and carvers use the same tools and techniques, the same methods and materials, to produce the same designs, the same quality, as did their ancestors. The carved designs, worked into the gebyok, the ventilation panels, the dodok besi, the railings and the tops of pillars, are common in Central and Eastern Java – a pre-Islamic aesthetic, similar to that found in Bali and further afield in India,

Nepal and Thailand.

By the end of the week it is all on site, stacked and ready for use. Tarno's crew, ten wiry Javanese men, have set up camp in the external kitchen structure at the rear of the main house.

'Do you think there'll be trouble?' I ask Agus on Saturday morning.

It's not the first time I have raised the issue. I am worried that the Sasak work crew might resent the foreigners from Java. They might see the arrival of the Javanese as an unwelcome intrusion on their territory. There could be trouble, violence even, if they feel the newcomers have been brought in to do jobs that are rightfully theirs.

'I hope not,' says Agus. 'I have talked to all the Sasak guys. They know what's going on. I think they accept it.'

There is another reason I am anxious about the arrival of the timber and the crew from Yogya. The whole thing has been planned and executed on two different islands by two different teams. Tarno and his men have been constructing all of the timber sections in Yogya, ready to fit together in Lombok. Here on the hill, Agus and his men have been constructing the foundations and framework. What is the chance of these two separate elements all fitting together as intended? What if mistakes have been made? What if the measurements are out? Or the panels don't fit together the way they are supposed to? The risk is high, or so it seems to me.

'Don't worry, we'll figure it out,' says Agus, once again in an effort to reassure me. 'It'll all be fine. You'll see.'

'Yes. We'll see, I guess,' I say. 'We'll find out when we start putting everything together. Can't do much about it until then.'

The weather today is wild. A gale blows in gusts from the north-west, bending the trees and tearing fronds off the coconut palms. A tall palm from above the top fence has blown over, it lies across a crushed fence panel and down the bank. The palm will be removed and the panel replaced.

'We will cut the lower two-thirds of the palm with a chainsaw,' Agus explains, 'we will plane it, dry it and turn into two-by-four lumber for use on site.'

'Is the timber good?' I ask. 'I thought we were using teakwood.'

'The timber from these palms is not bad,' says Agus. 'They have grown in the stony ground of the ridge, the quality is much better than the palms in the valley and by the sea. The palms grow slower and better up here. We might use it for the roof structure of the kitchen or the cottage by the creek. We don't have teak for those.'

My fears about conflict between the Javanese and Sasaks subside as I look around. The site looks orderly enough. Everyone seems to have a job to do and is doing it. Agus has split the teams while they settle in and get to know one another. The Sasaks are working at the joglo structure on the eastern terrace; a few are in the valley working on the second cottage site. The Javanese are on the main house site on the western terrace. A couple of fellows are busy planing thick teak floorboards, working their way steadily through the stack to prepare the timber for use. The timber smells leathery. All the pieces are individual and unique, different lengths and widths – but they must be planed to an even thickness for the floor. Where holes and knots in the timber need attention, these are plugged with spare pieces of timber cut to fit the holes precisely.

On the eastern terrace, Habib, the bricklayer, is building walls to fill the gaps between and beneath the old wooden panels of the cottage. He squats on a plank supported at each end by scaffolding and stacked bricks as they are thrown up one by one, from below. In front of the shed, two men are mixing concrete and mortar by hand; stirring the sand and water and cement together with a shovel and a short-handled hoe in a low concrete basin loosely constructed on the ground for this purpose. The petrol-driven cement mixer is in use on the western terrace.

Women trudge back and forth bearing plastic basins on their heads. A couple of Sasak carpenters are still at work on the joglo roof structure. A sweet little songbird keeps the workers company, jumping about in a rattan cage hanging from the rafters – and Rory and Harry are up the scaffolding and scrambling about on the roof structure like a pair of happy monkeys.

Karno has turned up and joins Agus and me where we stand in the half-built joglo structure. Eddy wanders up from the valley and joins the group. 'We should cut some more palms from the ridge below,' he says. 'We can use the coconut timber for the roof structure of the kitchen behind the main house and for the cottage by the creek.'

'It's true,' says Pak Agus. 'We will need more timber, and the coconut should do just fine. There are plenty of old palms down the ridge that are ready to fell. They don't fruit any more anyway and if we leave them, they'll end up rotting. We should do it.'

The four of us take a walk down the hill to pick out the older palms which need to come down and could provide decent timber. Karno says he will organise a fellow with a chainsaw and a portable circular saw, who can turn the palms into neatly sawn lumber where they fall. The wind whips up the valley and bends the palms as we make our way down the ridge.

Back at the building site, I discover that the seasonal winds have shaken a snake out of the crown of another palm. The pretty little vine snake is a bright green colour, rather elegant in a sinister kind of way. About a metre in length, with a long head and a thin spindly tail, it lies curled up in a corner of the kitchen area where the Javanese crew are camped. This is not the first time I have encountered a vine snake; it is mildly venomous, but its fangs are at the rear of its long upper jaw, rather than at the front as they are in vipers or cobras. This means that it cannot do us humans much harm – though it no doubt uses its venom to good effect on the little lizards, frogs and occasional rodents that form its diet.

'There's no need to kill it!' I say, as one of the Javanese carpenters reaches for a stick with which he intends to beat the creature to death. 'It's basically harmless.' I hope my confidence is not misplaced.

Five

The new principal for our school has arrived from Canberra with his wife and son. It is Sunday morning and I have arranged to take Gregg and his family for a drive to see a little of the island. They are staying with Peter and Ace while they sort out a house to rent. I plan to head south to Kuta Beach for the day and Peter has offered to lend me his car for the trip. The old hardtop is a character, but is not so comfortable for a day trip like this. Diane, the teacher who lives behind us in the village decides to join us. Together we drive to Montong to pick up the vehicle, a shiny Kijang – Indonesia's national car. The air is fresh and the sky blue. If we get going before the rains it should be a good day for an outing.

Gregg and Leigh are waiting for us at Peter and Ace's place – all handshakes and smiles. The group gathers around an antique table set among the pot plants on the porch in front of the house. Peter and Ace make the introductions. Someone appears with coffees and we talk about the school, about Lombok, about life in Indonesia, about Canberra, about Gregg's career and family. Gregg is a solid, affable man in his mid-fifties, and I like him immediately. This is his first overseas job. I watch the shifting expressions race across his open face; mixed emotions vie for control as we chat. He is well outside of his comfort zone. His features crease with worry and then relax with a smile – a raw, boyish excitement is quickly replaced by curiosity, then a nervous caution, concern for his family, anxiety about the job, confusion over the uncertainties and ambiguities of Lombok, and a more business-like appraisal of the situation. It is immediately obvious that Gregg's wife, Leigh, is his steady hand – an artist and trained teacher-counsellor, she manages to make light of the situation, taking some of the earnest worry out of Gregg's concerns, adding a little perspective here and there – and a dash of humour when required.

Then there's Jacob, a big eleven-year-old lad who will attend the school in the upper primary class, he is somewhere 'on the spectrum' as Leigh puts it. A mildly autistic boy, Jacob is different. He wanders out of the house to join us. He doesn't acknowledge me or the boys, his gaze is fixed on his mother; he looks agitated. Leigh takes him aside, speaking quietly, sorting out whatever the issue is. Jacob's voice rises and falls. He sounds very emphatic about something. The conversation ends with a hug. Jacob's speech sounds a little robotic, but when the issue is sorted his smile is wide and genuine. It might have been something to do with the colour of his board shorts for the day or something he was offered for breakfast.

'Autism,' Leigh explains, no doubt reverting to a familiar script, 'is a complex condition. It has an effect on brain development. Jacob has communication problems, normal social interactions are not easy for him; he has a tendency to repeat certain patterns of behaviour. It's like the record gets stuck in a groove.'

'He has a problem with the colour green, too, especially on

his plate,' laughs Gregg.

Gregg looks at Leigh. They both smile. Jacob, it is immediately obvious, is much loved. But living with autism, I reflect, must be a daily struggle, both for him and his family.

'Well,' I say, 'we've never had an autistic child in our school. But I think he'll be fine. We have always said that we are an inclusive school. If he needs extra help, we can sort it out, I'm sure. The kids are used to difference and diversity. And the school is like a family. He'll be fine, just fine.'

Coffees and conversations done, we climb aboard the Kijang. The boys pile in the back, Leigh and Diane sit in the middle, Gregg takes the front passenger seat, I take the wheel and we head out into the Sunday traffic. The drive takes us south through Ampenan and onto the coastal ring road, avoiding the city centre. Along the way, I chat to Gregg, pointing out the various places of interest, small and large. Leigh and Diane chat in the back. We turn off the dual carriageway at an intersection, which is dominated by a huge, shiny mosque, all decked out with bright blue and yellow ceramic tiles, an elongated dome reaching into the sky.

'Wow!' exclaims Leigh, a student of art and design, momentarily lost for words, 'it's so Arabic ... so ... Islamic.'

'Most mosques are Islamic,' says Gregg in a dry tone. The laughter that bounces around the car is not unkind. And she has a point. The old mosques of Indonesia look more like Hindu temples, with their peaked and layered rooflines. The newer variety, now springing up across Lombok and across the country, adopt a much more Arabic aesthetic with their tiled domes and arched windows.

We turn south, navigating through crowded villages and

mixed traffic. Trucks and buses hog the road, villagers wander precariously along the verges, bicycles totter at the edge, the occasional horse-drawn cidomo trots past, passengers perched on top of their market goods, or a cart laden with bricks, stacked timber or sacks of cement, motorbikes weave in and out, cars honk their horns, and we make our way south.

A lengthy stretch of road has been turned into an avenue, lined with golden shower trees. The trees drape across the two-track road, at places meeting in the middle. It is late in the season, but many are still in flower. Aptly named, the trees are completely covered, cascades of bright yellow flowers brush the air as we speed past, the roadside beneath is carpeted in fallen leaves and flowers. It is like driving through a long, long pergola, a golden garlanded tunnel.

Along the roadside, small stalls sell fruit beneath the trees. Trays of local papaya, clusters of hairy red rambutan and pale green mangos sit alongside imported apples and snake fruit from Java, bright purple dragon fruit, oranges, caramel kedondong and clusters of sweet little klengkeng. We pull over and stock up on bottled water and fruit.

The journey south takes us through small villages. Their markets spill out onto the road, blocking the traffic in a tumble of packing crates, plump women with bags of rice, horse-drawn cidomo, food carts, cigarette stalls, rotting fruit peel and muddy litter. We pass by expanses of terraced rice fields, bordered with rows of spindly *turi* trees, coconut palms, bananas, and the odd kapok standing tall, its branches bare and spread like a scarecrow's arms. The big dangling seedpods have already disgorged most of their fluffy white contents, a few remain clinging doggedly to the branches. The rice fields are mixed. Some are a solid sea of tall green, the heads beginning to dry off, yellowing for harvest. A mob of little birds flocks to the ripening grain. They circle in rapid spirals, rising and falling like a river, before alighting in a field, only to be chased off again by the village kids who guard the crop. Some fields have already been harvested – leaving behind a muddy square of stubble. Piles of discarded chaff smoulder in the corners, producing a dense fog. Following the harvest in Lombok, the rice husks are piled in the fields and burned – smothering the land with a thick white smoke. A buffalo is harnessed to plough these fields, turning the wet earth for the next planting. And in one or two fields, groups of villagers are gathered for the harvest.

Dark clouds are massing to the north, the sun shines on the south, and the little groups create vignettes, biblical scenes reminiscent of pastoral paintings from the nineteenth century. Women bend to their toil, cutting the stalks in the field with little curved scythes, which they hide, cupped in their hands, so as not to upset Dewi Sri, the rice goddess. The women carry huge rice-laden baskets on their heads to the centre, where two men stand before a giant stack of the harvested stalks. One wears a conical woven hat, typical of those worn by peasant farmers throughout the region, the other a rustic *blangkon*, a patterned cloth tied around the head with the knot at the rear. The two work together to thresh the rice, taking sheaves of the stalks and rhythmically striking them against an angled, wooden, slatted structure. The grains fall between the slats and onto the tarpaulin spread beneath. Another group sweeps them up, collecting the grain together into shiny brown piles ready for winnowing. The women all wear colourful sarongs wrapped around the midriff, some wear bright head-scarves and some have their hair tied back in a bun: each takes a basket of the rice, tipping a small amount onto a flat round woven tray and, following the rhythm of the threshers, throws the grains into the air, allowing the faint breeze to blow away the chaff, light husks and stray bits of leaves and stalk, leaving the heavier grain to fall back into the basket tray.

This glimpse of local tradition, of an old way of life, of communal endeavour now all but lost in the industrialized West, is special. I find myself smiling along with Gregg and Leigh as we make our way towards the coast. Half an hour or so on, a large lake appears on the left. The water level is high, but the lake is mostly covered in floating hyacinth, pale purple flowers nod above the glossy green carpet.

Not far beyond this we stop to visit a traditional Sasak-style village. Sade is designated as a tourist destination and, as a result, is less of a traditional village than it once was. A paved area out the front provides space for tour buses, and a uniformed official charges for entrance, issuing tickets beneath an arched sign announcing *Selamat Datang di Desa Sade – Obyek Wisata.* Welcome to Sade Village – Tourism Object. Indonesian style. After fending off the touts and would-be-guides who haggle for business in the carpark, we make our way into the village where narrow paved pathways are lined with tiny shops festooned with bright woven cloths for sale. Notwithstanding all this commercialism, it is an interesting and worthwhile visit. The village women continue to weave in the traditional way, producing beautiful cloth, and life goes on more or less as it always has – in amongst the commercial activity and gawping tourists. Gregg and Leigh are obviously absorbed in the whole thing. Jacob seems to take it in his stride. And, after peering into a traditional windowless Sasak dwelling – bamboo-framed, thatch-roofed, dark and shiny beaten-earth-and-cow-dung floor and a raised internal section for family treasures and unmarried women – we make our way back to the car, arms full of woven cloth and trinkets. The road winds up over a series of wooded hills. A plaited grass talisman hangs from a tree beside the road.

'It's probably there to ward off famine – I guess it's left over from the last dry season, or perhaps already anticipating the next,' I suggest – though I'm not really sure.

There is something unsettling about the sight – a primitive fetish, remnant of an ancient, dark religion; a puny, sad-looking attempt to ward off disaster, to move the unmovable forces of nature, to interrupt the inevitable cycle of famine that hits southern Lombok every few years.

Over the crest and through a gap in the trees, the ocean is suddenly visible below. Blue and shining like a promise. The road takes us down through the village and past the beachfront strip of homestays, grass huts and surfer hangouts along Kuta Beach, its coral sand and distant line of surf. The sun sparkles on that ocean – as if Mount Rinjani's dark clouds don't dare venture this far south. Mud-caked buffalo wander about – their dung decorating the broken tarmac – and the narrow coastal plain looks dry, as if forgotten by the rains – as if the wet season has yet to arrive here.

A little further on, a single-track road brings us out at Tanjung Aan, a wide crescent of a bay, deep like a wine glass, the beach of golden coral sand extending to either end. A fading sign hangs loose from its poles, 'Lombok Tourism Development Corporation', beyond which a sandy track leads to a small, abandoned building; it smells vaguely of urine, the roof collapsed, the walls crumbling in the muggy heat. Apart from this there is nothing; nothing at all, just coconut palms and sand. Blue ocean, hazy skies and dusky green headlands as far as the eye can see. The beach is not made for walking, my feet sink deep into the soft sand, making each step an effort. I reach down and pick up a handful of that sand to show the others, tiny spheres of polished coral, fragments, a myriad of shades, together they create a warm golden colour. Loosely clumped in my palm, the sand feels soft, gentle in a gritty kind of way, but it does not compact, the spherical grains refuse to stick together. A curiosity; beautiful, but not good for sandcastles or walks on the beach.

A half-hearted surf rolls in, petering out by the time it reaches the shore in tiny lapping waves, and we decide to go for a swim. The water is tepid and feels slightly oily, but is nonetheless refreshing. One or two pieces of grubby plastic swash around with discarded coconut husks near the shore, though it is nature's storm-washed flotsam that blackens the tide line: a loose mat of torn-off sea grass collects in eddies at this quiet corner of the beach, clinging as we wade in and out. There is no one much around, but by the time we are out and towelling off, a villager has turned up, an old man with a big bush knife and a pile of fresh green coconuts – an irresistible treat.

Leaving Tanjung Aan and its lonely, midday beauty, a fifteen-minute drive back through Kuta and up an impossibly steep road to the west brings us to a little restaurant. The style, a kind of chilled-out-eco-surfie chic, consists of polished, salmon-coloured concrete floors, woven bamboo walls, thatched roofing, low wooden tables and scattered floor cushions. We leave our sandals in the pile at the door. The polished concrete is pleasantly cool underfoot. A light breeze moves the air, open-sided windows creating a crossflow. Perched on an outcrop high about the coastal plain, the place offers huge, expansive views to the east. Beach after beach, bay after bay, headland after headland, it's all spread out like a painting.

'This whole area,' I explain over beers and *urap* – vegetables, toasted coconut and steamed rice – 'is earmarked for development.'

'What? Go on,' Leigh encourages. Diane, the teacher, raises her eyebrows. It's hard to know what lies behind that smile.

'Well, you can see the Novotel down there,' I press on. The collection of ethnic-styled thatched roof cottages is visible at the eastern end of the beach, just this side of Seger where, nearly ten years ago, I went to the Bau Nyale festival with Peter. We passed by there earlier today on our way to Tanjung Aan. 'That is the only five-star resort that was built here. But it was supposed to be one of many. Tommy Suharto, the president's son, was mixed up in the deal. They planned to open the whole area up – hotels, resorts, a marina, golf course, amusement park, shopping mall, all along the coast here.'

'A new airport is supposed to have been built near the lake we passed,' I explain. 'Water was to have been drained from the highlands to the coast here. Imagine the whole area as green and manicured golf courses and resorts. That was the plan. Of course, the government would have paid for most of the work, the military would have made sure the locals didn't object to having their land appropriated, and Tommy and the president's business buddies would have pocketed the proceeds. Ten percent to Madame of course!' I laugh.

'But that's crazy!' Gregg interjects, frowning. 'And why hasn't it happened?'

'Ah,' I warm to my theme. 'History intervened. Suharto lost power. And his family, including Tommy, lost all their opportunities with it. Tommy actually went to jail for a while, though I suspect his time there was quite comfortable. People say they used to let him out for gambling trips to Christmas Island. You have to understand that this family is mega-rich. Wealthy beyond imagining. Most of it is probably stashed away in Swiss bank accounts or in the Cayman Islands. But they could not continue with schemes like this one when *reformasi* happened.

'Now it just sits there waiting. Empty beaches and broken village roads. Every few years there is talk of reviving the plan. Perhaps the big investors will come from Dubai, or India or the U.S. Meanwhile the network of roads that was built to lead to hotels and resorts grows scrubby with grass and is gradually covered with cow turds and bush.

'The area set aside for the new airport was reclaimed by the locals,' I continue, 'although there is talk of the project being revived.'

'I heard that work will soon start on construction there,' interjects Diane. 'I suppose it's a good thing. Good for the economy, good for Lombok. But I worry about the impact on the environment, on the people here, on their way of life.'

The table falls silent, as I run out of steam and Gregg and Leigh digest all of this information. Gregg gazes off into the distance. Too much information, probably, I think to myself. My usual mistake.

'That's kind of how it is in Lombok,' I conclude. 'It's always about to happen, always the next big thing – but it never quite does happen.'

'Maybe that'll change,' says Leigh eventually. 'Maybe it will go ahead. I can picture it all now. It would be good for the people, surely.'

'Maybe yes, maybe no. We'll see,' I chuckle. 'This is Lombok. Nothing much happens in a hurry.' Gregg looks a bit worried. Leigh smiles in an ambiguous way.

Eventually, years later, the new international airport is built, the project is picked up by the Indonesian Tourism Development Corporation and work commences on the development of one-thousand-one-hundred-and-seventy-five hectares; Mandalika is designated as a Special Economic Zone and now boasts a number of international hotels and a MotoGP circuit.

With that it's time to rally the troops and head on. It was a late lunch and the boys are getting tired. We drive back the way we came. I would like to press on to the west. My favourite beaches are along this way, the beautiful crescent-shaped Mawun Beach with its huge shade tree, its pristine sands and rolling surf, and beyond that, the stunning Selong Belaneq, with its beach huts and wide stretches of shining sand that stretch away to the headlands, a silver ribbon by the sea – but the road is almost unnavigable in places, and I promised Peter I would take good care of his car and get back in good time.

Six

Back at the building site, the Javanese crew is making rapid progress. With nothing much else to do, they seem to be working from sunrise to sunset, seven days a week. Light scaffolding has been erected in the centre of the main building. To my surprise, the first story floor is in place: a solid expanse of timber flooring shades the interior of the building, a large mezzanine space left empty in the centre. Above this, the main frame for the limasan structure has been erected. Eight solid teak pillars – the soko guru – stand in parallel rows of four. A double row of giant collar beams forms a grid at the top of the pillars and spans the central void. Angled bamboo struts temporarily hold the whole thing in place.

***

Later that week I meet up with Gregg at Papaya, another Senggigi restaurant and bar. We chat about school and life over beers and noodles. Carl, a businessman from Senggigi and one of the school parents, unexpectedly joins us – curious to meet the new principal.

I have been thinking about the possibility of breeding local deer at our place on The Hill. I heard that Carl has a pair at his villa in the valley below our development. It would be nice to have them about, I think, and not a bad thing to breed them up in captivity. Perhaps I can learn something from him. I imagine a parklike garden, ornamented with deer and peacocks. Pak Mobin had told me that deer used to be quite common in the hills above Senggigi, but there are none to be seen these days. Hunted out by villagers, I presume. Like many of the larger birds and mammals.

I once witnessed a deer hunt, or at least the final moments of a deer hunt, on the island of Borneo to the north. We were travelling along an East Kalimantan backroad, somewhere inland from the mine site where I worked at the time, when we came across a commotion. Men were shouting, running across the road, disappearing into the weedy slopes between the clay road and jungle. Dogs were barking in the heat. We pulled over to the verge, stepping out to see what was going on. The men had cornered a large deer. The dogs circled, leaping, snapping. The deer, desperate, leapt this way and that, its eyes wide with terror. The men closed in on it, swiping at its legs, at its flanks, its neck and head. Then the beast was down. The men hacked at it with their *parang* – big bush knives, more like a sword than a knife. A reek of blood, sweat and adrenaline mingled in the moist air with the sweet stink of mud and crushed weeds. The deer struggled, a twisted, bloody mess, honking in distress. The men had it pinned down to finish the job. This image has stayed with me, a primitive brutality – nothing noble about the hunt, just bloody opportunism, mob-violence; nothing sporting, just the primal contest: man against beast, death and survival.

Carl was a hunter of another sort. A recreational hunter. The kind who hunts with a rifle, stalking his prey in the hills. There are two types of deer in Lombok and Sumba, the little barking deer, also called *kijang* or muntjac, which occur throughout South-East Asia, and the larger *rusa*, thought to be native to Java, Bali and Timor. Mind you, 'native' is a tricky term in this part of the world, where ancient migrations are known to have occurred and locals have been travelling back and forth between the islands for thousands of years, no doubt carrying live animals and birds with them – as they still do. Rusa are now found across the region, as far as Australia and New Zealand. Apparently muntjac are now widespread in rural England having been introduced on one country estate in the early nineteenth century before escaping to thrive in the wild.

Carl is tall, well dressed, with a calculated but casual urbane air. An affluent Eurasian with German and Indonesian parentage. He drapes himself across the wooden seat, leans on the table, and lights a cigarette.

'How are your pet deer doing?' I ask.

'You know about that?' he raises his eyebrows. 'Well, they're doing fine, I suppose. They take a lot of feeding, a lot of care. But I can't seem to get them to mate. They're Sumba deer, I brought them over from the island – a young pair, but they don't seem to get past first base,' he laughs. 'I don't know if I'm going to keep them.'

'I like to hunt,' he goes on. 'I usually go to Sumba to hunt rusa. They're just about finished here in Lombok.'

'Isn't it better to let them breed in the wild?' asks Gregg. 'It would be terrible if they became extinct.'

'Of course,' says Carl. 'I do it in a good way. I only take the adult ones. And I always leave some in the herd. They move about in small herds,' he explains. 'But if I don't hunt them, someone else will. The locals kill them for meat. You can't blame them for that.'

Carl takes a sip of beer, draws on his cigarette, blowing a cloud of smoke into the night air. I keep my thoughts to myself. I don't want to offend him. I heard from Andrew that he is investing on The Hill. We may yet need his support. Perhaps he will become an ally, a partner, a member of our little community up there? Perhaps I can take his pet deer and give them a larger run? Apparently, they are kept in a very small compound behind his villa in the valley. Perhaps.

'There are still some Lombok deer about, you know,' he says. 'I heard that there is a pair of them in the hills to the north, up behind Mangsit somewhere. I'm going to go for them.'

'What? You want to hunt the last remaining Lombok deer?' asks Gregg, incredulously.

'Of course,' says Carl. 'Why not?'

I'm not sure if Carl is just winding us up or if he really means it. With that, he leaves us, and heads on to another table. Doing the rounds. I look at Gregg and shake my head. 'You'll find that not everyone shares your views and values around here,' I say. 'You just have to get used to that.'

But the conversation has unsettled me. I am still thinking about it as I drift off to sleep later that evening. The images drift and blur. I think about Laras in Hobart. I picture Carl stalking the last deer in the coastal hills of Lombok. I picture that bloody scene in the jungles of Kalimantan. I think about the pretty little Indian deer on the lawns of the state palace in Bogor, West Java; about the big herd of local deer grazing in front of the electricity plant we passed by on the coastal ring road on Sunday; about the lonely tame deer I encountered in a decaying villa complex on the old Dutch road to Pusuk, about how it ran through the bushes to greet me, trailing a loose tether rope, assuming I was there to feed it.

And I reflect on our perversity as a race, the human race – about how we are systematically destroying the planet, hunting our fellow creatures to extinction, about the arrogance and hubris that lies behind it all. Is it me that is out of step, I wonder? A dreamer with his head in the clouds; a snowflake, or a 'soft cock,' to use one of Andrew's expressions; a man who doesn't understand the harsh realities of life? That night my sleep is restless, disturbed.

Seven

On Friday evening I catch up with Peter, Ace, Gregg and Leigh at Stammtisch. Sakinah is there as usual. Harry and Rory have disappeared out the back to play pool with their friends. And, as usual, it's a good chance to unwind after the week – and a good chance for Gregg and Leigh to meet a few of the local characters. The family is already becoming part of our community. They will be fine.

**

On Saturday morning I drive up the hill again for what is becoming a routine weekly check on progress. Agus meets me on the western terrace. The place is a hive of activity. Four or five of Tarno's men are up high – really high; they sit precariously straddling the limasan roof framework and applying a traditional shellac treatment to the raw timber, way above where I stand among the piles of sand and bricks below. Pots of the mixture are perched on the beams as the men paint the timberwork. The dodok besi – big, ornately carved, ridge beams – are in place, running the length of the structure in an east-west direction. From a structural point of view, I see that these are not really ridge beams at all. The dodok besi perform an ornamental and symbolic function. The real ridge beam will be an insignificant stretch of timber placed where the rafters meet, somewhere high above the dodok besi.

Agus explains. Following Tarno's instructions, the shellac mix is created by dissolving shellac flakes in methylated spirits with a pinch of ochre tint. The shellac, I subsequently discover, is derived from a resin secreted by the female lac bug on trees in the forests of India and Thailand. In all things, Tarno favours traditional methods and materials.

On the ground floor below, the remaining members of the Javanese crew are fitting the centre section of the three-piece gebyok from Tuban, the one I first encountered at Tarno's workshop in Yogya. Like a triptych, the three sections have been separated and will now form part of a five-piece gebyok that spans the length of the front of the house. Two new pieces have been carved to match the old sections. The central piece is an ornate wooden archway. This will become the main entrance to the house, flanked by two more arched doors, so that the whole downstairs room can be opened up onto a front veranda during the day. The men are positioning the panel, securing it with angled bamboo stays. It appears to be floating in empty space.

'How is all this going to work?' I ask Agus.

'Don't worry,' he laughs. 'Once all the panels are put in place, we will fill in the empty spaces with brick walls. When it's all finished it will be solid enough, and it will look great, you'll see!'

Prior to fitting each section, the panels are sanded smooth and painted with the shellac solution. The alcohol is burned off as the panels lie on the ground in what looks to me like a rather hazardous procedure. Over the hour or two I spend on site, I watch the crew fitting these panels, one by one. Simple plumb lines, consisting of a weighted string hanging from above, guide them as they place each piece. Behind the panels, the concreted ground floor is still full of timber sections, carved panels and pillars and rafters, all stacked and ready to install.

* * *

Later in the evening, Pak Tarno arrives from Yogya. On Sunday morning we all meet on the site to check on progress. By the time we get up to site, it is around ten in the morning. Karno is there with Tarno, Rani and Agus. Tarno greets us with a big smile. It is good to see him, to hear his soft, rounded Yogya accent on the hills of Lombok. Together, the four of them are checking the inventory; looking, one by one, through the big pieces, the panels, windows and doors, making sure that all the pieces are there and will fit together as planned. There seems to be something wrong.

'What's up?' I ask, my heart beginning to sink.

'Well, it's strange,' says Agus, 'no one can understand why, but we seem to have one more gebyok panel than we need!'

The remaining panels, those that have yet to be installed, have been stacked up against a tree at the side of the terrace. There is a bunch of doors, windows, frames and carved sections. Tarno's face creases in consternation. He and Rani go through the list one more time, comparing Tarno's inventory with Rani's house designs. Agus and Edy look on. Karno comes and goes. The kids are running about and the workers mostly carry on with their work.

Finally, it is decided.

'It's true,' says Agus. 'There's definitely one too many!' We wander around to the rear of the building; there is much shaking of heads accompanied by nervous laughter.

'Well, never mind, it's happened. There's no use in crying over spilled milk,' I laugh. And then find myself having to try and explain the expression in Indonesian. It doesn't translate well.

'Where can we use it?' I ask finally. 'Better to have one too many than one too few. And I'm sure we can use it somewhere.'

The contrary piece, surplus to requirements, is an antique gebyok panel. A beautiful piece with a double door frame, above which is a carved ventilation panel, featuring a rustic design of spears converging at a central point. After much discussion it is agreed that it will fit at the rear of the small bedroom – where it will lead onto a small courtyard at the rear of the house. The piece which had been prepared for this position, another antique panel, can be used upstairs, with a little refashioning, as a double window panel.

I walk about, wanting to get a feel for things. The separate kitchen structure at the rear has been turned into an accommodation for the Javanese crew. The walls, now closed in with woven bamboo bedeg, together with the tarpaulin roof, keep out the worst of the elements.

Looking up from inside the main building, the roof structure looks quite extraordinary. A complex web of golden-brown teak, reaching high – ten or eleven metres – into the heavy grey sky. Tarno's workers are visible here and there. All are in bare feet, a sensible way to improve grip as they clamber about in the heights. A couple of the lads are on the outside of the structure, near the peak, busy fixing wafer-thin planks of recycled teak to the rafters. These will form a ceiling, with that wonderful roof structure exposed beneath it.

And then I spot Rory. He stands on the second floor, hanging onto the scaffolding, peering down at me with a cheeky grin from beside the central void. I scramble up a wobbly bamboo ladder and join him. For the first time, I get to fully appreciate the view from the second floor. Looking over the top of the trees to the south and west, the ocean view opens up – Bali is clearly visible to the west, shrouded in midday cloud. And the view up the wooded valley to the hills in the north-west is equally impressive. Below us, work is still underway to terrace the lower corner of the block, near where Karno has planted a little citrus grove.

***

Over the next few days I manage to meet up with Tarno, Agus and Rani several times on site. The build seems to be continuing as expected. Some details are getting sorted with Tarno. The weather is generally calm, though the daily rains continue.

On Wednesday I meet with Pak Abu. Another Ampenan Arab. We meet at the house Abu built for his English-Indonesian family. I find him out the back tinkering with something mechanical, happily lost among his collection of Volkswagen kombi vans and vintage Vesper motor scooters. We chat over muddy coffees and kretek cigarettes. We meet again the following day, this time on the hill after work. Abu and Agus talk about waste-water systems and Abu says he is impressed with the standard of work he sees.

'It's great, Mark,' he says with a gruff smile. 'I love it. I really do.' He means it.

The month of March seems to disappear in a blur of kids and work and report writing and house building and school governance – and all the business of life. Tarno returns to Yogya. We have agreed on some extra pieces to complete the jigsaw puzzle that is to be our home. Harry recovers from a local illness. Rory surfs on weekends. And I stay vaguely sane with Friday evenings at Asmara and Sunday afternoons at Café Alberto. Laras seems to be doing fine in Tasmania. We track back and forth with emails and phone calls – the odd Skype hook-up, which is always a bit fraught, given the vagaries of Lombok's internet service.

In amongst it all, we seem to have secured the sale of three plots of land – the first land we acquired, the block that Andrew showed me all those years ago when we stood on that windy ridge, the one where we originally intended to build our house. The proceeds from all this will go a long way to paying for our house construction. Sometimes, just sometimes, the cards fall your way, I think to myself with a smile. And Harry's mythical little Javanese brother has now been adopted by a Catholic from Flores and a Balinese from Lombok. Dewi, our erstwhile secretary is back, and she and her husband have bought a block from us.

The rains continue throughout the month, although with lessening intensity. Occasional blue skies and dramatic sunsets lighten the mood. I am up and down to the site whenever possible, and there are various meetings with Agus and sometimes Rani, to discuss details of design and materials as the project progresses.

Andrew and I meet with Will, a New Zealander who has a Balinese wife and villa in the valley. Will is a friend of the Arab fellow who acquired another of our top blocks. It was Will that introduced me to Agus and Rani. An energetic young man, a family man with a good heart, Will works in the mining industry and, like all of us, has become a land developer in his spare time. He has big plans for acquiring and developing the higher slopes of The Hill for housing. We decide to meet at our building site. Both Andrew and Will are keen to take a look. But by the time we get together it is late afternoon, already turning dark. The sky to the west does its thing, turning a beautiful shade of orange-blue, I take a cool box from the car and pass out some cold beers; we sit around and talk business.

As the three of us sit there chatting, clouds of flying termites appear from the darkness. Attracted by the dim lights perhaps, or by the piles of timber; something in the changing seasons, warming weather and fresh rains must have triggered the swarm. Whatever it is, as we sit there, the termites fill the air like flying ants, their thin brown wings fluttering this way and that before they drop to the floor, seemingly exhausted to the point of death. By the time we leave an hour or so later, the floor is littered with their little bodies. Is this an attack, I wonder? An advance party? Are they moving in, looking for mates, creating their own colony, before the house is even finished? Termites are something for the builder of a timber house to dread. A serious threat in the tropics. Left unattended, houses can collapse in a few months, eaten from the inside out. I have been trying to find an organic solution, a way to keep them out without introducing pesticides and poisons. But have had no luck as yet. Supposedly teakwood is unattractive to termites, but I am not convinced of that either.

Eight

On a Wednesday in late March, I take the boys to see the *ogoh-ogoh* parade. Tomorrow is Nyepi, the Balinese New Year, the Hindu day of silence, and another public holiday. The Indonesian people do like to party. We leave after school, pile into the hardtop and drive up to town. Diane joins us to see the parade. Information is a little scarce, but I am told it will take place in the main street of Cakranegara. The place is bedlam. With the main street blocked off, the side streets are clogged with traffic and parking is at a premium. Eventually, after sitting in traffic and driving around in circles for a while, we find a spot, not far from the tomb of General Van Ham. From there we walk through the park with its giant trees, its weedy graves and dripping greenery, emerging on the main road near the shopping mall.

The Balinese are forever downing tools and taking off to meet their religious and social commitments – the two are really inseparable. Starting with daily prayers and morning offerings, the spiritual dimension is rarely far from the temporal. Family temples, house shrines, village shrines, local temples; all demand their cycle of activity. Temple festivals take place at various times, dictated by the phases of the moon, a different schedule in every village, but the big annual festivals, Nyepi, Galungan and Kunginan, are celebrated en masse. The gist of this endless round of activity seems to be an effort to appease the gods, to sway the fates in favour of good, and ultimately to celebrate the triumph of good over evil, light over darkness, life over death. Not a bad thing, I think to myself. Especially given the aesthetics of it all. The temples, the festivals, the ritual clothing, the gamelan music, the dances, the floral offerings and smoking incense, the paintings and carvings. All of it is beautiful, just beautiful – at times painfully so.

By the time we get there, the streets are lined with spectators. The parade is under way. A great, noisy, colourful carnival, it stretches as far as the eye can see in both directions. We find a vantage point on top of a low brick wall out the front of the mall, from where we can get a good view of the spectacle. Rain comes and goes, light afternoon showers which do little to dampen the spirits. The street is already full of the ogoh-ogoh, huge statues built for the parade, the monsters represent a host of mythological beings, mostly demons. Huge fanged creatures, brightly painted, with bulging eyes and protruding bellies, their clawed fingers reach for the spectators as they waggle past. The procession begins in the east, at the Mayura temple and waterpark, where the Dutch were ambushed a century ago. From there they parade down the main street, past where we stand in the drizzle, and back again in a big circuit, until finally they are apparently burnt to ashes as a symbol of self-purification.

One by one the ogoh pass by, each standing four or five metres tall on a bamboo frame, lifted and carried by eight or more young men. The teams, representing their villages, wear matching black t-shirts, most with their village insignia printed in white; *udeng* headscarves and black-and-white checked sarongs complete the uniform. The lads are spruced up for the parade, many with slick hairstyles and dark sunglasses, cigarettes dangling from moist lips: this is obviously a good time to show off your cool. Many are accompanied by drums and clashing cymbals, a processional village gamelan orchestra creating a happy din in the damp air.

Just west of where we stand, as they pass the crossroads, each ogoh is rotated three times counter-clockwise, the bearers running in circles, alternately lifting their monster high and then plunging it back down in a giddy effort to bewilder the evil spirits, to persuade them to leave and stop bothering the people. The event has something of the tradition of Halloween or the Mexican Day of the Dead about it. The whole thing is about frightening away the bad spirits ahead of the holy day of Nyepi and the start of a new year on the Balinese calendar.

The village youth organisation, *Seka Truna Truni*, in each Balinese village is responsible for designing and constructing the ogoh ogoh. The creativity of these young people is extraordinary; each year they produce bigger, wilder and more grotesque monsters in an effort to outdo their competitors from neighbouring villages. Most are constructed from elaborate frames, and a mix of carved Styrofoam, cloth, fiberglass and papier-mâché – all painted up in lurid colours. A range of influences is evident in the designs, from classical Balinese Hindu iconography to contemporary comic-book superhero references. Some are male, some female – often with huge dangling breasts and witchlike features. Some breathe fire, some sport protruding forked tongues. Some have multiple arms or legs. Some tangle with snakes or dragons, some ride mythical beasts; some are naked, scaled like green aliens, some wear flapping sarongs. Some are black, some bright red, some pink, some orange, some blue. The variety is endless. All are equally fearsome.

Apparently, the tradition – as currently practiced – is relatively recent, having begun in the 1980s. In the early years, Suharto's thought police were kept busy monitoring the event to ensure that the Balinese youth did not use it as excuse to poke fun at the president and his regime. The parade seems endless, over an hour passes as we stand and watch, until eventually the boys tire of the show and we make our way through the crowds to the mall where I buy ice creams, and back past the general's sad little tomb to where the old car is parked.

The next day is Nyepi. The village of Baruna Shanti is silent. The streets have been swept clean. Nothing stirs. Even the dogs have ceased their incessant barking. The day is set aside for self-reflection. From sunrise to sunset anything that might interfere with that is restricted. The lights are off, no TVs, radio or music, no fires are lit, and for the Balinese villagers there is no work, no entertainment or pleasure, no reading, no travelling, and, for some, no talking or eating. I take the opportunity for a little reflection of my own. The silence is pleasant. Lombok is a mixed community, however, and there is nothing to stop us from getting on with a normal day. Karno and I go for a walk up the hill, to take a look at some more land that is on offer.

On the neighbouring island of Bali, where Hindus are the majority, the prohibitions of Nyepi are taken much more seriously. The entire island is silent. But for the occasional birdsong or breath of wind in the trees, the place is totally quiet. It is eerie and strangely beautiful. The normally busy streets are empty. The beaches and bars and restaurants are deserted. The shops and markets are shuttered. The only people outdoors are little groups of black-and-white saronged *pecalang*, traditional village security guards who patrol the streets to ensure that the restrictions of the day are enforced. When once I arrived in Bali's international airport on Nyepi, I found myself stranded at the airport with a crowd of bewildered tourists. There were no officials there to advise, no hotel representatives to greet the guests, no taxis, no buses, no restaurants or food stalls, nothing – and no way of getting to the hotel at all. Eventually the problem was somehow resolved, and I found my way to my hotel – but not before having to explain myself to some bolshy young men on guard in the quiet streets outside the hotel. These days, the airport is closed for the day.

Having restored the balance between heaven and earth, between humanity and the natural world, having cleansed the mind, the body and spirit, normal business resumes on Friday, the first day of the Balinese new year. In the evening I meet again with Will and Andrew. There is some discussion about negotiating with the Balinese banjar, the community organisation that owns and manages land in the valley below The Hill. We catch up again with Sakinah before Stammtisch and chat about developments on The Hill. There is a plan to establish our own community association. A number of others, including Andrew, have started construction of villas.

Pak Tarno has returned for another inspection visit and on Saturday morning we meet with Agus. Tarno walks about in a business-like way, talking to Agus and to his foreman, chatting with Karno, looking at details. The front and back verandas have been built. The roof has been edged all around with fretted teak bargeboards. Some of the Sasak crew have begun work on plastering the rough brick walls. The great staircase with its heavy polished timbers is being put in place. All goes well with the installation until, when they put it all together, we discover that the bottom pillar does not quite reach the floor. Something must have gone astray with the calculations. Tarno and Agus confer and an extra fifteen centimetres is added to the lowest section.

Laras arrives from Tasmania on Sunday. After three months apart it is time to reconnect as a couple, as a family. The boys are beside themselves. We all meet at the airport and head directly for the hill. The feeling, standing there together in the upstairs open galley, is hard to put into words. With the afternoon sun low in the sky, the vast panelled teak roof-space glows, a beautiful soft, warm colour. The great carved dodok besi in centre stage and the elaborate limasan roof structure exposed above. The floor is littered with sawdust and timber offcuts, with pots and tools and sacks and electrical cabling. A couple of Tarno's men are busy installing the final sections of railing around the central void. The place is a building site, a workplace, but already it feels like a palace!

The boys scamper about. Laras and I take a few moments, together, leaning on that outside railing and looking out at the view – trying to take it all in. Not just the view, but the enormity of what we are creating here. Immediately below us, the front veranda's timber ceiling is exposed. This section has not yet been tiled and we are looking at the reverse-side of the timber panelling, an odd patchwork of colours, of shapes and sizes, faded paintwork from other buildings, remnants of other people's lives, from other islands. Beyond that, the valley is carpeted with palms and the ocean stretches away to a hazy distance.

'So far, so good,' I smile at Laras.

'What do you mean?' she asks.

'I mean, think of all the things that could have gone wrong. All the hassles that others have had building villas. We seem to have had a very good run. No major issues. No major hurdles. We have a good team. The work is basically on schedule. So far, no one has tried to rip us off. The quality of the work is fine. And look at what we have. It's amazing!'

Laras smiles back. 'That's because we set things up in the right way, I guess' she says knowingly.

Over the following days we catch up with the finances. Laras spends her days at the cottage, with Karno and Rina, poring over the numbers; spreadsheets and notepads sprawled across the big table; checking prices, market rates, quantities and timesheets. I look on with concern, but at the end of it all she emerges with a smile on her face. 'We're okay,' she says. 'A little over, but close to budget.'

Laras looks good. Student life must suit her, I think. The sky is clear. The garden is a vivid green. Lush and vibrant after months of rain and the recent sunshine. The day's heat haze evaporates in the cooling air. A late afternoon sun casts long angled shadows from the west. Across the straits, Bali's conical Mount Agung appears. And the sun begins to settle behind it. The call to prayer drifts up from the little mosque in the valley. I glance at my wife. Her hair is gathered back in a casual, Javanese-style bun. She looks into the distance, tired after the travel. But her smile is irrepressible, and a small tear of joy gathers in the corner of her eye.

THE SEASON
OF THE SEA

One

Nothing compares with the feeling of setting out on a journey. Some say it is our primitive nomadic instincts. For others it is simply an escape from mundane day-to-day existence. Whatever it is or it isn't, for me the feeling is quietly euphoric. Cares of home and work are cast aside, responsibilities are left behind, and, as the anchor is weighed and sails unfurled, there follows a moment of surrender. What lies ahead, what mysteries or disasters, what new experiences, joys or challenges; it is all in the hand of the fates now. We are on the way!

***

April merges into May, May into June. The monsoon rains leave, the grass on the hill becomes dry and brittle. The leaves fall from banten trees like crumpled brown paper, the bare earth is carpeted with yellow bamboo leaves, and rusty-looking seed pods hang off the tamarind tree in front of the house. As the earth tilts towards its sun, the great land masses of the northern hemisphere heat up, drawing in cooler air from the oceans; the winds have turned around and are blowing from the dry south-east. In the words of Lombok's fishing folk, the wind is coming home.

Laras has returned to Tasmania to continue her study. Work

continues on the build, and I take off with Andrew and the boys for a sailing expedition to the east.

A few weeks ago, we were chatting at a Friday-night Stammtisch. 'Are you interested in joining a trip to Sumbawa?' he asked. I smiled and turned it over in my mind – could I justify a few days away? Andrew went on to explain that he had arranged to charter a wooden-hulled ketch and planned to sail to Sumbawa, combining some pleasure with a chance to survey coastal land for a potential agricultural project. Of course, I was interested, but could I take the time off, leaving the build and my work in Jakarta? And what about the boys?

'Why not join us?' Andrew asked again over a beer a week later. Derek, the Australian teacher, and I both signed up. I could do with a break from it all. I managed to sneak a few days off work and, at the last minute, as I was preparing to leave and about to say goodbye to Rory and Harry, I phoned Andrew.

'How would it be if the boys come along?' I asked on a whim. A couple of days off school wouldn't hurt, they could bring their books with them and the informal learning would more than compensate.

'Sure!' replied Andrew, after only a moment's hesitation, 'Why not? Good show!'

***

It is late morning when we gather at Teluk Nare, an hour's drive around the beautiful coast road from our home near Senggigi. The *Antares* lies at anchor about a hundred metres offshore. A rather scruffy looking eighteen-metre wooden-hulled ketch, she sits well in the glassy water.

Teluk Nare is a sheltered bay on the west coast of Lombok. Overlooked by the Buddhist hillside village of Pemenang, the harbour is home to a gaggle of craft, beautiful wide-hulled *pinisi*, Bugis schooners adapted for live-aboard cruises, sleek white catamarans, locally built and fitted out for international travel, and Sasak outriggers, used for fishing and ferrying passengers back and forth to the Gilis, the three small islands which lie a few kilometres to the west. Rows of shiny black buoys stretch offshore, a pearl farm creating strange geometric patterns in the milky calm. The thin beach is lined with coconut palms, a mess of flotsam and jetsam, broken masonry juts from the creamy white sand, plastic rubbish and coconut husks bob around in the low waves that lap the shore, and the late morning sun bathes it all in a bright heat; a thick and sticky honeyed light.

We heft our luggage out onto a floating wooden jetty as a tender makes its way from the *Antares* to meet us. Andrew's boatman bumps gently into the jetty in a black zodiac, kills the outboard motor and, smiling a wide greeting, clambers onto the decking and begins to load our bags. We are six in all: Andrew and his wife, Felicity; Derek; me and the two boys. Then there is our French skipper, Fabien; his mate, Matt; and their local crew of three, a mix of Bugis, Javanese and Flores sailors. There is much smiling and shaking of hands. Everyone shuffles about, taking stock – of the boat and of their fellow passengers and the crew. Greetings are exchanged and, one by one, we poke into cabins and explore the deck. The *Antares* was built, like many of her kind, by the Bugis people of South Sulawesi on the beaches of Bira, using traditional materials and traditional methods. At eighteen metres, she is not a large vessel, and, unlike the new generation of high-end live-aboards, she is not equipped for luxury travel. But she was solidly built with a *bangkarai* hardwood hull, and she will be comfortable enough for the trip we have in mind.

We plan to sail eastwards. Tracing the north coasts of Lombok and north-west of Sumbawa, we will call in at Moyo Island before heading south to explore the vast, sheltered bay of Teluk Saleh. Fabien stands in the wheelhouse, an airy arrangement at the stern, and we make for open water, heading out of the bay, bearing north through the strait that separates the Gili islands from the west coast of Lombok. With his hands on the wheel and his eyes squinting into the glare, he looks typecast for the role of skipper. A scruffily handsome and sun-bleached Frenchman in his late thirties, Fabien is tall and thin, with an open face and an ambiguous smile. A wispy beard and blonde top-knot ponytail complete the picture. A few years prior, he had sold up in Paris and put his savings into the boat, taking his chances on a business running charters in eastern Indonesia. But, I have begun to suspect, his spirit is perhaps too free and his heart too generous to ever really make a success of business.

Fabien's sidekick, Matt, provides a contrast and a foil for Fabien's whimsy; short and full of nervous energy, Matt is in his mid-twenties. Closely cropped dark hair and a three-day growth frame an impish face. Matt grew up on the French Reunion Island out in the Indian Ocean east of Madagascar. He is living an alternative kind of life, dividing his time between the ski season in Japan and the diving season in Indonesia, and dreaming of settling down to organic farming and holistic retreats. Andrew gave him some work at one time, creating a compost system by the creek just above our building site.

The midday air is hot and still. But the boat's movement brings instant relief. Bright sunlight glitters across the water and the group assembles behind the open wheelhouse. The boat is fitted with a cantilevered platform which sits out over the stern. The space is covered with a canvas awning and fitted with a thin mattress, a perfect spot in which to while away the days at sea. Behind this, a narrow bench is fitted across the rear, and a woven hammock has been slung so that passengers can sway out over the open water. Cool drinks appear and we join Fabien as he steers the vessel into open water. Andrew raises a beer can, smiles, and proposes a toast: 'Here's to a successful trip!' And everyone, in their own way, surrenders to the simple joy of travel.

Two

An hour or so up the coast from Teluk Nare we drop anchor in order to explore a local curiosity. Gunung Rinjani is perpetually cloaked in cloud, its foothills lush and green. The west of the island is thickly forested. When, between October and March, the annual monsoons sweep in from the north-west, the mountain sucks up that warm moist air and rains fall daily in great steaming deluges, drenching those steep western slopes. But the southern and eastern parts of the island miss out, and the people there suffer from routine famine cycles. Like most of the eastern Islands, once beyond Rinjani's rain shadow, Lombok is very dry. The fields are bare and dusty for much of the year, the children wide-eyed and hungry. This need not be the case. Hidden rivers run beneath the parched surface of the land, and broad subterranean aquifers, fed continually by the moist uplands, drain slowly to the sea. I was once shown hydrogeological survey maps of the island, which illustrated in bright navy blue these vast reserves and flows of groundwater which could so easily be tapped.

A bleary late-night conversation with an Australian geologist some months ago taught me much about the island's anatomy. His vision sounded simple enough after a few beers. He sees the dry plains of central and south Lombok as a green and fertile rice-bowl, dotted with windmills – simple mechanical devices which harness the winds that blow in the dry season and pump water from the aquifers to irrigate fields and quench the thirst of villagers. As with so many elegant solutions to the problems of poverty and development, there seems to be no real reason why this cannot happen – or indeed why it has not already happened. Windmills like this are found all over Australia and southern Africa. Fifteen years ago, he demonstrated that it can be done in Lombok. The windmills he installed are still producing water.

Along the north-west, north and north-east coasts, Gunung Rinjani drops almost straight into the ocean. Sharp valleys funnel rainwater to the sea over sparkling waterfalls and through picturesque, forested gorges. Beneath these valleys and ridges, running along fractures and fault lines, lie deeper rivulets, hidden from the eye by layers of volcanic rock and shingle. Fabien was looking for a point at which, around a hundred metres offshore, one of these subterranean rivulets finds an outlet, creating a freshwater spring beneath the sea.

The *Antares* circles for a few minutes, Matt peering into the blue and shouting directions, when, without warning, he leaps off the boat and disappears in a splash. As the water settles, he can be seen scurrying about beneath the water, hovering above the sea floor, legs flailing, arms wide, as he noses this way and that like a playful seal pup amongst the coral. After an improbable length of time, Matt surfaces and, with a broad wet smile, declares 'I've found it!"

I had heard tales of this offshore spring and imagined villagers paddling their canoes out and fetching buckets of fresh water from the surface of the sea for use in the home. It isn't quite like that. But before long I am in the water with Matt. The simple joy of diving off a wooden boat and into warm tropical water has never left me. Having grown up on the island of Tasmania, surrounded by icy seas where bathing was an act of bravery, foolishness, or childhood exuberance, the novelty of swimming in warm, clear water remains – even after over twenty years in Indonesia. I take a gulp of air and plunge beneath the waves, dragging myself down through that water to the spot that Matt has identified. The coral garden is only a few metres beneath the surface. I find the spring after a few floundering attempts. It isn't immediately obvious. But, with the benefit of a mask, the fresh water is faintly visible as a kind of bubbling vertical flow which distorts the sea as it emerges from beneath the coral and seeks the surface. Reaching into that flow the temperature difference is immediately evident. The fresh water is much cooler than the salt. But my attempt to drink a draft of the water, to taste that underground, underwater flow, is less successful. I simply cannot persuade my mouth to open when four metres under the surface of the sea.

The remainder of the day consists in a leisurely cruise up the coast. As the muddy grey-green hills slip by to our east, the lowering afternoon sun glitters over the sea to the west. Intermittent chatter alternates with periods of silence, the grumbling of the motor and swash of the sea a constant soundtrack to private reveries. Like a warm bath, the quiet atmosphere soaks in. I sip on a drink and, grinning at nothing in particular, drift in and out of focus. A dozy contentment washes over, the day wears on, and we make our way northward. Even the kids settle down eventually, their initial bubbling excitement subsiding into easy warmth, as each finds a corner of the deck to snuggle into. Everyone wears a quiet smile. And the day wears on.

* * *

It was at Teluk Nare, from where we set off that morning, that poor Gert's ashes were scattered. The German was one of a kind. A Lombok character. He came out to Indonesia years ago, a young man looking for adventure, and ended up running a dive business in Lombok. Gert's death was a result of heart failure, which, in turn, was a result of lifestyle, a heady but ultimately lethal mix of alcohol, cigarettes and hedonism. He was well-loved and I guess he died happy. I was called upon to give a short speech at his funeral, on behalf of the Senggigi community. Actually, it was Sakinah's job – but she was feeling too emotionally raw, and turned to me for help at the very last minute. I struggled for words, but in the end it was not so hard. Gert was a long-term member of our community, a regular at Stammtisch; he will be missed, but he made his own choices. He lived life to the full. And his remains were returned to the place he loved, merging finally with that great body of water which covers seventy per cent of our planet, with the element that connects us all.

'You're a *jilpie* now, Mark,' whispered Derek, who was there among the mourners.

'What?' I asked.

'A *jilpie*,' Derek explained quietly, 'is a tribal elder. Someone who is called upon at times like this.' Derek had spent many years working with indigenous people in the Northern Territory of Australia. My greying hair and beard apparently qualified me for the role.

We make our way slowly northwards. Seen from the *Antares*,

the coast of Lombok is a dull green pile, all the colour and drama of cultures, histories, celebrations, conflicts, wealth, poverty, births and deaths irrelevant, washed away by time, distance and the late afternoon heat haze. Sparks of light occasionally flare from the foothills as the sun catches the tin roof of a village house. Otherwise there is nothing to indicate life. The seascape to the west is somehow more dramatic in the absence of features. Bali crouches like a giant frog, its heights now diminished by distance and swaddled in mountain cloud. But it is the expanse of ocean to the north which draws the eye, for it is there and to the east across that vast, unknown and empty plain that adventure may lie.

'Ayo. Let's sail!' It is Fabien, who had just appeared from the aft cabin, bare-chested and wearing a sarong. A light wind is blowing off the island, an afternoon sea-breeze. In earlier days all travel was under sail; today most vessels travel under motor. Sails are used to gain a little efficiency when there is a following wind, and to steady the boats in choppy seas. The operation involves a fair bit clambering about and good-natured shouting on the part of the crew, but before long the sails are up and after Fabien kills the motor we are left with the sounds of the sea and the occasional flap of canvas or creaking of timbers as accompaniment.

We are running with the following breeze, goose-winged, like a gliding gull, the mainsail is spread wide to the starboard and the jib to the port. The big sail clings to the mainmast – a single white-painted tree trunk – and its base to the boom, a narrower trunk ending in a natural fork that loosely hugs the mast like an elbow joint. A smaller jib or foresail pulls on the forestay, stretched tight from the bowsprit to the mainmast and set wide to the portside with a wooden spinnaker pole at its base, to catch the light southerly breeze.

A guitar appears from somewhere and I find myself sitting at the stern and picking out a few old tunes while Derek plays the harmonica. It may not be concert-standard music, but it is gentle and, I think, appropriate. Andrew and Felicity sit quietly.

'I admire anyone who can play music,' Andrew says at one point. 'I really do.'

I sing a couple of sea shanties, old songs, and then an Irish rebel tune, sad and lyrical to reflect the mood. Andrew raises his eyebrows. His Irish ancestors were probably on the other side of that political fence.

Three

From this vantage point, on board the *Antares*, not a great deal has changed in the one hundred and fifty years since Alfred Russel Wallace passed by here on his way to Ampenan. Having noted the substantial differences between animal and bird species in Bali and Lombok, the British naturalist developed a theory and proposed a boundary, which became known as the Wallace Line. Our first day's travel takes us directly along Wallace's line, which runs up the Lombok Strait, between Bali and Lombok, and continues northwards between the islands of Borneo and Sulawesi. To the east of the line lies Asia and to the west Australasia. On one side, tigers, rhinos and squirrels. On the other, cockatoos, gum trees and kangaroos.

Wallace's invisible line and the Lombok Strait now hold a poetic fascination for me. I can stand on the unfinished deck of our new home on the Hill in West Lombok and look across that line to the continent of Asia. And now we are sailing along it.

Wallace must have looked a bit like Fabien at the time, tall, skinny and bearded, he was then in his thirties. I became a big fan of Mr Wallace when I learned of his exploits, his extraordinary life and achievements. Wallace travelled throughout these islands over a period of eight years, collecting specimens of insects, butterflies, birds, animals and plants (over a hundred and twenty-five thousand in all, one thousand of which were newly identified species) and making copious notes, which he later published in his book, *The Malay Archipelago*. Wallace is notable for his resilience, his ability to cope with hardship and move on from setbacks. After spending four years collecting in the Amazon basin, wandering alone amongst the tribal people on his first trip, he lost the lot, and nearly his life, when his ship caught fire on the way home. But what makes him such an attractive figure is not only his extraordinary achievement, but his humility.

Wallace, like Lombok where he spent some time, has until recently been overlooked by history, overshadowed by more popular places and people – in Lombok's case, the better-known island of Bali to the west. In Wallace's case, Charles Darwin, with his better connections in London's scientific establishment, is credited with the theory of natural selection, which, arguably, Wallace first proposed. Reportedly he formulated what later became the theory of evolution while suffering from a malarial fever in Ternate, North Maluku, though some say he was actually in the field near Jailolo.

Wallace described his journey across the strait from Bali to Lombok in his book as follows: 'It was on the 13th of June, 1856, after a twenty days' passage from Singapore in the "Kembang Djepon" (Rose of Japan), a schooner belonging to a Chinese merchant, manned by a Javanese crew, and commanded by an English captain, that we cast anchor in the dangerous roadstead of Bileling on the north side of the island of Bali.

'Leaving Bileling, a pleasant sail of two days brought us to … the island of Lombock … We enjoyed superb views of the twin volcanoes of Bali and Lombock, each about eight thousand feet high, which form magnificent objects at sunrise and sunset, when they rise out of the mists and clouds that surround their bases, glowing with the rich and changing tints of these the most charming moments in a tropical day.'

***

As I think of Alfred Russel Wallace, I am reminded, again, of his namesake in Bali; Wallace, the buffy fish owl. Next to Wallace's perch at the ecolodge was a magazine table. On one my visits I picked up a *National Geographic*. The magazine fell open at a foldout map of the world which illustrated the rather different shape of continents and land masses during the last ice age, when the sea was about a hundred and twenty metres lower than it is today. Britain was part of the Continent, Canada's Hudson Bay was dry, the island of Papua and New Guinea was part of mainland Australia, as was Tasmania. And the Malaysian peninsula extended south-east in a wide continuous land mass as far as Bali. But there it ended.

What Wallace could not have known is that, corresponding to his theoretical line between the Asian and Australasian regions, there lies a physical barrier to the spread of species. The Lombok Strait averages about a thousand metres in depth, though in places it is far deeper – nearly twice as deep in places. We are sailing over a deep, deep trench. And not only is the strait deep, it is treacherous. The southern entrance to the Lombok Strait is guarded by Bali's Nusa Penida and Lombok's wonderfully named Bangko-Bangko, where the Japanese positioned their big guns in the Second World War. Today's surfers pit themselves against the big waves of Desert Point, described by a friend as one of the longest breaks on the planet and an 'evil place'. At this entrance to the strait a sill reduces the depth to around two hundred metres, creating racing currents and dramatic conditions as the warm waters of the Pacific rush through to join the cooler Indian Ocean in the south.

The Lombok Strait is the only deep-water passage from the Indian Ocean to the Java Sea in this part of eastern Indonesia and was very strategic in the Second World War. Most underwater passages by U.S., British, Dutch and Australian submarines from the big base at Fremantle were made through it. The fast and turbulent currents sometimes forced these submarines to surface. The Japanese navy knew this and patrolled the channel. The Japanese guns, manufactured in Germany, were positioned at Bangko-Bangko (also known as Cape Pandanan) where they could pick off sea traffic as it negotiated the treacherous passage. Similar gun placements on Gili Trawangan and Bali enabled the Japanese to triangulate their defence of the channel.

This was the route taken by the *Krait* on her passage to attack the Japanese fleet in Singapore, during Operation Jaywick in 1943. The *Krait* travelled slowly through the channel disguised as a local fishing boat. Its crew of white sailors and the fourteen Z Special Unit commandos aboard changed their skin colour with dye and boot polish to look like local natives. The operation was an outstanding success – the commandos sank or disabled seven Japanese ships in Singapore harbour before returning the way they came. There was one tense moment as a Japanese patrol approached the *Krait* in the Lombok Straits, but she made it back, undetected, to Australia.

The seas around Bali and Lombok were the scene for many such encounters. In the final months of the war, a band of four young men Australian and British Z Special Unit commandos – Lawrie Black, Alex Hoffie, Malcolm Gillies and James Crofton-Moss – went behind enemy lines to reconnoitre the south of Lombok. Four went and two returned. An air operation had attempted to destroy the three six-inch Japanese guns, located on the point. The mission aimed to determine the condition of the guns, to gather intelligence on enemy defences, and, if necessary, to lay the ground for a demolition team which would follow to destroy the guns. The operation, code-named Starfish, was a partial success.

In March 1945, the men travelled from Australia to Lombok on the *Rook*, a US submarine. Tensions and youthful spirits were high when a fight broke out between the Australian commandos and the American seamen in the confined space aboard. The battle apparently involved a lot a talcum-powder and ended with a few bruises, a little blood and sore heads – but no disciplinary action. The team was dropped south of Cape Sara, near the beautiful Selong Belaneq Beach. While the submarine waited in the dark, the Australians floundered across the reef and made it ashore to the east of the point in a rubber dinghy, getting thoroughly swamped in the surf along the way. Stores were buried in pig holes, where reportedly the Japanese did not find them, though it transpired that the local Sasaks were well aware of the cache. The team returned to the submarine. After a second landing at Pengantap Bay, to the west of the first landing, more stores, the rubber dinghy, outboard motor and fuel were stowed in a sea cliff cave and the team set off to explore the area, finding water and making camp before heading inland and north-west towards the gun emplacements.

The four men spent around six weeks on the island, managing to make friendly contact with the locals, with whom they met frequently, exchanging propaganda leaflets and cash for information and fresh supplies in the form of chickens, eggs and vegetables. A substantial amount of information was gathered and later reported back to Command in Darwin. After around three weeks, they moved camp to Batugendang Point, just south of the gun placements at Pandanan Point. A replacement radio was requested after the power pack for the first set burned out; it was duly delivered with more stores in a night-time airdrop in the bay below the new camp. About a month after they first arrived, the party divided, Black and Hoffie heading off with some locals on a recce, while Gillies and Crofton-Moss returned to the first camp to collect stores and make radio contact. At some point, these two became separated, getting bushed in the thick scrub. James Crofton-Moss never saw his friends again.

The remaining three managed to avoid the Japanese until the end, when they were finally discovered. They were sitting around their camp in the early morning, cleaning up their breakfast dishes when a snapped twig alerted one of the men. The alarm was raised, there was a clatter of dropped dixie bowls and, as the three ducked, grabbed for their weapons and ran off into the bush, a storm of gunfire followed them. Malcolm Gillies was wounded and captured. The remaining two, Black and Hoffie, made it out a few days later, having found their way back to the first camp and south to the coast. After several attempts they made radio contact with the base in Darwin. Recovering the rubber dinghy from the cave, they rendezvoused with a Catalina seaplane offshore, and were safely returned to Darwin.

Alex Hoffie died fifty years later in 1996, Lawrie Black in 2009. Malcolm Gillies and James Crofton-Moss lie in the Commonwealth War Cemetery in Ambon. Both were captured and beheaded by the Japanese. The remains of the Japanese guns can still be found, covered in tropical vines and rusting away on the ridge at Bangko-Bangko, though the exercise involves some serious scrub-bashing. The headland is thickly covered with low, dense and thorny scrub; little wonder that Crofton-Moss and Gillies got disoriented.

A studio portrait of Gillies in uniform can be found on the Special Forces 'Roll of Honour' website. The pensive-looking young man stares off to the right of the frame. One wonders what he endured during the month between his capture and execution. Tales of derring-do, night-time escapades in rubber dinghies and talcum-powder battles; all of this pales somewhat when you look into the eyes, as it were, of this young man. So much pain and waste – and all to feed or fight the hubris and ridiculous ambitions of wartime leaders. It was only three months later that the Americans dropped their bombs on Hiroshima and Nagasaki, ending the war and the lives of one hundred and twenty nine thousand Japanese civilians.

The memory is kept alive and the sacrifice of these men is honoured in a modest way in an annual ANZAC Day ceremony held on the beach in Senggigi. On April 25th this year, a small group of expatriate Australians and New Zealanders gathered in the cool pre-dawn at the Beach Club restaurant, where preparations included a table on the beach draped with three flags: Indonesian,

Australian and New Zealand. The dawn service was casual but solemn. A short speech from a Vietnam veteran, singing of national anthems, reciting of old poetry, a lone bugle playing the last post, and a long two-minutes' silence. I led the singing of Eric Bogle's lament, 'The Band Played Waltzing Matilda', and Rory was one of a two children from our school chosen to lay a wreath at the edge of the sea, where a gentle wash dragged it out and scattered the petals as the day gradually lit up. As tradition dictates, the brief ceremony was followed with a 'gunfire breakfast', sausages and eggs washed down with rum and milk.

They shall grow not old, as we that are left grow old:
Age shall not weary them, nor the years condemn
At the going down of the sun and in the morning
We will remember them
Lest we forget ...

Four

The day is ending. The sails have been furled, and we motor quietly northward, following the coast, the ketch's bubbling wake fading with the light in the south-west. The three Gilis eventually disappear behind a headland, the low islands merging with the sea, their surf breaks a hint of white in the dim gold.

Once again, I find myself watching the sun set across the Lombok strait. Just as Wallace did all those years ago, I watch as the world turns, draining the light from the sky and, for a short time, painting it with a deep orange wash. The two volcanoes, Rinjani to the east and Agung to the west, still dominate the scene. As the mountain mists evaporate in the cooling air, their peaks appear in the day's final glow.

Gunung Rinjani's dun-coloured foothills rise from the sea in a tumbling, clambering heap. In the last of the day's light, the volcano's peak emerges high above the mists. The mountain comes and goes as we pass by on the wooden ketch, our journey, our worries and ambitions, a silly irrelevance. West of Lombok, the sea is a vast shimmering plain. The island of Bali is afloat, alight. Shafts of light pierce the mountain clouds as it passes from view. A mirage. A dreamscape. A glimpse of the glass islands.

To the north, nothing. A thin glimmer, emptiness, the sea stretches away to a distant imagined line. Lost in a haze of golden light, tiny sailboats, local dugouts, outriggers, appear to float on air, their triangular sails caught in the sea mist, suspended between heaven and earth.

* * *

That night, we sit on the open deck and look at the stars. The air is pleasantly cool. Motoring around the north-west coast of Lombok, we are far from the distraction of urban light and the sky is magnificent. Derek points out the various constellations to my sons and together we ponder the mysteries of time and space. Fabien explains that his boat, *Antares*, is named after a star, the brightest star in the distant constellation of Scorpio. After several attempts, we identify it hanging over the dark shape of Rinjani to the south-east, one of a vast multitude of light points in the high darkness, Antares, the heart of the scorpion, glows a dull red.

'I'm told that the Antares star no longer exists,' says Fabien. 'She probably burned out years ago. What we are looking at is the light of a dead star. I thought it would be good to name my boat after something that doesn't exist, an illusion...' he chuckles.

Although I'm not entirely sure that this is true, it makes a good story. In our concrete and neon-lit human world we tend to forget how small and fleeting we are in the scheme of things. I am keen for my boys to see what I see, to feel what I feel.

'It's so far away!' Rory observes, lying back and gazing up into that vast distance.

'It sure is!' Derek replies, always ready for the teachable moment. 'Antares is probably about fifteen-million years old. I guess it's five or six hundred light years away. That means the light from the star we are looking at now took over five hundred years to reach us. Fabien could be right. Maybe the star was already dead before the light reached us. So, we could be looking at something that doesn't exist.'

'As if we're looking into the past,' says Rory. I turn towards him. He wears a thoughtful expression, his young eyes reflecting the lights of the aft cabin.

'It's like a ghost,' says Harry, still focussed on the star.

'Like a ghost,' I repeat. There is a brief silence. The motor rumbles on. Seawater slaps against the side of our boat in the darkness. We all gaze up in the same direction at that distant sky and its curious, milky ghosts.

'You know, there is a moral to Fabien's story,' I say eventually. 'In the end we are tiny, insignificant, nothing really. Those stars, each one of them is huge. There are millions of them up there – and that's just the few that we can see. Some of them are a thousand times bigger than our sun. And our sun is a million times bigger than the earth. And you know how big the earth is. It would probably take us a year to sail all the way around the earth on this boat...'

'Some stars are so far away that we haven't seen them yet,' comments Derek. 'The light hasn't reached us...'

'We're tiny, like tiny grains of sand on the beach,' says Rory after a pause for thought.

'Like ants!' adds Harry.

'Yep, we're like ants,' I say, looking again for the star. It has shifted position in relation to the boat as we gradually round the north coast and bear east. 'And what we see is gone before we even see it.'

'If the star is not real, how do we know anything else is real?' asks Rory, still staring up into the dizzy void.

'Good question,' I reply. 'People have been asking that question for thousands of years. Some people say our world is an illusion. The Buddhists think that.'

'Scientists say it in a different sort of way,' says Derek. 'Our world is made of atoms, of sub-atoms, but mostly it's just a lot of space and tiny, whizzing atoms. Clusters of energy, nothing more, really.'

I lean back, looking out at the dark sea, glancing every now and then at my sons. Harry is nodding off. So much wonder. So much love. But we like to overlook the ephemeral nature of our existence. We forget how irrelevant we are. How big the natural, non-human world is. How small we are. How we are composed mainly of empty space. How quickly we will be gone, forgotten.

'When the light we are now looking at left its home in the Scorpio constellation five hundred years ago,' I muse, speaking quietly to no one in particular, 'my ancestors were farming somewhere in Devon, I suppose. They left no trace. No record. I have no idea who they were, their names, their passions. What was important in their lives. We become so self-important in our cities, in our careers, and our petty concerns. None of it matters, really... none of it...'

The boys have found a spot to sleep on top of the rear cabin. Beyond that, at the stern, Andrew and Felicity have already made their nest on the overhang behind the open wheelhouse, the quietly rushing water beneath them. It will be more pleasant, all had agreed, to sleep out in the open than in the confined space of the cabin beneath. A final beer and Derek drifts off to sleep on the foredeck. I claim the remaining space on the port side between the two masts and beneath the lashed boom which stretches between them. Sounds of shuffling sleepers, each in his own world now, keep me company in the dark.

As I lie down and gaze up into that night sky, something about my sense of self begins to slip away. The rhythmic rock of the boat, the steady chug of her engine, a faint whiff of diesel fumes, salty air, and the recent discussion, all come together in a seductive way. It is like a drug. With the afternoon heat haze long gone, the great dome of the night sky is alive, filled from horizon to horizon with bright stars. The sweep of the Milky Way is visible as a long cloudy mass of distant light at the centre of my vision. Boundaries begin to dissolve. With no visual clues beyond the swaying masts and rigging above, the unfamiliar vastness begins to take hold. It feels a little weird, a little scary. You could drown in that sky.

I drift off to sleep thinking about the old people. Little wonder that they sought meaning in that sky, finding gods, spirits and signs among those wheeling stars. People have been navigating by those same stars for many thousands of years, finding their way across the oceans with only the sky to guide them. Many still do.

***

The *Antares* makes steady progress. Light seas across the sheltered north coast of Lombok become a little choppy when we reach open water between the islands of Lombok and Sumbawa. I once took a 'fast boat' from Lombok to Sumbawa and recall hitting a standing wave halfway through the crossing. The long narrow vessel reared up and then crashed back down with a most unnerving 'whack' before we continued on our otherwise uneventful passage to the port of Maluk in West Sumbawa. The string of islands that makes up much of Indonesia, stretching in a wide loop from Sumatra in the west to Timor in the east, separates two oceans. To the south-west lies the wide Indian Ocean and to the north-east the Pacific Ocean merges with a handful of seas bordered by the islands of South-East Asia: the South China Sea, the Java Sea and the Banda Sea. These vast bodies of water are subject to differing tidal pulls as the moon and the earth spin across the heavens. Sometimes the two oceans can be as much as a metre different in height. At such times the rush of water through the narrow straits which separate the islands produces strange phenomena: racing currents, standing waves, white water rapids, and whirlpools in the open water.

Some hours later, a light rain begins to fall. We make our way downstairs, dragging thin mattresses and light blankets back to the communal cabin below. Sleep is uneasy but not unpleasant on that first night.

Five

One by one, the passengers emerge, shaggy haired, blinking in the bright morning light and wiping the night away from sleepy eyes. Derek is up first. He stands beside the open wheelhouse, nursing a mug of coffee and staring into the middle distance.

'Ahoy!' he cries in a jolly, nautical sort of way, when he spots me.

'Indeed,' I mutter and shuffle about in an effort to collect my wits, before thinking about coffee and the day ahead.

Andrew is the next up. 'Beautiful morning!' he manages as he clambers up through the galley from the forehead cabin. And it is. The sun shines low from the east across a perfect sea and a cloudless sky. It is the dry season and the weather is kind.

Felicity, not far behind, is the only woman aboard. Like Andrew, Felicity is from Africa. Wearing a habitually quizzical expression and a china-pale complexion, she speaks with a mild middle-English accent, as if she is slightly puzzled about the world.

My wife is far away in Tasmania. But, having grown up south of Yogyakarta in Central Java, boats and the sea are not really her thing, anyway. Stories of Ratu Kidul, and the South Sea Queen's mischievous habit of stealing away foolhardy bathers, have programmed Ibu Laras for a life on the land. I have some sense of this. My earlier visits to the southern Javanese beaches of Parangtritis and Samas added a dose of practical reality to the mythology. Wide, windswept stretches of hot sand, the beaches were battered by an Indian Ocean which, to me, felt distinctly unfriendly and best left alone.

Soon, Rory and Harry are up. The boys' view of the world differs from their mum's. Having spent their lives thus far on the islands of Lombok, Flores and Sulawesi, with occasional spells in Tasmania, the two are well-acquainted with the sea, both of them strong swimmers and budding surfers. Rory recently earned his junior diving ticket and is keen to get into the water. The two boys are bronzed a healthy brown by sun and salt, and Rory, in particular, sports a mass of curly hair to complete the image of a beach boy.

'What's for breakfast?' mutters Rory.

The answer is soon provided. An aroma of fresh baked bread emanates from the galley. The boat is equipped with a gas oven, and Fabien's star turn, it transpires, is to produce bread, a different type of loaf each morning. Before long the children are crowding below, a clatter of plates and shrill chatter, a busy smearing of butter and jam on thick, warm slices of bread. The day is looking good.

The coast of Sumbawa slips past to the south, several kilometres off our starboard side. Dead ahead and sitting low in the distance is Moyo Island.

'How long till we get there?' I ask, like an impatient schoolboy. Fabien's Bugis skipper sits on a high stool and grips the wheel, a cigarette in his hand and an easy smile on his face.

'An hour or two,' he replies.

I sip my coffee – good strong Lombok coffee – and look

across at Sumbawa. The truncated crown of Mount Tambora, some distance away to the south-east, is backlit by an early sun. The sea is a deep grey-blue and choppy, a light and steady breeze follows us from the west, cresting the occasional wave with foam. White horses prance in the morning light and I sip on my coffee and think about the world.

I look across at Andrew as he sits at the stern. He wears a pensive expression, gazing out to sea, frown lines etched on his forehead. Several years younger than me, but well into middle-age and perhaps contemplating what remains of his future, he looks a little worried. Life has dealt Andrew some serious blows and it shows on his face. Over the years he has fought back. And this morning on the boat he sits in apparent ease, but somehow poised for action like a predator on the African plains. A head of cropped curly hair crowns a handsome face, bright eyes and a complex set of features.

The man is a puzzle, I think. We have been friends for over ten years, since I first arrived in Lombok; we have worked together to create The Hill, to realise a dream, we have drunk together, on occasions we have run around a coconut field with a bunch of kids and a rugby ball; at other times we have laughed at the absurdities of life; we have argued about politics, and we have fought over plans and developments on The Hill, sometimes bitterly. I won't forget the time Andrew decided to shape our land while the heavy machinery was handy nearby, without bothering to tell us. Or the time he decided that the best place for an electricity transformer was on our block, rather than his. But, for all that, I have to admire his ability to get things done – and we always manage to make peace at the end of the day. And yet, I think, I barely know the man.

And then it hits me. The key to Andrew's character. Andrew was raised for a world that no longer exists. The boat sways steadily in the light breeze, making its way towards Moyo Island, and I think of the other white Africans I have known. There was my old friend, David, whom we buried in Tasmania, an African once removed. And then Alan and Meryl from Bali. All share some common characteristics: a generosity of spirit, a bigness in their view of the world, old-fashioned values, followers of traditional sports, cricket and rugby, conservative in politics, courteous in company, and open in a generous way to new friendships; an inclusivity borne, perhaps, of life in far-flung small communities, but contradicted by a tendency to divide the human world up into leaders and followers, to assign status according to ethnicity, nationality and the school one attended. These are men and women of honour, of sundowners and gentlemen's agreements, men and women with a can-do attitude, who don't suffer fools easily, who are little constrained by the expectations of others, who work hard and play hard. Andrew can be awfully bloody-minded. He can be infuriating. He can also be generous to a fault.

I reflect on my own background. I, too, have roots in this nineteenth-century colonial world, great-uncles in South Africa, relatives in British India, a missionary in the highlands of Papua, an uncle in Sarawak. But these are long gone. Like my parents, I grew up in Tasmania, an island with its own dark past, its own distinctive version of brutality. This colonial family history is a generation or two removed from my life, recast as quaint sandstone cottages, sea shanties and period dress. My grandmother used to reminisce about how she and her new husband took the stagecoach to Tasmania's east coast for their honeymoon. It was 1917. The coachman stopped at the top of Black Charlie's Opening and Bust-me-Gall Hill for a smoke and perhaps a nip of whisky, while the horses took a rest and the gentlemen passengers toiled up on foot. But sometimes I find myself wondering how far, really, is this history removed? Scratch the surface and the old colonial attitudes, values, beliefs are probably still there. Sometimes the cheery Indonesian greeting for Westerners, 'Hello, Mister!' can sound suspiciously like 'Hello, Master'.

I am reminded, too, of the books I grew up with. Tales of British adventurers, images of natives in loin cloths and paternalistic white men. Robinson Crusoe and his faithful man, Friday. On Sunday nights I would listen with my brother to a radio play called *Jungle Doctor* ('Koh', said Baruti. 'Yoheeey, Bwana ...'), my favourite comic was not *Superman*, or *Archie and Jughead*, with their urban fifties-America references; it was *The Phantom*, and his romanticised colonial world, an imagined early twentieth century of seaplanes, steaming jungles, pigmy tribesmen, colonial administrators in pith helmets – and roughnecks in stilt-house kampungs and seedy port towns.

***

It is late morning when we drop anchor off a Bajau fishing village on the west coast of Moyo island. Like the Bugis and Makassar peoples, the Bajau – sometimes known as sea gypsies – are originally from the south of Sulawesi; Indonesia's seafarers. These sailors, boat builders, traders, fisherfolk and occasional pirates, have settled on offshore islands and coasts across not only Indonesia, but the islands of the Philippines, up into the Gulf of Thailand and as far west as Myanmar and even Madagascar – and the north coast of Australia, where they traded for three hundred years with the local people, until the Australian border force started burning their boats.

The entire island of Moyo is a national park and traditional hunting reserve. Cloaked in forests which reach to the sea, the island sits off the north coast of Sumbawa to the west of the huge volcanic Mount Tambora. The village is just up the coast from an upmarket resort, where the rich and famous come to holiday away from cameras and bothersome stares. Guests fly in on a seaplane direct from Bali and are put up in glamourous tents in the coastal jungle shade. The island is home to long tail macaques, wild cattle, pigs, deer and a great many birds and bats, including flying foxes. The remainder of the day is turned over to exploring. The village straggles along, a couple of rows of timber shacks and a dusty track between a white sand foreshore and the jungle behind. The beach is strewn with bleached shells, broken coral and debris. Smiling kids leap about in the late morning heat, swimming off the concrete piers and kicking a can about on the beach. Little white-tailed Balinese cattle look up idly, their pretty faces covered with flies. A tethered monkey snarls and watches our arrival with interest. A small shop sells cigarettes, packaged foodstuffs, and local honey in recycled plastic water bottles; a thick dark liquid with the scent of the forest, it will go well with Fabien's fresh bread.

After an obligatory visit to the sandy village office, we hire motorbikes and head inland, riding pillion behind local guys along a bush track. We are off to check out a series of low waterfalls and jungle swimming holes now known as Diana's Falls, after the English princess, who once visited. My driver is up for a chat. 'I worked in Lombok for many years,' he tells me. 'I used to drive a car for tourists. Made some good money.'

'Why did you give it away?' I ask. But I already know the answer. It's a common story.

'I missed my island home,' he laughs in a sad, resigned sort of way. 'There is no work here. Nothing much to do. No money. But it's my home.' And we bounce our way into the jungle.

Along the way to the falls, Derek spots a large nest mound of an endangered Tanimbar megapod bird. The nest is a heap of sand, litter and forest debris. Heat generated by decomposing organic material incubates the eggs, a nice synergy between life and death, birth and decay.

Diana's Falls turn out to be a beautiful series of shallow pools in a small stream, shaded by jungle giants and fringed with fallen leaves, mossy rocks and ferns. Each low fall is defined by a crescent-shaped limestone rim, which contains a pool ideal for swimming, and over which the river gently flows. The water feels soft, silky, tinged with the green of the jungle but refreshing in the heat of the day. It's probably just my imagination, but the falls seem aptly named; a place of delicate beauty, of rest and calm, that smells faintly of death, perhaps of tragedy.

***

A few months later, Derek, Fabien and I came this way again, this time with my brother and his family from Tasmania. From Moyo, we sailed north-east to the extraordinary little island of

Satonda, which boasts an inland sea, separated by less than a hundred metres from the beach. On the *Antares* again, we shared the sheltered anchorage with two luxury yachts. An odd contrast in this remote place. The *Ocean Victory* was the plaything of a Russian oligarch and operated by a mainly New Zealand crew. More like a small cruise liner than a yacht, the vessel is listed among the top ten super-yachts in the world. At one hundred and forty metres, she apparently boasts seven decks, six pools and a fourteen-metre tender in a floodable garage; not to mention the thirteen luxury cabins, on-deck jacuzzi, elevator, beach club, anchor stabilisers, gym, helipad, cinema, beauty salon, barbecue, helicopter hangar, underwater lights, bathing platform, study, underwater observation lounge and quarters for fifty crew. Not long after dropping anchor, a flap dropped open on the side of the vessel, and two zodiac dinghies popped out, James Bond style, and sped towards the shore, where crisp-white liveried crewmen stepped out and carried the owner and his family to the beach. Our polite request to the crewman for a bottle or two of spare New Zealand wine was unfruitful: 'Perhaps a Sauvignon Blanc? Or a cheeky Pino Gris? Surely no one will notice?'

The second vessel, though hardly less impressive, was closer to what I regard as a real yacht, an oversized catamaran, called the *Douce France*. At forty-two metres, she reportedly has a fore and aft sail area of five hundred and thirty-five square metres, enabling her to skip along at a constant twenty-two knots in a twenty-eight-knot breeze. Other features include a two-hundred-and-fifty-bottle wine cellar and a choice of three dining areas: a spacious cockpit, an intimate interior lounge or the aft teak deck.

The *Antares* felt distinctly downmarket in this company.

'We must look like a boatload of asylum seekers,' quipped my brother at the time. The seas of eastern Indonesia, it seems, have become a playground for the world's wealthy elites. Some years after this, a friend of mine, an American musician and writer based in Yogyakarta, joined a cruise in these waters with Peter Gabriel, Sting, and a bunch of Britain's musical royalty in search of some eastern authenticity. When my son, Harry, and I visited the remote Banda Islands, we discovered that Mick Jagger and Princess Diana had been that way before – though not at the same time.

From Satonda, we sailed further east, passing a massive flock of fruit bats which filled the sunset sky, stopping the next day at the volcanic island of Sangeang, where we dived on steeply shelving reefs to see sulphur gases bubbling up in little rows from the black sands in crystal clear waters. From there, it was south into the colourful seas and scattered islands of Rinca and Komodo. Giant manta rays swooped about, underwater pillars were patrolled by schools of circling sharks, a scattering of dug-out canoes marked a fishing ground, and prehistoric-looking frigate birds wheeled overhead, occasionally diving to scoop up a fish from the swirling waters. We stopped and lit a bonfire on a beach. The odd heron flapped past, a lone sea eagle circled above the island, pods of dolphins played in the sun, and flying fish skimmed the waves.

The Komodo national park is an extraordinary place, a place of abundance. White water surges in the middle of the sea and in passages between the islands, warm waters wash onto pink beaches, a profusion of corals decorates the underwater landscape – and giant Komodo dragons lie in the sun and drool, the closest thing to a living dinosaur that we will ever see.

The dragons, the world's largest lizards, range the islands and hang around the rangers' huts on Komodo. At around three metres in length, they drag their plump, scaly bodies across the sand on extended clawed feet. But mostly they just lie in the sun, long forked tongues flickering, black-rimmed eyes following the visitors' movements, perhaps looking for prey. The dragons dominate the ecosystem on these dry grassy islands, preying on birds and mammals, especially the local deer – and on rare occasions unfortunate humans, including one Baron Rudolf Reding von Biberegg, who disappeared on the island in 1974, presumed to have been taken by a dragon. Fossils of similar giant lizards have been found in Australia and dated at nearly four million years old. A visit to the Komodo dragons is a visit to another time: the Pleistocene era when megafauna, like giant wombats and kangaroos, huge flightless birds, giant crocodiles and a marsupial lion wandered the forests and savannas of this part of the world – east of the Wallace Line.

* * *

But that was all in the future. Back on the *Antares* and following Andrew's plans to survey Sumbawa's coastal land, we sail south-east from Moyo, leaving behind its royal waterfalls, its jungles and megapods, and into the huge sheltered bay of Teluk Saleh. As we round the southern coast of Moyo and head into the bay, the mountain of Tambora, at nearly two thousand metres, now dominates the scene. Derek, who subsequently wrote a book about 'the mountain that changed the world', regales the boys with stories of Tambora, and its famous 1815 eruption.

'It doesn't look much like a volcano,' says Harry. We all peer at the distant mountain, purplish in morning shadow.

'See how it's flat on top?' asks Derek. 'Well, it used to be shaped like a proper cone – more like Gunung Agung on Bali, but bigger. It was four thousand three hundred meters high then, more than twice as big as now. But it blew up in 1815 – nearly two hundred years ago. People say it made the loudest noise ever heard by people. It lost its top. Hundreds of cubic kilometres of rock and dust were blown up. Can you imagine what that must have been like?'

'You wouldn't want to be here in this boat when that happened,' says Rory. The boys squint at the mountain, making little peaks with their fingers to picture its original height.

'That's for sure,' says Derek, warming to his theme. 'There were tsunamis and enormous floating islands of pumice – you know that rock that floats? Boats wouldn't have been much good to you then.'

'The eruption caused the "year without summer" in the northern hemisphere – an ash cloud covered the earth and blocked out the sun. Europe and America froze. They couldn't grow food, so people starved and rioted and there were all sorts of problems. Some people called it "the year eighteen-hundred-and-froze-to-death".'

'Oh, and Frankenstein's monster was born,' he adds.

'Really?'

'Well, Mary Shelly couldn't go outside all year, because it was too cold and wet where she lived in Switzerland, so she stayed indoors and wrote the novel, *Frankenstein*.' We chat for a while about how everything on earth is connected, about how a volcano in Indonesia can make it rain in Belgium.

'Apparently, Turner's famous sunset paintings are another result of the eruption,' I add. 'And Tambora helped the Duke of Wellington defeat Napoleon in the Battle of Waterloo.'

Fabien looks up, his eyebrows raised. This is his history as well as mine. Derek looks a bit sceptical.

'Well,' I continue, 'apparently, the eruption changed weather patterns, causing heavy rains which gave an advantage to Wellington and his troops.' A few years earlier, the duke had devised the now-famous, waxed leather Wellington boot, which meant his cavalry did better in the soggy conditions. So, Napoleon lost the battle in 1815 and was exiled to the island of Elba. The Napoleonic wars were over and, as part of the settlement, the British handed Java, the Banda Islands and Kupang back to the Dutch.'

'Oh, and Mount Wellington in my hometown of Hobart got its name,' I add for good measure.

'There is some debate about all this, actually,' says Derek, adopting a scholarly tone. 'For a start, I'm sure Mount Wellington had a name before the British arrived.'

'Well, that's true,' I say. 'I think the locals called it kunanyi.'

'There is a sign on Mount Tambora that mentions Napoleon,' continues Derek. 'It's possible that the eruption influenced the outcome of the battle, which happened two months later. The year without a summer wasn't until 1816, but there was definitely a lot of rain about in 1815, when the battle took place. According to some, Napoleon was worried that the mud would bog his soldiers and artillery down, so he delayed the advance of his troops until the ground was dry. This gave Wellington time to unite the

Prussian and British forces – and as a result they trounced the little emperor's army.'

'Well, either way, we should never let the truth get in the way of a good story!' I say with a grin and a wink at the boys. Derek frowns.

'I agree,' laughs Fabien. 'We might all be speaking French if it wasn't for that mountain.'

'Maybe, or Indonesia might have been British, and we'd all be speaking English and playing cricket,' adds Andrew, in a dry tone.

'True,' I add. 'But at least Raffles instituted British road rules while he was in Indonesia. Peter told me that. Before Raffles, it was "Out of the way, I'm coming through!" and that's why we drive on the *correct* side of the road to this day,' I laugh.

'I've always wondered why Indonesians drive on the left,' says Derek. 'Now I know!'

* * *

There is something rather magical about sailing these eastern seas. I am reminded of *Gulliver's Travels* and of the *Dawn Treader*, and her voyage to the edge of C.S. Lewis's mythical world of Narnia. Like Lemuel Gulliver, and the *Dawn Treader*, we go from island to island, from sea to sea, encountering ever-more fantastical creatures, as we venture further from the known world. Beyond Lombok and Sumbawa, with their fire-breathing mountains, flying fish and underwater springs, lie the islands of dragons, and beyond there, Flores, with its megalithic culture and fossilised hobbits, little people who fifty thousand years ago co-existed with Homo sapiens and pigmy elephants. Heading south-east across the wide Saleh Bay towards a group of little islands and pearl farms, we sail into a shallow pink sea – the ocean is carpeted with pale pink jellyfish for as far as the eye can see. Magic!

Eventually, after a night out on the islands, it is time to go home. We clamber aboard the zodiac tender, leaving the islands and the *Antares* for another time, another adventure. An overpowering stench of rotting seafood greets the senses as we approach a fishing village on the mainland of Sumbawa. The annual jellyfish harvest is underway. Local fishing boats cruise the pink seas, the sailors scooping up jellyfish in long handled nets. On shore, a makeshift processing plant is in operation. A lone Chinese overseer stands amongst huge vats of salted jellyfish, while a team of local women remove the bells, tossing them into the sea where they slosh about and wash onto the beaches. Jellyfish deteriorate rapidly in the heat, so processing starts as soon as they are caught. After the dangling oral arms are separated from the bell, they are washed in seawater before being scraped to remove the gonads and muck. The little body and arms are salted, and, as they dehydrate, heaped up to drain, turned several times and left to dry. The jellyfish are destined eventually for dinner tables and fine dining in China, Japan and Korea, where they have apparently been regarded as a delicacy – and an aphrodisiac – for nearly two thousand years.

After a while, waiting in the lazy heat behind the processing plant, we are met by Andrew's driver in a pickup. A couple of off-road motorbikes are unloaded – Andrew plans to go exploring the coastal lands with Matt. Derek and I climb into the cabin, leaving the boys with big grins to bounce around with the luggage in the open flat tray at the rear. An hour or so through the dry lands of

Sumbawa takes us to the town of Sumbawa Besar, with its huge ironwood sultan's palace, and from there around the north-west coast past the little island of Bungin, reputedly the most densely populated place on the planet. The low coral atoll is entirely covered with a Bajau sea-gypsy village, most of the stilt houses now sitting out over the shallow surrounding seas. At the harbour of Poto Tano we board an inter-island ferry back to Lombok. Passing by some low flat islands, sipping on sweet milky coffee and chatting with a travelling salesman from Java, we approach from the east; Mount Rinjani dominates the island.

THE SEASON
OF THE SUN

One

July and August are the dry months in Lombok. The acacias are flowering in yellow swathes across the slopes of the hill. Red ants build nests in the mango trees, stitching leaves together and swarming on the branches. The fleshy frangipani are beginning to flower – perfect little blooms, a splash of yellow framed by creamy white petals. Now that they have taken root, maturing from the sticks we planted earlier this year, the frangipani will grow into small trees, producing new blooms each morning for Balinese offerings and Javanese graves. A birdwing butterfly flaps lazily amongst the trees, and a lizard flicks out its yellow throat, spreads its lateral wing-like flanks – and glides in a long swooping arc from one palm to another.

Diane and I go for a walk up the hill. After sweating our way up to the little school, an hour or so from our building site, we follow a track down into the forested valley where we cross the creek above a big waterfall. Heading back down the north-western ridge, we stop to chat to an old woman who is preparing a meal in her tiny home, a single grass-roofed room, barely big enough to stretch out in.

'Come and sit, take a rest, share my meal,' she calls. We chat about life and taste her thin broth made with bamboo shoots, conscious that this is all she has.

'My husband is gone, and my children live in the city. I'm all my own now,' she says with a smile. But when we offer to pay for the few mouthfuls of soup, she refuses.

'No!' she cries. 'It's my treat, I'm happy to have the company for a few minutes.'

In the valleys and across the southern plains, the rice has been harvested, the husks have been burned, and the farmers are growing soybeans, peanuts or tobacco, the big leaves beginning to ripen in the dry heat. On the beaches and in the beachside bars, in the streets of Senggigi and out on the Gili islands, European tourists smile and sun themselves, the beach sellers are busy with woven blankets, t-shirts and trinkets, and the masseuses do a brisk trade.

A troupe of long-tailed macaque monkeys makes a daily visit to our house site; following the tree line to the west they make their way down from the hills in search of fruit and water. Leaping from branch to branch, swinging off the palm fronds in a splash of foliage, the little creatures shriek at one another, sometimes descending to the ground, where they scamper about, the big males glaring from the shadows, the mothers carrying their babies and chasing the youngsters. In later years, the animals become increasingly cheeky, coming closer and closer to the house, though they do not enter the villa or the open kitchen at the rear – which is my fear as we build the house. Bush mangos ripen on the trees and the monkeys take advantage, feasting on the fruit and scampering up lanky palms to pick the coconuts, which they drop, cracking them open and exposing the flesh and sweet water inside.

In the early evenings on the hill, we hear the distinctive call of an owl. The birds call to one another across the valley, a melodious hoot in the darkness. At the time I didn't know that it was the Rinjani scops owl. In fact, the bird was yet to be identified by science. It is not every day that a new species of bird is discovered. Especially one as large as an owl. And especially one that is living, literally, in your backyard.

It was a year after our villa was built when a visitor from Tasmania told me he had heard an owl in the tree behind the joglo where he was staying. And then, one evening, Harry and I saw it swoop across the dam and over our heads into the forested area below. A year later, I received an email from another guest. Alan, a Scotsman, had been staying for a couple of months in the joglo with his Swiss wife, and was recording his observations of birds and butterflies. Owls, he explained, are most easily identified by their distinctive calls at night.

Alan wrote to me: 'An owl can be heard every evening and early morning in the wooded area (100 m altitude), around the Studio, The Hill, Batu Layar, near Senggigi, Lombok, Indonesia, from our arrival on the 6th of November, 2012, until today, 5th December. The voice is a single note repeated at a few seconds (often 8 seconds) interval.'

But the owl's call was unlike any of those mentioned in the scientific literature on birds in Lombok. Alan, like the Tasmanian birder in the previous year, was surprised at how little-studied was Lombok's birdlife. A recent academic survey found that only fifteen serious studies of Lombok's birds had been conducted, beginning with that of Alfred Russel Wallace, one hundred and fifty years ago. Alan had found a bird which did not match the description of any known species. 'It needs some more research to identify the bird in question,' he wrote.

Two months later, headlines around the world announced the discovery of the Rinjani Scops Owl on Lombok. A group of scientists published their findings in the *Scientific American*. The owl, unique to Lombok, is apparently common in Rinjani National Park and coastal foothills. The researchers recorded the bird's territorial song in five locations, including Senggigi. After an exchange of emails with one of the scientists from Stockholm University, we confirmed that the bird in our garden, identified by Alan, was indeed the newly discovered Rinjani Scops Owl. Alan recorded the owl's call and we sent it to a bird authority in Bogor for verification. The challenge then was to get a photograph of the elusive bird. Derek was keen to try.

Derek arrived that evening with a couple of bottles of beer, and the two of us set up with cameras and a loudspeaker. The front terrace of the joglo is ideal for bird watching, located at tree-level in a wooded area of the garden. After waiting quietly for around half an hour, the bird called from somewhere in the darkness. We replayed the bird's call through the speaker, and, in a few minutes, the owl responded from nearby. In this way we hoped to attract it. If it perched in a tree in front of the joglo, we would be ready with a flashlight and a camera. After a series of lively conversations between the real owl and the recorded owl, the beer was finished, and we packed up for the evening. 'Play the recording too often and the bird will become suspicious,' we had been warned.

The next night, a phone call sent Alan scurrying up the hill to Andrew's newly built home, a hybrid Asian-villa-cum-African-planter's-bungalow with extra wide verandas for outdoor living and a lap pool that divides the house down the middle in two. Andrew had spotted the owl perched in a raintree. But the bird flew away before a photograph could be taken. Alan did, however, get a photograph of a juvenile Rinjani Scops Owl, a fluffy, grey bundle in the hands of a teenager at a warung on the hill. Not what we hoped for.

***

The joglo is now complete, a small team is finishing the painting. And the cottage by the creek now has two storeys, interior walls and roof framing made from coconut timber cut on site.

A truckload of beautiful pink stone is dumped beside the big house, a locally quarried basalt slate. A specialist stonemason has been brought in to work the stone and sits chipping away at the raw rocks creating roughly evened edges which he will fit together like a jigsaw puzzle to create a series of stone-faced walls around the pool decking. Alan, the Scotsman, later told me he thought the stone might well be gold bearing.

Meanwhile, Karno has managed to source a load of ironwood from an old rubber factory in South Sumatra. The plan is to use the recycled timber for pool decking. Sticking to our principles, Laras and I insisted that there would be not a scrap of rainforest timber in the project. All the timber is to be recycled or grown and harvested locally. Coconut wood is already in use to frame the roof of the outdoor kitchen. But tougher timber is needed for outdoor decking in the tropics where the humidity, heat and rain will destroy softer timbers in a season or two.

The timber turns up, a truckload of massive ironwood beams

– *ulin* wood from the old forests of Sumatra, the beams have been sitting beneath the rubber factory for a hundred years or more. Around fifty large pieces of varying lengths are dropped in the sandy area by the beach, while Karno sets about finding a sawmill to turn them into planks for decking. One by one the local sawmills turn him away. The timber is simply too old and too hard. It will wreck the circular saw blades. Eventually, the last local mill agrees, reluctantly, to give it a try.

'We'll cut one beam, one only,' Karno is told. 'If that goes okay, we'll do the rest. But if the saw is broken, if we hit an old nail or a bolt – or if the timber is just too hard for our saw and it breaks, if that happens, you pay.' We agree, and the next day Karno tells us that they won't do it. The saw blade is wrecked. The timber is too tough.

Laras's resourceful brother comes up with another plan and hires a chainsaw operator. The timber is delivered up the hill to our house site, and the operator begins the painstaking job of cutting the big beams into narrow planks. Each plank is then planed smooth. For a week or two, the air is filled with the whining din of a chainsaw and then an electric plane. By the time he is done, at least a third of the original timber is gone – turned into sawdust. And we are left with a stack of planks, all a slightly odd length, width and thickness. In due course, these are turned into decking and we have our recycled timber decked pool – but at what cost?

***

I manage to fit in a trip with the boys to Tasmania to reconnect with Laras at our small home in the foothills of Mount Wellington. Borrowed boots, mittens, scarves, windcheaters and beanies; mid-winter bonfires and communal singing in Salamanca Place; evenings with family and friends; red wine and woodfires; fish and chips by the dock, visits to the public library, the art gallery and the museum – all the things that Lombok does not offer. I have arranged a few days at the old Waldheim cabins in Tasmania's wintry highlands; the puddles are frozen and ice hangs in snowy sheets from the eaves; the boys break off icicles and chase their breath, great clouds of white in the brittle air. We celebrate Laras's birthday with steaming enamel mugs of tea, card games and candlelight. Here I can breathe it all in; the dark green of moss and myrtle forests; the smell of sassafras and cold, damp earth; wombats, pademelons and currawongs in the shadows; morning walks across the moor to Dove Lake and Cradle Mountain before the tourists arrive; the stillness, silence and pale light of a morning after snow – Tasmania!

Along the way, I become a grandfather. Charlotte Rose is born on 12th July at the Royal Hobart Hospital, a little pink bundle with a fine head of fuzzy blonde hair. My daughter is everything a new mum should be: overwhelmed, overjoyed, overprotective. Rory and Harry get a brief cuddle each, before the new-born is returned to the safety of mum's arms. Laras takes care of the boys and I take my son-in-law to a nearby pub to meet my son and wet the baby's head. It is a bitterly cold Tasmanian evening. In that crowded bar, with a roaring log fire, a yeasty beer in hand, my son and my son-in-law as companions, I reflect on life, birth, the pain and the joy, and on the strength of family that makes it all worthwhile.

Two

Back in Lombok the days drift on, hazy and hot. Laras continues her study in Tasmania. My life proceeds as a kind of juggling act: trips to Jakarta and occasionally to Bandung, Aceh, Makassar, Surabaya and Semarang; stints working at my desk in the cottage in Lombok; Friday nights at Stammtisch, catching up with Sakinah, Andrew, Derek, Gregg and Leigh; late nights at the Happy Café, where the beers are cold and the band pumps out rock standards, the shouted conversations, snake-skin boots and wild lead breaks; lazy Sunday afternoons at Café Alberto, the children running about on the beach, while I chat with Gregg about school and with the Belgians, who are also constructing villas, about The Hill.

Work continues on the build. I arrived back from Tasmania armed with photographs and designs for some new garden features: a Tasmanian-style wood fire barbecue, a garden pathway constructed with natural stone. A few weeks later, two splendid barbecues are built. When we experiment, lighting a decent fire in the hearth, the structures perform magnificently, the chimneys drawing the smoke in a satisfying column into the air and the fire heating a sold plate. I was worried that the smoke from the barbecues below the pool area might be drawn into the open-sided second story of the big house – but thankfully this is not a problem. We also end up with a natural stone stepped path leading from the creek crossing by the cottage up the slope to the joglo cottage.

The big pillars and concrete beams in the main house are clad in more recycled teak. Plastering is finished and the villa is painted – a classic plain white throughout. The combination of dark timber panels, unglazed windows, white walls, the open upper-storey galley, shady trees and green lawns outdoors, not only looks fantastic but keeps the house cool. It is not only the shade, but the *breath* of trees, I learn, that reduces temperatures by one or two degrees; the combined effects of shade and transpiration can reduce temperatures by around five degrees. We decide to retain as many trees as possible in the garden and around the house – and avoid solid paving which radiates heat. Instead we grow lawns and use hexagonal, donut-style concrete pavers with holes for grass planting. The slopes and flat lawns are planted out with grass ahead of the rains, a fine creeper for the paved areas, something called *rumput mutiara,* or 'pearl grass', for the little lawn along the front of the main house, and regular grass dug up in tufts from the fields in the valley everywhere else. Rows of tall lemon grass are planted along the verges. Lotus flowers, lifted from flooded fields in the valley, are now well-established in submerged planter boxes at the corner of the dam.

* * *

In Jakarta for work, I take the time to visit Jalan Surabaya and its permanent flea market, searching for antiques – real or manufactured. I am particularly keen on finding cast iron chandeliers of the type that were made in Europe and brought out to furnish the homes of Dutch and Javanese aristocrats in the nineteenth century. We plan to suspend three lamps from the big carved dodok besi beams, high in the rafters of the main house. After walking the length of the street, with its rows of hole-in-the-wall 'antique' shops, I am none the wiser, and still without what I'm looking for. Eventually, Pak Tarno supplies what we need from Yogya – the ornate cast iron chandeliers weigh a ton but look grand in the villa. Meanwhile, Jalan Surabaya takes me back to old haunts in Jakarta: Jalan Jaksa, where backpackers come for cheap accommodation, street food and Bintang beer and where dodgy policemen conduct sting operations to catch unwary foreign kids buying marijuana – and fleece them.

Three

William is dead. I hear it from Laras, who is back in Lombok for a study break and heard it from the neighbours. We knew it was coming. But it is still a shock. Will, the New Zealander who introduced us to Agus and who has been a partner on The Hill project; young, fit, healthy Will, who once lived up the lane from us in the little Balinese village of Baruna Shanti; Will, husband of Tari and father of a gaggle of bouncy children, a member of our school community; for months, he had been back and forth to Singapore for chemotherapy, each time returning a little older and a little weaker, but each time with renewed commitment to life. Will's recipe for recovery was to take the chemo and fight the cancer through hard work and denial. His schemes became ever larger, ever grander; he set about building a wide paved road up the steep high slopes on the hill, opening up new areas for development, carving great swathes of raw yellow earth out of the side of the green hill. A few days after his last return, Laras saw him driving an excavator high on the hill, a look of grim determination on his face.

But it didn't work. He is gone. Tari is Balinese – a member of the banjar that owns the valley land – the funeral will be Balinese style, a whole-day affair. Early in the morning we walk to Will's home in the valley – a sprawling Balinese bungalow designed by

Rani and built by Will and Agus. The body is laid out in the main room, an airy space that opens onto a green courtyard and pool area. Friends and family stand about, sipping coffees and chatting in subdued tones – an odd mix of Australian surfers, international miners and Balinese villagers.

From there we drive in convoy into the city and to the Balinese temple of Karang Jangkong, where, a hundred years ago, the Dutch staged their last defence in that first failed assault on the Balinese, and where General Van Ham is buried in that forgotten tomb. The cremation site is open; low brick walls in a dusty space; the tall green backdrop of an overgrown forest reserve in the middle of the city. A bonfire has been prepared, Will's wrapped body is laid on top and Tari reads a brief statement in English, a very personal eulogy, before putting a match to the pile. The fire catches and I wince. This is raw. Flames creep up, licking the body before crackling and leaping into the morning air. As the heat grows more intense, the mourners step back a few more feet, all watching with grim fascination as their friend's mortal remains are consumed. I stand with Laras in the shade of the giant trees, with only the sounds of shuffling feet and uncomfortable conversations for company; the hum of the city in the background. A couple of old faces from my Kalimantan days are there in the crowd. It takes a while to burn a body. One by one the mourners creep away, leaving a few close friends and family members to see it out and gather up the ashes.

Later in the afternoon, we reconvene at the beach below our house site, just up the road from Will's home – a sign indicates that this is a designated spot for Balinese to dispose of ashes. A Hindu priest, dressed in white robes and headdress, intones prayers; a little cloud of fragrant incense smoke drifts into the sea air, a piney scent of sandalwood and salt; a group of Will's surfing mates paddles a little way offshore and forms a circle on their boards; someone scatters the ashes into the ocean. A distant sun sets behind the surfers. A fitting farewell. Laras and I sit on the sand and chat to Agus. A cock crows in the kampung behind, children run about on the beach, and a hawker wanders amongst the mourners selling snacks and cigarettes. The look of relief on Tari's face is contagious. It has been a long day, a day that brings a three-year ordeal to an end, for the still-young Balinese wife.

In the evening we meet again at a villa in Senggigi, to drink beers and reminisce. Will's brother is puzzling about how he will manage to get a portion of the ashes back to New Zealand, with a transit stop in Sydney. Will his brother's remains be confiscated by customs or quarantine officials? Should he declare them – or just take the risk?

* * *

The month of Ramadan has come around again, eleven days earlier than last year. Once again, we shift gear and slow down for thirty days of fasting, daily prayer, and festive fast breaking events. It is September. Cooling breezes blow in off the ocean and the sky is a high blue. In the mornings, a flock of pigeons, released from their cages in the village, whirls about in great circles, little whistles fixed to their legs creating music in the sky.

Laras returns to Tasmania after the big Islamic festival of Idul Fitri. But before she does so, another little ceremony is performed in the valley – at the southern border of the banjar land, where we hope to one day build a road to provide access to property we have acquired below our house site; the area across which I walked all those months ago with Diane, Agus and a heavily pregnant Rani. Laras has made friends with a Balinese priest. The colourful Hindu ritual serves both a spiritual and a practical purpose, firstly to enlist the support of the gods and local spirits in the construction of our intended road, and secondly to buy a little more goodwill and credibility within the Balinese banjar community, whose support we may yet need.

Across the border, to the south of the banjar land, is a large block enclosed by the seasonal creek, and occupied by an old Balinese gentleman, Ketut, his ancient wife, and around thirty yapping kampung dogs. Ketut is not interested in selling land for a road – though his sons might be, according to Karno. He is, however, interested in seeing the last of Wayan, another old Balinese man, who lives across the creek, where he runs a tin-shed brothel and sly grog shop. Wayan is a small-town thug, and has, in the past, threatened both Will and Karno. While the little ceremony may not have convinced Wayan, it does help us to build a coalition to move him on in due course. His presence, where we hope to one day build an access road, is a problem.

Meanwhile, the Sasak builders and labourers are on holiday. Work on the build has ceased. Nothing will happen now, until after Lebaran Topat. I take a week off over the holiday period. Laras and I take a brief trip to Bali, where we see her off to Australia again. A few days in Kuta and Ubud provide a good chance to reconnect as a family before she leaves. The trip also provides a chance to check out design features of villas, gardens, planting, paving and statuary. In Ubud we take the boys to see a village dance performance.

We are seated on low wooden benches in a courtyard. The performance begins, and, as we watch good, once again, triumph over evil, I think about Will, about The Hill, about our building project. I think about humanity, our arrogance, our vain attempts to build a legacy, to construct a bulwark against mortality, to leave a mark on this earth. The glittering Barong dragon-lion once again conquers the demon queen, Rangda, and her army of evil witches. The terrifying, child-eating Rangda leaps about, bug-eyes staring, feathers trailing and long nails flashing in the dim evening lights; a clash of cymbals and the beat of a village gamelan announces her entrance and eventually celebrates her defeat.

Four

The rains arrive this year in fits and starts. The winds have turned and are blowing from the west. Dark clouds roll in from Bali and across the Lombok Straits, but the big rains have not yet arrived in earnest. Light showers brush the dry earth and the grass begins to green.

September turns into October. The mangos ripen on their trees, and bowed duwet trees begin to drop their purple fruits. Big pods dangle from the tall, green-trunked kapok trees, their fluffy insides beginning to burst and litter the ground. Mushrooms and fungi spring up in the damp and shade of the creek area; but when Laras's sister picks a bag of what look like edible mushrooms and cooks them up for the family, everyone is violently ill. The holiday season has passed and the work resumes. Nyoman, a Balinese businessman from up in town, arrives one day to discuss plans for a bore. The banjar has given us approval to use their land and so the drilling equipment is set up by the creek in the valley to the west, around eighty metres below the house site. There is no way of knowing whether or not we will strike water, but the signs are good, and it makes sense to bore in the valley close to the creek, where the subterranean flows are likely to be found. Andrew had previously tried boring in the high valley, just above our house site, but the crew failed to find water – and the drill bit, an expensive item, was broken in the attempt and now lies abandoned somewhere beneath the earth. His second and successful bore is located at the foot of the hill in the valley to the east.

Nyoman's Sasak technician turns up on site. Supri has a dark complexion, a round, weathered face and a wide smile. We discuss terms and possible locations for the bore. Supri seems amused to be dealing with a foreigner.

'We will share the risk,' he says, 'fifty-fifty. If we strike water, you pay the full fee. No water and you pay half.' Fair enough. Supri decides to hedge his bet, using a local water divining technique. He places some leaves on a patch of bare earth; it is apparently a good sign when the next morning the underside is moist.

'What do you think?' I ask Pak Mobin.

'Mudah-mudahan,' he laughs. 'Hopefully, hopefully ...'

A few weeks later a great gush of water rises into the valley air. Success! Agus collects a sample from the new bore and takes it up to town to be tested at the government's mining and minerals office. No organic or other contamination is found. The mineral content is all within safe levels. A slightly higher than standard level of zinc is found. I research this and it turns out that zinc, in small quantities, is not a bad thing – it may even improve the libido. All in all, a pleasing result.

The water system is complicated, but effective. The water stored beneath the villas does not go green, as I feared. the cool and dark space prevents the growth of algae, as intended. And the delight I later experienced when first taking a shower and knowing that the water was a gift from the earth and the sky – and was heated by the sun – has never left me. Meanwhile, a new ionisation unit bubbles away, producing metal ions which are dispersed into the water and keep the swimming pool clear and clean. And the solar-powered DC pool pump does its thing, quietly cycling seventy-five cubic metres of pool water through the sand filter each day.

Over coming years, I collect monthly records of water usage, using meters installed at various strategic locations. The gravity system produces a low-pressure flow, and water usage proves to be modest. In a year, around a third of our water is rainwater, ten percent is recycled, and the rest comes from the bore. I also collect daily rainfall records. Derek scoffed at the makeshift gauge I had fashioned from a Perspex tube marked off in centimetre intervals with a felt pen and placed on a wall behind the main house – but it served its purpose. The year after we built the villa was a wild one. Some days we got a hundred millimetres of rain. The record, according to my rough gauge, was a hundred and eighty in a day – a big fall! Our new tiled roof, guttering and downpipes held fast, water flooded into the underground tanks – and the network of stormwater drains that Agus had designed and built, channelled water in great torrents into the creek. The water rushed down the valley, carrying leaves and debris with it, over the dam and around the roots of trees, scouring the hillside as it made its way to the sea. Something went awry with the seasonal cycle that year and we received more rain in the dry season than in the wet.

By the time the water system is functioning in November, the rains have settled into a daily or two-daily pattern. The monkeys have retreated to the hills and the row of big banten trees along the western border is bright green with new growth. The new raintrees are growing fast. Rambutan and mangos are fruiting in the valley, and on the plains the fields are flooded and thick with new rice, lush and green. The recently planted grass areas around the villas are soon green, too, and before long rows of lemon grass are thick and healthy looking. Little brown toads appear in damp corners of the garden and croak rhythmically through the nights. The fingerling fish we had emptied into the dam earlier this year have grown, and the pond is alive with Nile perch and bottom-feeding catfish. Frog spawn collect in the shallow water amongst the lotus flowers, little pond skaters sit on the surface, and squadrons of red dragonflies dart about in the sun. In the daytime, swallows swoop across the pond, replaced at night with little bats – both of them scooping up any mosquitoes or bugs that the fish have failed to eat. A metre-long monitor lizard has taken up residence and feeds on the fish, slipping in and out of the murky water with barely a ripple. Rory christens him Monty – and, now that Monty has a name, Pak Mobin's efforts to persuade us to catch and kill the lizard fall on deaf ears. There seem to be plenty of fish to go around.

* * *

Yesterday I had a difficult conversation with Laras. We've been living apart now for nearly a year, while Laras works on her doctoral thesis, and it's beginning to take a toll. Our lives have become defined by distance, I told her. In a way, we're tempting fate. Nothing terrible has happened to shake the foundations of our relationship, but I had a creeping sense that not all was well. We have been apart for too long.

I stood, leaning on the railing of our new home, looking out from the second-storey galley across the wooded valley, across the greening hills, across the Lombok Strait to Bali. The house smelled of wet paint. It was late afternoon. The workmen had packed up for the day, the tiling of the pool was finished, a deep ocean blue, and the surrounding slopes and terraces were green with newly planted grass. The air was cooling and the sky beginning to take on the tints of another Lombok sunset. The teak floor felt silky beneath bare feet. Lombok's day-end sounds reached me from below: a distant wallop and thump of waves breaking on the far shore, dogs barking in the Balinese kampung, Pak Mobin's geese cackling at one another, the high-pitched voice of a boy calling the faithful to prayer from a little mosque in the valley, and a steady stream of traffic along the coast road – the roar of motorbikes with knocked-out mufflers reduced to a harmless hum by distance.

I called Laras. Three hours' difference at this time year. I wondered what she would be doing in Tasmania – sitting at her desk at the university with a pile of books and photocopied journal articles for company, the silence and smells of academia, of dust and ink, or packed up and walking through a long Spring twilight to catch the last bus home, the crisp air perfumed with magnolia blossom, a late afternoon sun disappearing behind clouds or streaming through a filter of blue gum trees, the bulk of Mount Wellington looming in the western sky.

'Are we okay?' I asked, trying to keep my voice steady.

'I think so,' replied Laras.

She will be home soon. This morning I sit on the barugaq outside our little home in the Balinese village. An early glare forces me to squint, as the sun lifts above palms and bounces off tiled rooftops. I pick up my old guitar, the nylon-string I grew up with, and play around with a few minor chords, composing a song for my wife, trying to sort out a complicated set of feelings through music and words – an attempt to create order out of chaos, turning the clamour into song, as I have done in the past.

'Look out on the ocean,' I sing to no one, conjuring up a mental image of Laras on the beach in Sandy Bay, bare feet, toes in the lap of cold water, 'feel the sand, and breathe the air. Think of me from time to time, and I'll be there.'

Five

In December, Laras is called home to Yogya. Her father is dying. The family home is busy. The children have gathered. Now middle-aged and living different lives in different places, one by one they have returned to the village: the teacher, the soldier, the scholar, the cook and the administrator. The grandchildren scamper about. Mother busies herself in the lean-to kitchen out the back. The siblings sit together on the veranda, breathing the village air, chatting in subdued tones, catching up on family news. Each has a story to tell, a life to share. The talk goes on late into the night.

The old man lies on a pallet. A low-wattage lamp hangs bare from the rafters. Sacks of rice are stacked on the polished concrete floor, the family's meagre wealth. A rusting bicycle leans against the rice. The old man no longer eats. He probably weighs no more than fifteen or twenty kilograms. He's had enough of life, he says. It's time to move on, time to go home.

The old man lives in another time now, another world. He chats about his brother who was lost in the violence of 1965. He talks about escapades with his youthful friends; he tells stories as if it were today. From time to time he remembers who he is, where he is; from time to time he can recognise his children. But mostly he just lies there, sleeping, dozing or muttering to ghosts.

Laras's younger sister wears a dark robe. She peers at her father from beneath a black veil, her big eyes bright and watery. Laras wears light city clothes, her hair is free. The two sit with the old man. He looks up from his pallet, his eyes childlike, a faint flicker of recognition in his smile. Santi holds his hand. Sometimes it feels cold and she wonders if he has already gone. And then the life returns, feeble but warm and real. She begins to recite verses from the Qur'an, her voice strained but pure as she invokes the Almighty.

Laras takes her turn, holding her father's hand, looking into his eyes. She, too, begins to recite. The old man joins in. Together the three of them recite the more familiar verses that she remembers from childhood. Their voices blend; there is comfort and companionship in the well-worn liturgical Arabic, in the rhythm of prayer. And then the old man reverts to high Javanese; perhaps the old language better expresses his humility as he seeks forgiveness and an easy passage.

'*Arep mulih*,' he says quietly. 'I want to go home.' Eventually the prayer falters, the old man's muttering becomes incoherent, and he is once again asleep. The sisters look at one another and, with the hint of a nod and a smile, take their leave. It is late. No more words are needed. Santi makes her way down the village lane to her home, where her husband and children are already long asleep. Laras unrolls a thin tikar mat and prepares to sleep.

Two or three hours later, the village is woken by *adzan*. A crackling speaker declares that it is time for the pre-dawn prayer of *subuh*. 'Come! It is better to pray than sleep!'

The old man sleeps on as his wife and daughter ready

themselves for prayer. Deep splashes of cold well water wash away the night as they perform the ritual cleansing. Like white shrouded ghosts in their prayer robes, the women walk the few steps to the village mosque, Laras's mother shuffling as she makes her way, bent from a lifetime of toil. The two nod greetings to friends and neighbours in the darkness.

The morning mosque fills with a scattering of worshippers, the old folk of the village. Together they perform the ritual prayers, standing, bowing and prostrating in unison, the women at the back, the men at the front. Looking around, Laras notes that she is by far the youngest member of the congregation. Except for the imam. The younger man who leads the prayer advertises his piety with the uniform of the fundamentalist; his baggy pants are cut to calf-length – just above the ankles, his white shirt has no collar. He wears a white *kopiah* cap and a wispy beard; his forehead is marked with two dull grey smudges, as if he spends his life in prayer – his forehead forever bruised against a prayer mat.

As the congregation settles down, cross-legged on their prayer mats, the young man preaches his sermon. Following some formulaic Arabic by way of introduction, he begins to speak in Javanese of foreign ideas, of far-away places, of distant conflicts. Laras looks perturbed. 'What is this?' she asks herself. Looking about she sees that none of the old people appears worried. Most stare absently at the floor as the young man's voice rises in a hectoring tone. Their eyes glaze over, as they nod off to sleep or begin to think about the day ahead.

'We must stand together with our brothers in the Middle East!' the young man exhorts, switching to Indonesian. 'Do you know who is killing our brothers? We must unite. We must establish a caliphate. We must fight the infidel!'

The old people doze. Laras becomes increasingly agitated.

'I wanted to stand and walk out,' she later says to her sister. 'I wanted to make a stand against this nonsense!' But she doesn't walk out. Instead she sits quietly, her face creasing in anger as she listens to the foreign rhetoric. It seems only yesterday that the preacher was a little boy running about the village. She thinks of the old people, of her mother. She thinks about how they want to live their quiet lives undisturbed.

'What did you think of the sermon?' she asks her mother as they make their way home to begin the day; to sweep the yard, to cook the breakfast.

'The sermon?' the old woman chuckles, 'I don't know. I don't worry about all that.'

Later the family gathers for breakfast. A big pot of fresh rice porridge is on the table, the aroma of stewed coconut cream fills the air. A jar of homemade *emping* crackers is opened. One by one the children emerge from the different corners of the house, of the village. The old man sleeps.

'What's going on in the village?' Laras asks, as they begin to eat. Santi looks up, sensing something in her sister's tone. 'What are you doing?' Laras accuses her sister. 'What are you doing to these old people? They don't want your nonsense. I don't want it either!'

'It's the right thing,' Santi explains patiently. 'How can you resist God's law, Sister? We should all struggle for what is right. For a caliphate. It is the only choice. It is stated in the Qur'an. It is God's law.'

'Listen to you!' Laras says, her voice becoming sharp. 'You sound like a propaganda machine. You should stop going to those prayer meetings. You're trying to change everything. It's not right!'

The young imam is a local leader of Hizbut Tahir Indonesia, the Indonesian Liberation Party. A well-educated young man, he has studied science in Japan. Santi has been attending his meetings and prayer sessions. There, she sharpens her faith, she studies the dogma, politics and propaganda of an imported brand of puritanical Islam. In this new world, Javanese ritual has become an evil. She has joined the struggle to create a caliphate, ruled by sharia law.

Santi's new beliefs have already brought her into conflict with her parents and her siblings. When, some time ago, her husband's grandmother died, she refused to follow the customs, the traditional Javanese Islamic funeral rites. The home of the deceased is normally a busy place on the day of a death. The village women arrive with food and offers of support. With flowers and leaves from the graveyard. Prayers are recited, stories are told, the body is bathed, wrapped and interred, and the traditional prayers commence. Much of this, she reasoned, was un-Islamic. No announcements were made. The house remained dark and silent. Her parents were distraught.

'Don't you dare to treat me like that when my time comes,' the old man said at the time, on the edge of tears, an unusual intensity in his voice.

'Well, even if I don't believe, I will take part this time,' says Santi, when her sister presses her on the issue. 'I don't want to upset my parents. I don't want to upset you all.' Her younger brother, Budi, remains quiet. Aisyah shifts in her seat. She is not comfortable with this friction in her family home. She is not sure what to believe.

'It's not my Islam,' says Karno, eventually breaking the silence, his voice quiet but firm. 'I try to be a good Muslim, like you, but I am also Javanese; Indonesian. And I don't believe in an Islamic state. I believe in Pancasila. Our country will fall apart if you carry on like that. Is that what you want?'

'Answer this,' says Laras, looking hard at her sisters. 'Do you really want to live in a world where you can no longer go about as you please? A world in which you must have your husband or your brother with you – just to leave the house? Is that what you want?'

'All I want is to do God's will,' Santi responds.

'Well, you do what you like,' snaps Laras, 'but don't disturb these old people with your foreign ideas. You'll break their hearts with your nonsense!'

'And don't mess with my nieces,' she adds. Santi has been taking her younger brother's daughter to a kindergarten that is affiliated with an Islamist political party. Budi looks up. He doesn't want this conflict. He doesn't want his children indoctrinated either. But he is not sure how to deal with it. What to do. His older sister remains quiet.

'I spoke with the mosque committee,' says Laras. 'I talked with Uncle. He told me they didn't realise that your radical preachers have taken over. He promised they'd stop it. Everyone is supposed to have a turn at preaching. It's wrong to spread hatred and division. The mosque is for compassion, for fellowship. If our nation's founders had wanted to establish a caliphate they would have done so, he said.'

Laras begins to weep. Tears of anger, tears of frustration. It is not right for conflict to be allowed to surface like this in a Javanese family. But she cannot ignore the problem. 'I am a Muslim, too,' she says quietly, between sobs. 'There is nothing wrong with my faith. But my Islam is not political. I don't want your Islamism. None of us do!'

'I'm not sure,' says her younger sister. 'I don't know what to believe.' Santi raises her eyebrows. Breakfast is over. The old man wakes eventually. And eventually it is time for the family to return to their various lives, their various homes. It is not the old man's time yet.

One by one they take their leave. One by one they sit with their father, one by one they hold his still cold hand, look into his eyes, ask for his forgiveness, for his blessing. One by one they pray for an end to his suffering. One by one they clasp their mother's hands. One by one they seek her blessing, reassuring the old woman of their love and loyalty.

And one by one, they part from their siblings, from their nieces and nephews, from their village.

Laras and Santi hug. It is a fierce hug. Pulling back, they look into one another's eyes. Their eyes are moist but clear.

***

There are several more false alarms before the old man finally passes away.

'Prepare the shrouds!' he demanded one day, prompting a flurry of consternation. But nothing happened. At one stage, he was admitted to hospital, and diagnosed with fluid on his lungs. I returned to Yogya. The family was gathered together in the hospital room. There was some discussion about whether or not to administer further treatments. The old man no longer spoke. In between Qur'anic recitations, prayers for his release, the brothers and sisters chatted in hushed tones. I could see little recognition in Father's eyes. A few days later he was returned home. And a few weeks after that he was gone. One morning he just didn't wake up.

The funeral took place in the family home. When we arrived, the place was busy. Harry was put to work with Laras's younger brother, Budi, arranging chairs in the front yard. The body was laid out in the front of the house in a spare room that was sometimes used for a playgroup. Laras's brothers had washed the body and wrapped it in a plain white cotton cloth. Villagers and family arrived in twos and threes, and, at some point, when it was deemed that the time was right and everyone was present, proceedings began with prayers and recitations of the prescribed Qur'anic verses.

The shrouded body was placed on a frame draped with a prayer cloth, and carried aloft – down the laneway, across the village road, and to the small cemetery, where a plot had been dug in preparation. Big trees shaded the corner plot. The congregation followed along, and the old man was laid to rest in the earth. Karno climbed into the grave, carefully positioning the shrouded body, as if his father was sleeping on his right side, with three fist-sized balls of soil for a pillow – one under the head, one under the chin and one under the shoulder – his head facing sideways towards Mecca. Mother, sisters and others each threw three handfuls of loose soil into the hole, and the shrouded body gradually disappeared under the earth; the earth of the village where he was born, where he was married and where he raised a family; the same earth that he had spent his entire life tilling. As each threw their three handfuls of soil, the mourners muttered a verse from the Qur'an.

Minha khalaqnakum wa fiha nu 'idukum wa mihha nukhrijukum taratan 'ukhraa.

From the earth we created you, into it we return you, and from it we will raise you again.

When my turn came, I peered into the hole and thought about the darkness, the nothingness of death – and the importance of a good farewell. More prayers were said, asking for the old man's forgiveness, reassuring him of their faith. Eventually the villagers left. The brothers got busy shovelling loose clay into the hole, patting it into a respectable shape. The family remained to sprinkle bright flower petals and perfumed rose water over the mound of raw, red earth.

When it was all over, a simple but dignified procedure, and when all the guests had gone, we sat together on the steps of the front porch back at the family home. The sense of a job well done, of a life well lived, and of a good ending, was evident in the smiles and quiet laughter that rippled around.

***

It was some years since my brothers and I had laid my father to rest. He died unexpectedly of pneumonia, fluid on the lungs. Like Laras's dad, he simply went to sleep and didn't wake up. I was there, in Melbourne, the next morning.

'He promised he wouldn't go before me!' complained my mother, a muddle of tears and muted rage.

Everything was organised by a funeral director, the body was washed, dressed and laid out for viewing for a few days before the funeral. It all seemed rather unreal. The old man was gone; skin and bones, thinning hair and sightless eyes, his mortal remains seemed frail and insignificant as I thought of the big character that once inhabited them. My brothers and I gathered on the back porch and talked long into the night, laughing and weeping as we recalled old stories and misdemeanours.

'The boys like their beers, don't they?' said my aunt to my mother.

The funeral was a modest church affair. A contrast to the pomp and grandeur of my father's ordination as a bishop at the cathedral down the road, twenty-eight years earlier. Laras flew in from Indonesia. Harry was in a stroller, Rory was a toddler. 'Who killed Grandpa?' he asked quietly, trying to make sense of it all. My brother and I played some music as the worshippers took communion, a sip of wine and a wafer in memory of the living flesh and blood of Jesus, the man whose two-thousand-year-old teachings had defined my father's life and work.

'Well the sun is surely sinking down, but the moon is slowly rising, so this old world must still be spinning round, and I still love you.' I played guitar and sang the old James Taylor song, a song the musician once described as a secular hymn. Pete played the flute and sang harmonies. The familiar phrasing came easy, the sound echoed around that high vaulted space.

'So, close your eyes,' we sang together, 'you can close your eyes, it's alright. I don't know no love songs, and I can't sing the blues anymore. But I can sing this song, and you can sing this song when I'm gone.'

My mother lived on. Her stubborn heart wouldn't let go. But her spirit was diminished. She moved back to Hobart, back to the town where she was born and grew up, the town where she made a family, where she raised four rebellious boys. Eventually mum's time came. It was ten years after my father died. I was back in town for a brief visit. We hung out together in the nursing home, her life by then reduced to that which could be fitted into a single small room, her conversation reduced to a few muttered words. The room had a pleasant view out over the Cascade Rivulet. She could watch the seasons come and go, the yellow leaves fall from poplars, oaks and plane trees; trees from the old world. When it was time for me to return to Indonesia, I knew that this was the last goodbye. My mother looked at me as I left the room, her eyes sad and resigned. Is this how it ends? I peeked back into the room, reluctant to leave, and she was still looking at the space I had left behind. Like a lost child. We locked eyes and she managed a small smile. She knew.

My mother's funeral took place not long after. The service was held at her parish church, All Saints, in South Hobart, a stone's throw from where she died, the church in which her mother, my grandmother, was married a hundred years earlier – before heading off on that honeymoon to the east coast. The autumn sun streamed in through old stained glass, making colourful patterns on the wooden parquetry and the sandstone walls. I was elected to give the eulogy and managed to put a few words together. But how, at the end of the day, do you make meaning of a life, of a death?

'Dust thou art and unto dust thou shall return', says the Book of Genesis, written around two and a half thousand years ago.

Six

It is December in Lombok; the flame trees are flowering in the valley – a mass of bright orange-red along the coast road – and I plan to move into the new house with the boys. Laras should join us soon, and my brother and his wife are coming to stay.

'We need to be in by the middle of the month,' I tell Agus. 'Laras is coming home. We have visitors for Christmas, and I have invited everyone over for a Boxing Day barbecue. They all want to see the new place, to see what we've made of it: Peter and Ace, Andrew and Felicity, Gregg and Leigh, Diane, Pearl, Sakinah, Iwan – everyone!'

'Right,' says Agus, with a smile, never one to get his feathers ruffled. 'Don't worry, everything will be ready.'

'Are you sure? We really need to be sure that everything is finished in time,' I say, looking into his eyes, looking for reassurance. But I have no reason to doubt Agus. The building has gone to plan over the last year or so. We are on budget and on time – more or less. There is no cause for concern.

Since then, Agus, Eddy and the crew have redoubled their efforts to get everything in order. I am back and forth to Jakarta. The pool decking gets done – not quite how I expected it, with various odd sizes and thicknesses of timber – but nonetheless it is done. The railing will have to wait. The garden is all in place.

And paving is completed for driveways and paths. Steel grates are added to the stormwater drains. One day a carload of government officials turns up at our door. They are here to inspect the house and to issue a building permit, known as *Ijin Mendirikan Bangunan*, or IMB. The men look around with interest, we answer a few questions about the water system and building design, everyone gets a cup of sweet tea and an envelope with some pocket money, hands are shaken, and the building permit is issued – eighteen months after we started building.

The following weekend, I go fossicking among the nurseries along the road to the airport and acquire four gigantic shallow pots. With the exception of fruit trees, which we paid for, our gardening to date has involved seeds, seedlings, cuttings or suckers obtained from other gardens or culled from the wild hills. That and retaining the existing trees. Placed on the edge of the terrace in front of the main house and above the pool area, the new pots add a little casual formality to the scene. We plant large-leaved aquatic plants that send out long stems decorated with beautiful, tiny white flowers which open in the evenings or on cloudy days and disappear in the sunshine. Last weekend I managed to acquire a little specimen from Sakinah's garden at Asmara. But today I purchase four big plants from the nursery.

Sakinah and Iwan call in for a look. Iwan wanders about wearing a silly smile, while I tell the story and explain the meaning of the big house. Eventually, he stops me, we are standing on the second-storey galley; he takes hold of my arm, looks me in the eye and says, 'You know what, Mark? You haven't built a villa, you've built a home, a real home.'

A few days later, a flat-tray truck turns up with some stone statues we have acquired from Magelang, in Central Java. Magelang is a centre for carving; the volcanic temple stone cut from the slopes of Mount Merapi is the same black andesite that was used to build the nearby Borobudur Temple twelve hundred years ago. Today's stone carvers are likely descended from the men and women who carved Borobudur, the world's largest Buddhist monument. Row upon row of carved black-stone statues are on display along the sides of the main road – huge Buddhas, standing, sitting, lying, fat and skinny; figures of Christ and his mother, the Virgin; Hindu gods and goddesses with beatific smiles and multiple limbs; holy cows, frogs, and elephant gods; pissing boys and breasty women to adorn pools; little meditating monks, Chinese lions and dragons to guard temples, homes and businesses. Some time ago, Laras and I went for a drive north from Yogya and picked out some things for the garden: a Borobudur-style meditating Buddha, a contented-looking Hindu cow, an image of Dewi Sri, Java's pre-Hindu goddess of fertility, and a pair of tough-looking Javanese gate guards.

The statues are unloaded onto the newly paved carpark, where the crates are removed and they sit beneath the overhanging duwet tree, an odd little congregation of gods and demons. It takes a good day, ten men, two bundles of stout bamboo poles and a length of sturdy rope to manoeuvre the three-hundred-and-fifty-kilogram Buddha into position, where he now sits on the flat rock by the well beneath the giant waringin fig tree. Dewi Sri sits among the ferns nearby, the two of them merging into the jungle reserve and adding a little spiritual class to the garden. Not far away, the cow sits, as if chewing her divine cud, surveying the scene and contemplating the universe.

At the entrance to the cottage by the creek, a quartet of painted little wooden wayang characters stands, as if in earnest conversation – the Punokawan clowns, Semar and his three sons. Semar, is a complicated character, and much loved by the Javanese. Posing as a commoner and an ordinary mortal, Semar is known to some as Batara Ismaya, the brother of Batara Guru, the king of the gods. He apparently made himself ugly to blend in with earthly humans, and often plays the role of a servant. Whatever his status, Semar is a wise old soul with a flat nose, double chin, huge belly and bulging rear. There, on the porch of our cottage, he holds perpetual court with his sons, Gareng, the cunning cripple, Petruk the lanky, long-nosed middle child, a bit of a joker, but a good listener who can keep a secret, and Bagong, the baby of the family, cheeky, chubby and a bit wet behind the ears.

Our complex is now guarded by a pair of Dvarapala statues. The two demons sit on small pedestals placed on either side of the entrance gates, there to ward off malevolent spirits. The little Javanese characters are stout and rather chubby, but wear a fierce demeanour, with glaring goggle eyes, protruding fangs, curly hair and splendid moustaches. Both wield fearsome looking clubs. In contrast, across the stream, on either side of the entrance to the joglo cottage, stands a pair of Balinese figures. Beautifully carved from fine, creamy sandstone sourced from Yogya, the figures were created by a father and son in Batubulan village, near Ubud in Central Bali. The statues represent Rama and Sita, lovers from the Ramayana epic.

**

On a blustery weekend in mid-December, we move in. Karno manages the move, organizing trucks and directing the workers. The storage shed is unpacked, and, over several trips, all the furniture is shifted to its new home up the hill. I bring a few personal items up in the hardtop – and then stand outside, like a conductor, explaining where each piece is to go. The rains hold off until late afternoon.

After a brief but heavy fall, the rain clears – and it is a beautiful clear evening. The stickiness and heat of the day are gone, the air is balmy and fresh. We have been invited to a Christmas party at Villa Quisia, up the coast. The villa is part of the Qunci villas family, owned by another of Lombok's great characters: Scott is American, and a kind of Great Gatsby type, who loves nothing better than to throw a party. The more lavish, the more flamboyant, the better. Scott's villa, which, like ours, sits on a hill overlooking the sea, is lit up with candles and fairy lights. Early in the evening, a group from our school performs. Fifteen girls wearing tailor-made white feathery dresses, fluffy halos and angels' wings, sing carols. Scott doesn't hold back on the hospitality; the drinks flow free, the crowd – most of Lombok's international community, family and friends – mingles happily in the balmy evening, the kids fool about in the dark, a jolly Santa makes an appearance, and a drag queen struts about in a series of elaborate costumes and huge wigs, hips swinging, lip-synching raunchy songs.

A week or two earlier, Scott had turned up at Café Alberto on a Sunday afternoon with a cool-chest full of cheeses and smoked meats that he had bought from an exclusive delicatessen in Rome and hand-carried back to Lombok. On another occasion, he threw a massive birthday party at Villa Quisia, invited the entire community, and made it his coming-out event. The villa complex was awash with light and fun. Nubile young women and muscled boys – borrowed from the local gyms and fitness centres – stood about in togas, all oiled and shining. Endless drinks were served, huge food platters passed around. Indonesian pop stars from Jakarta performed alongside the Australian drag queen from Bali. A massive birthday cake was carried in on a litter by six-foot-plus black Nubian slaves, and – the piece de resistance – when Scott blew out the candles, simultaneously the entire traditional fishing fleet, scattered across the wide bay below, turned off their twinkling Petromac lamps, and plunged the ocean into darkness.

* * *

The following morning, a Sunday, we complete the move, clearing out the old cottages in Baruna Shanti. Mbak Rus and the team organise the linen, making up the beds, putting clothes away in new cupboards and fresh towels in the bathrooms. Boxes of glasses, crockery and cutlery are unpacked, unwrapped and put away in the new kitchen. Books are stacked on shelves. Tonight is our first night sleeping in the new villa, the first night in our new home. The feeling is not quite real. The boys eventually get to sleep, worn out from the weekend's excitement, and as I slip between freshly laundered sheets in our newly made bed in our newly made home, I try to grasp the enormity of it all. Lying on my back, I fold my arms behind my head, look up at the beautiful timber ceiling, feeling its warm glow, and listen to the night sounds; frogs croak, distant waves crash, and an as-yet-unnamed owl hoots in the darkness. A gecko has already taken up residence somewhere in the rafters and adds an occasional rhythmic croak to the night song.

A few days later, the school holds its final assembly for the year. Gregg gives a fine speech. Peter and Ace are there. Parents mill around, a happy mix of aspirational middle-class Indonesians, small-business people, retirees, miners, tattooed surfies, and expatriates who have dropped out of the mainstream. The children perform a series of skits and traditional dances, a melange of multicultural celebration: there are ballet dancers, break dancers, Acehnese hand-percussion dancers, and hula hoop dancers; painted donkey masks, Chinese dragons and carol singers; a drum band bangs on plastic gallons and cardboard boxes, angels play violins, and everyone sings the school song. Every child, from pre-school to high school, is involved. And the school semester finishes with smiles and a pot-luck meal.

Laras arrives back in Lombok on Friday and we spend the weekend pottering around, putting things in place in our new home, and getting reacquainted. It is time for Agus to sign off, to hand over the project. There are a few things to finish, but basically the build is done. We sit on the terrace with Agus and Karno and go over the books. The final figure is pleasing. Unlike some others, we have come in close to budget. Costs did not blow out, we are still friends with our builder (and with one another), and the sale of those three blocks where we originally intended to build has largely paid for the construction. I should remind myself not to appear too smug when sharing this information with friends and neighbours. Life has not always gone to plan, as it seems to have done this time. But, for now, I am grateful that the fates are smiling on us.

My brother and his wife arrive a few days later from East Timor, where they are currently stationed. Pete is an Australian diplomat. The joglo cottage has been prepared and, after gin and tonics on the galley, they settle in, while we make preparations for Christmas and the Boxing Day barbecue. It's going to be a busy few days, Laras has explained to our family and friends. 'Don't worry, Christmas is a family tradition,' she says. 'It is my husband's culture. We are still Muslims.' No one seems to mind.

Karno and his family are moving into the cottage by the creek. That evening he has invited a bunch of friends around for a selamatan, to bless his new home. Twenty or thirty soldiers wearing short-cropped hair and plain clothes arrive on motorbikes, take a look around, and file into the cottage. Laras and I join the group with Pete and Sue, who reluctantly dons a headscarf for the occasion. Everyone is seated on floor mats, Karno makes a brief welcome speech, prayers are recited, Qur'anic recitations, and a meal is shared – rice, chicken, water spinach, *tempe* and chili sambal.

The next day is Christmas Eve. Karno turns up in the morning with a potted Javanese pine tree. The tree, around three meters tall, is placed in the main room where it reaches up into the open space beside the stairs and makes an excellent Christmas tree. I set too with the boys to decorate the tree, pulling out an old box of mixed decorations – tinsel and strings of bud lights, baubles, stripy candy canes, and little painted papier-mâché balls that my older children made twenty years ago, at school in Kalimantan. Rory's friends from our old Balinese neighbourhood join in, along with Karno's wide-eyed five-year-old daughter. It's a team effort.

And there is something a little magical about decorating a tree. Finally, a foil covered cardboard star is placed on top and its done. After Christmas, the tree is planted out in the yard – where it is now around twenty metres tall.

The pool is declared fit for use; but it takes all day to fill with our low-pressure water system and it is still filling the following morning. The insect world seems not to have realised that our home is no longer their home. Trails of little black ants find their way across the tiled floor and up the big teak-clad pillars; clouds of flying termites turn up at night, huge long-legged wasps bat around the lights, and spiders take up residence in the eaves. In time they will find a new home, I think wishfully, as I apply anti-ant chalk to demarcate the border along the front steps. In the afternoon Sue helps me hang the paintings while the children play board games. Some of the Balinese boys from the village are here. The Belgian boys have turned up, too. Laras and I have accumulated an eclectic collection of artwork over the years: Tasmanian watercolours, landscapes, a Dayak *huduq* mask from Borneo, a charcoal portrait from Chiang Mai, an ink sketch of a nude from a women's art co-op in Ubud, a tryptic screen print called *Three Queens*, from American artist, Symon, also in Ubud, and a huge, wicked-looking red dog painted in acrylics by fellow Tasmanian, Khan, who is teaching kindergarten at our school in Lombok.

* * *

Preparations are well underway for Christmas dinner. Diane will be joining us, along with Gregg, Leigh, their grown-up daughter, who is visiting from Australia, and Jacob – so there'll be ten for dinner, including the boys. Pete and Sue brought some duty-free Champagne with them and Laras hand-carried a set of wine glasses from Australia on one of her return trips. Diane comes with me to pick up the turkey we have ordered from a supplier in Mataram. This will be the first test for our new gas-fired oven. On Christmas morning I am up early and preparing stuffing for the turkey. Santa has been to visit overnight, filling the big socks that the boys left hanging on their bed ends; a collection of little toys and nick-nacks, chocolate snacks, coloured crayons, a tennis ball, and a fresh orange each. Similar to what he brought me and my brothers fifty years ago.

Someone has contributed an old-style Christmas pudding from Australia, a sticky concoction of suet, minced dried fruits, nuts, figs, eggs, lemon rind, apple, flour, breadcrumbs, rum, stout, sugar and spices – all wrapped tightly in a muslin cloth, and ready for steaming.

'We'll need brandy for the brandy sauce!' I insist, despite Diane's protestations.

'You can't have Christmas pudding without brandy sauce – and you can't have brandy sauce without brandy!' I declare, and head down to a bar in Senggigi where the Chinese owner keeps a stock of wine and spirits.

Back in our open kitchen and in the courtyard at the rear of the house, preparations are underway for dinner – and for the Boxing Day barbecue. A team of local staff is at work, cutting, chopping, slicing, stacking, steaming, grinding and mixing. The air is full of laughter, Sasak banter, and fresh aromas: coriander, little knobbly limes, broad green kafir lime leaves, red chilis, black pepper corns, bright yellow ground turmeric, nutmegs, little red shallots, woody ginger and galangal. Mbak Rus sits on the floor, grinding spices in a wide stone mortar with the stump of a black pestle. Her little daughter hovers about, holding things and trying to be helpful. Her husband sits with a huge pile of green coconuts cut from the palms in our garden, and a big bush knife. Coolboxes are filled with smashed ice blocks, beer and wine. Laras is in the thick of it, directing the whole affair in a business-like way. Harry helps his mum prepare bruschetta for pre-dinner snacks – fresh chopped tomatoes with garlic, basil, olive oil, and vinegar, served on toasted slices of French bread from Senggigi. I cut the limes and prepare the gin, tonic and bitters for pink gins – and sticks of fresh lemon grass for swizzle sticks.

Pak Mobin is preparing kindling and dry wood for the barbecue.

'How's it going?' I ask.

'Mudah-mudahan,' he laughs in reply. 'It should be fine. Hopefully ...'

The newly installed oven performs admirably, everyone pitches in, and with much merriment we produce a splendid Christmas dinner. The big teak dining table we acquired from Bill in Jakarta is laden with platters of baked vegetables, steamed green beans, turkey and gravy. The turkey is judged to be moist and well-cooked. The children are seated at a separate table. Leigh makes sure that Jacob is happy – no greens. I found some Christmas crackers in Jakarta, so everyone winds up wearing silly hats. Beneath the tree, a big pile of presents beckons, and after dinner the children open their gifts while the adults watch on – a surfboard, a game of Monopoly, books and puzzles, a volleyball and a badminton set, science kits and toy aeroplanes. At some stage, Karno and his family join in, there are presents for his children too.

'Time for some music?' I ask.

'Sure,' says Pete, with a grin. 'Why not?'

I tune up my old guitar and pull out a box of instruments; everyone gets something to rattle, shake or blow. Pete plays his flute, a lovely sound in that open, airy space with its cathedral-like timber ceiling high above. Everyone finds a comfortable spot, glasses are charged, and we spend a pleasant hour or so singing Christmas carols; songs about snow and reindeer, about angels and shepherds, about medieval kings and goodwill to all men. The music is a little rough and unrehearsed, but it serves its purpose.

'Isn't this what music is for?' I laugh, after a particularly dodgy rendition of White Christmas, a song my mother once loved and that I first learned from a scratchy seventy-eight record, played on a wind-up gramophone with a rose thorn for a needle.

Eventually, we all retire to the front veranda for coffees. Freshly painted white rattan chairs have been arranged along the terrace, recreating that scene in Singapore. The children bob about in the pool, which is still not quite full, and I reflect on the meaning of all this festivity; a secular Christmas celebrated by Muslims, Christians and atheists in the tropics. Of course, many of the traditions we have been observing pre-date the birth of Jesus, that we are ostensibly celebrating. Trees and turkeys, lights and decorations, Santa Claus and gift giving, steamed puddings, brandy and old songs; all are echoes of the mid-winter solstice in Western Europe, a pagan festival to honour the gods of winter, to observe the changing of the seasons, the birth of a new year, to pray for an end to cold and darkness, and a return of the sun.

Like the big festivals of Islam, Christmas has its roots in that old world, a world in which men and women were at the mercy of nature, a world in which we knew our place. We knew the importance of humility – and of family and kinship. For without this understanding we would not survive. We forget that old world at our peril, I think. As humankind evolved, so too did these traditions, these patterns and rituals for strengthening communal bonds, for reaffirming loyalty and for making meaning out of it all, out of birth and life and death, out of pain and pleasure, hunger and plenty, suffering and celebration.

'I do like the Christmas story,' I say to Laras, who is sitting beside me in one of the refurbished cane chairs. 'I am a Muslim now, but I still love Christmas, I love the traditions – and I think it's a wonderful story, too.'

'What do you mean? What story?' asks Laras.

'I mean the religious story,' I reply. 'The birth of Jesus, the story of his virgin mother, and of Joseph, the carpenter. Of how they travelled rough to the village of Bethlehem for the census, Mary heavily pregnant, Joseph leading the donkey. The three wise men following a star from the east. The shepherds and angels. The story of how they all ended up camped in a stable, because the inns were all full by the time they got there. And of how the baby was born in that stable. The one the Christians call a King, King of the Jews, the one they call the Messiah, the promised saviour, son of God, God made man, whatever; he was born there among the animals, among the smells of rotting straw and cow shit. Don't you love the irony of that?'

'I guess so,' says Laras, looking a little puzzled. 'It's your story, really. You grew up with it.'

'But it's your story, too,' I say. 'Jesus is a prophet in Islam, right?'

'Yes, we call him Isa.'

'And the story of the virgin birth is repeated in the Qur'an, too,' I add. 'Isa was the final prophet of the Jews, yes? The Messiah – and his mother was a virgin. He's an important figure in the Qur'an. So is his mother. Too many Muslims like to forget that. It doesn't suit the narrative in their political struggle with Israel and the Christian West.'

'All true,' says Laras, after a pause for thought. 'But it's not really the story that's important for you, is it? It's the tradition, the family ritual. That's what you grew up with. That's what's really important to you.'

'You're probably right,' I reply with a smile. 'For me it's all about family and friendship. It's all about reconnecting, reaffirming those ties, gathering together, sharing a meal, giving and receiving gifts. Christmas marks the passage of time, too. Another year passed. It's not so different to Idul Fitri, Nyepi or Chinese New Year, really. But still, I do love the old stories.'

I reach across and take Laras's hand. Her grasp is firm in response. She looks at me and smiles. A world of meaning is contained in that look, that grip; a lifetime of stories, fifteen years of shared experience, and a promise for the future. The sun is low over the island of Nusa Penida. Distant rainclouds form a dark backdrop and the ocean sparkles with late afternoon light. The boys are laughing in the pool, shining wet, and silhouetted against that bright orange sky. A new ball is tossed around. I look at my children, and I look again at my wife, my brother and his wife, our friends from school; a contented little community on the veranda of our new home. And I smile.

* * *

And so, the wheel turns. It rains overnight. A good heavy downpour. The next day, over a hundred people turn up for the barbecue: young and old, children and babies, family and friends, old and new; all the usual characters; Australians, Brits, Dutch, Germans and Belgians, Italians, Chinese – and Indonesians of all descriptions. Agus and Rani come to see their handywork put to good use. The afternoon rains hold off and it is a proud day for us all. A couple of Karno's soldier mates arrive to help with the barbecue. A huge pile of corn cobs is grilled, sticks of battered *tempe* sate are passed around, oily little mackerel are barbecued on skewers, and marinated legs of goat are slow cooked over a low fire, churrasco style. Great bowls of steamed rice and creamy potato salad are set out on the table with platters of fresh rambutan, sliced watermelon, sweet tomato-chili sambal and urap. Fresh coconut drinks are poured, and the beer is on ice.

* * *

The people of Lombok live their lives like people on any other island. Babies are born, children are raised, young folk flirt and marry, old folk grow old and die. Each day the sun rises and falls. The rains come and go. The tides pull back and forth. The rice is planted, bright and green. Four months later it is harvested, fat and golden. The village folk go about their business, sweeping their yards, feeding their ducks, scolding their children and arguing with their husbands. Each day is punctuated with simple meals, temple offerings and the call to prayer. And in this way the business of life is negotiated. There is comfort in the sameness of this life, in its slowness, its routines and familiarity. And life, for me, is measured in the changing of the seasons, the falling of the leaves, the coming of the rains – another Christmas and another Ramadan.

Some things never change. The love of a man for his wife, for his children; his need to leave a mark on this earth; to build, to plant a garden, to make a home; his urge to write, to sing songs, to tell stories; his fear of death, his love of life.

crazy little heaven

by Mark Heyward

When Mark Heyward first went to Indonesia, to teach at a small school in East Kalimantan, little did he realise how life changing his decision would prove to be. Within three years his Australian life would be behind him and he would be travelling, with fellow adventurers, across remote Indonesian Borneo. The story of that remarkable expedition – a true travel adventure – coalesces with the author's longer journey into the complex heart of Indonesia. It is a journey that spans two decades, that takes the reader from a treasured childhood in Tasmania to a new life in the world's most populous Muslim nation. Along the way the author travels from one end of the archipelago to the other, from the jungles of Kalimantan to the riots and political turmoil of Jakarta. When he meets and falls in love with an Indonesian girl, he must make another life changing decision.

Books set in Indonesia, published by Monsoon Books

Bali Raw by Malcolm Scott

Bandit Saints of Java by George Quinn

Cigarette Girl by Ratih Kumala

Harvesting the Storm by John Waromi

In the Footsteps of Stamford Raffles by Nigel Barley

Island of Demons by Nigel Barley

Island Secrets by Alwin Blum

Jaipong Dancer by Patrick Sweeting

Jakarta Undercover by Moammar Emka

Mataram by Tony Reid

Not a Virgin by Nuril Basri

Olivia & Sophia by Rosie Milne

Radikal by Olivier Ahmad Castaignede

Raffles and the British Invasion of Java by Tim Hannigan

Rogue Raider by Nigel Barley

Shaman of Bali by John Greet

Snow over Surabaya by Nigel Barley

The Glass Islands by Mark Heyward

The Man Who Collected Women by Nigel Barley

Toraja by Nigel Barley

Twilight in Kuta by David Nesbit

You'll Die in Singapore by Charles McCormac